Creating Sustainable Work S

Promoting competitive and sustainable growth is an issue throughout the industrialized countries. While the need is well-recognized and urgent, solutions have emerged and disseminated only slowly. Furthermore, many of the experimented remedies for lagging competitiveness have increased work intensity, but have not met the competitiveness requirements of even the immediate future. The increased intensity of work is not only claiming a human toll but is also having an adversary effect on the quality of operations and business. New work organizational approaches are obviously needed to save companies and jobs, and to enhance employees' well-being and employability.

The book is organized in four sections: Framing, Perspectives, Illustrations and Attainment. The Framing provides a grounding in the key research issues and the historical evolutionary dimensions of work and work intensity. The Perspectives section presents a range of paradigms, concepts, conceptual frameworks, ideas and lenses from different academic disciplines to examine the emerging practice. The Illustrations are intended to provide a few examples of work systems in a variety of contexts, national and industrial, that show how different aspects of sustainability may be realized. The Attainment section attempts to indicate potential solutions coupled to the stages in development and learning processes, for sustainability is a process, not a state.

In this book the authors provide a much-needed vision of 'sustainable work systems' which can viably reverse current trends: this innovative form of work organization is based on the idea of regeneration and development of human and social resources. *Creating Sustainable Work Systems* sheds light on emerging work systems and describes the existing problems and paradoxes. Based on a four year collaboration by nineteen researchers representing different academic disciplines and ten nationalities from the United States and Europe, this is a timely exploration of viable alternatives to intensive work systems.

Peter Docherty is Professor in Services Operations Management, Royal Institute of Technology, Stockholm, and Senior Researcher, National Institute for Working Life, Stockholm. **Jan Forslin** is Professor in Operations Management and Industrial Ergonomics, Royal Institute of Technology, Stockholm. **A.B. (Rami) Shani** is Professor of Organization Behavior and Change, California Polytechnic State University, San Luis Obispo, and Visiting Research Professor in the FENIX programme, Stockholm School of Economics, Sweden.

Creating Sustainable Work Systems

Emerging perspectives and practice

**Edited by Peter Docherty, Jan Forslin
and A.B. (Rami) Shani**

London and New York

First published 2002
by Routledge
11 New Fetter Lane, London EC4P 4EE

Simultaneously published in the USA and Canada
by Routledge
29 West 35th Street, New York, NY 10001

Routledge is an imprint of the Taylor & Francis Group

Typeset in Baskerville by M Rules
Printed and bound in Great Britain by
T.J. International Ltd, Padstow, Cornwall

British Library Cataloguing in Publication Data
A catalogue record for this book is available from the British Library

Library of Congress Cataloging in Publication Data
A catalogue record for this book is available from the Library of Congress

ISBN 0–415–28575–5 (hbk)
ISBN 0–415–28576–3 (pbk)

Contents

Figures

Tables

Contributors

Tomas Backström is D. Eng. from the Lund Institute of Technology and a sociologist at Stockholm University. He is a senior researcher at the National Institute for Working Life in Stockholm. He is conducting research on sustainable work systems, organizational development and complexity. tomas.backstrom@niwl.se

Palle Banke is a sociologist from the University of Copenhagen. He is head of the section for Organizational Development in the Human Resources Development Department at the Danish Technological Institute. This conducts action-oriented research and consultation in private and public organizations. His key interests are the improvement of productivity and competitiveness in companies through an integrated development of work organization, qualifications of the labour force and the quality of working life. Palle.Banke@teknologisk.dk

Monica Bjerlöv has a Ph.D. in educational psychology. She is a senior researcher at the National Institute for Working Life and is affiliated to the Department of Education, Stockholm University. Her main research interests deal with workplace development and sustainable work systems with special focus on the processes concerning sense-making, dialogue and learning. monica.bjerlov@niwl.se

Peter Brödner is D. Eng. from the Technical University of Berlin. He is head of the Production Systems Department at the Wissenschaftszentrum NRW, Institute for Work and Technology (IAT), Gelsenkirchen. His research addresses work-oriented design and implementation of computer-supported production systems, organizational changes and change management. Broedner@iatge.de

Peter Cressey is Senior Lecturer in Sociology and Industrial Relations, University of Bath. His research interests all have a European or international dimension. They include developments in social dialogue and industrial relations and the related field of employee participation, employment, labour market and industrial relations trends in the banking industry and, finally, research on work organization, corporate strategies and learning. hsspc@bath.ac.uk

Peter Docherty has a Ph.D. in organizational psychology from London, and a D.Sc. in business administration from Stockholm. He is Professor in Services Operations Management at the Royal Institute of Technology, Stockholm and a senior researcher at the National Institute for Working Life in Stockholm. He is conducting research on the couplings between individual, group and organizational learning and on the impact of new information and communication technologies on individuals and organizations. peter.docherty@niwl.se

Marianne Döös has a Ph.D. in educational psychology and is a senior researcher at the National Institute for Working Life and adjunct professor at the Department of Education, Stockholm University. Her research deals with the processes of experiential learning in contemporary settings. Recent projects concern conditions for learning and organizational development and change. mdoos@niwl.se

Frans M. van Eijnatten is associate professor at the Institute for Business Engineering and Technology Application at Eindhoven University of Technology, the Netherlands. His main research interest is socio-technical systems design. Currently, he is exploring the application of chaos and complexity theories to this field. F.M.v.Eijnatten@tm.tue.nl

Jan Forslin has a Ph.D. in organizational psychology from Stockholm University. He is Professor in Operations Management and Industrial Ergonomics, Royal Institute of Technology, Stockholm. His research interests include socio-technical systems and work organization, social aspects of automation and technical change, organizational learning, leadership and management philosophy, action research and organizational change, and industrial relations. fosse@lector.kth.se

Bob Hancké has a Ph.D. in political science from MIT. He teaches European political economy at the London School of Economics and was a senior research fellow at the Wissenschaftszentrum Berlin from 1994 to 2000. His research interests include comparative labour relations and work organization, as well as institutional analysis of macro-economic policy-making. r.hancke@lse.ac.uk

Armand Hatchuel is Professor of Industrial Design and Management at Ecole des Mines de Paris, and Deputy Director of CGS (the Centre for Management Science). He is also guest professor at the Swedish FENIX programme. His research has been in the field of the theory, history and development of industrial models of management and design and more recently on what is now called in France 'the revolution in design and engineering management' and specifically on the new knowledge dynamics related to that long wave of change. armand.hatchuel@paris.ensmp.fr

Annemarie Holsbo has an M.A. and is a researcher and head of the competence development and learning section in the Human Resources Development Department at the Danish Technological Institute. This conducts action-oriented research and consultancy in private and public organizations. Her key interests are the improvement of productivity and competitiveness in companies through an integrated development of work organization, qualifications of the labour force and the quality of working life. Annemarie.Holsbo@teknologisk.dk

Mari Kira has an M.Sc. and a Lic.Sc. (Tech.) from Helsinki University of Technology. She is currently conducting research in the Industrial Work Science group of the Institute for Industrial Economics and Management at the Royal Institute of Technology, Stockholm. Her research interests include organizational development towards regenerative work and compensation systems of developing organizations. Mari_Kira@lector.kth.se

Martin Kuhlmann, a sociologist from the University of Göttingen, is working at the Sociological Research Institute (Soziologisches Forschungsinstitut, SOFI) at the University of Göttingen. He is doing research in the field of industrial sociology covering work organization, employee participation and the role of unions in workplace reorganization. mkuhlma1@gwdg.de

Manfred F. Moldaschl has Ph.D.s in psychology and sociology. He is Professor in Economics at the University of Chemnitz, and leads the Innovation Research Centre, Munich. His current research focuses on organization theory and network studies, concepts of change, group work, mental workload, social capital, and reflexive modernization. Manfred.Moldashl@sozielogie.wiso.tu-muenchen.de

James B. Sena has a Ph.D. in management information systems from the University of Kentucky. He is Professor of Management Information Systems at California Polytechnic State University at San Luis Obispo, California. His main research interests are on the organizational and individual impacts of network technologies and in CSCW and DSS. jsena@calpoly.edu

A.B. (Rami) Shani has a Ph.D. in organization behaviour from Case Western Reserve University, Cleveland, Ohio. He is Professor of Organization Behavior and Change at California Polytechnic State University at San Luis Obispo, California, USA and Visiting Research Professor in the FENIX programme at the Stockholm School of Economics, Sweden. His most recent work has focused on emerging forms of partnership between academy and industry, action research methodologies in the pursuit of actionable knowledge creation, and creating the learning organization. ashani@calpoly.edu

Michael W. Stebbins has a Ph.D. in business administration from the University of California at Berkeley. He is Professor of Organizational Design at California Polytechnic State University, San Luis Obispo. His research interests include utilization of ICT and the design of product development processes. mstebbin@calpoly.edu

Lena Wilhelmson has a Ph.D. in educational psychology and is a researcher at the National Institute for Working Life. She is also affiliated to the Department of Education, Stockholm University. Her research deals with individual and collective learning in renewal processes in working life. lena.wilhelmson@niwl.se

Foreword I

Are people to serve work or is work to serve people? This question is highly relevant today when early retirements due to injury and ill-health are increasing in working life. 'Burnout' is a new word we acquired in the late 1990s. At the same time we still have our 'traditional' problems with us such as noise, repetitive movements, heavy lifting and chemical risks.

Improvements in the work environment and participation took second place in the recession years. We are seeing the effects of this today as more and more people at work are feeling unwell, are sick and even suffer permanent injuries. We can also see that these negative developments have a clear class and gender dimension. Workers, especially women, face much more serious health risks than other groups in the labour market.

Fortunately, this development is not determined by fate. On the contrary, it can be reversed. It is possible to create a working life that develops and enhances, instead of injuring people and breaking them down. As President of the Swedish Trade Union Confederation (LO), my goal is that all work should offer employees development and participation.

Everyone can and must have the right to rewarding work, even care assistants, hotel cleaners and textile workers – a few of the groups that have practically no room for personal initiatives at work and for whom sickness and injuries are commonplace.

A prerequisite for a sustainable working life is that the will exists to make changes and, not least, a belief that individuals can and will develop and take responsibility for their own working lives. The words 'personnel are the company's most important resource' must become a reality for all employees, not just a few. Everyone must be treated as a responsible adult, even in the workplace.

Many different measures are required to meet these demands. The issues of influence, power and participation are central in this context. We must improve the prospects for employees' control over their own work.

The organization of work is thus something that has a very high priority on our agenda. Everyone – employees, employers and society – has something to gain from a changed work organization in which every employee feels secure, has real influence in his or her daily activities and has the opportunity for continual competence development. Such an environment stimulates creativity and promotes constructive employee contributions to innovative improvement. Such an environment strengthens team spirit and generates a healthy loyalty to the company. Investing in this is among the most important things a company can do. It increases productivity, thereby creating positive conditions for growth and employment security; at the same time, it reduces the costs to society of sickness benefits and early retirement.

It is important that there is an ongoing debate on conditions influencing working life. We must generate and exploit new knowledge. This book is a contribution to the debate. It illustrates the issue of a sustainable working life from many angles. Nineteen authors with experience from ten countries describe the emergence of current problems, and present different scientific perspectives and practical examples from working life where different facets of sustainability have been realized. By weaving together scientific knowledge and practical experience, they have increased our insights so that we are better prepared for the important discussions on a sustainable working life.

Wanja Lundby-Wedin
President, Swedish Trade Union Confederation
Stockholm, December 2001

Foreword II

How might business organizations create a work system – the system of roles, responsibilities and relationships for getting work done – that achieves the proper balance between involvement and engagement on the one hand and life–work balance on the other? How might organization and work be designed to ensure both high performance and employee growth and development? Organizations that are able to do this are likely to be sustained over time. What mechanisms can organizations design to enable a conversation to take place among stakeholders about the many trade-offs that are involved in ensuring that the interests of various stakeholders are brought into decisions? These are some of the very important questions about which the authors in this volume have been thinking and doing action research. The impact of work system design on people's motivation and well-being is an issue that has been of concern to academics and practitioners for approximately four decades.

In the mid-1960s, I received a request from an instrument manufacturing plant at Corning Glass Works (now Corning Inc.), where I was employed as an Organizational Psychologist, to help the factory implement the ideas of Douglas McGregor. What evolved was a five year organization development effort that focused on redesign of the work system. Assembly lines were torn down and, following the ideas of Frederick Herzberg, whole jobs in which workers were given responsibility for assembling the total instrument and doing their own inspection followed. Communication practices were totally overhauled. Employees received information from physicians about how the product was used with patients and from management about the performance of the organization, its revenues, costs and profits. High levels of employee engagement and satisfaction as well as plant performance made this instrument factory a model, at the time, for other organizations inside and outside the company.

This plant-level organization development effort reflected the major concern of the time. Work in most organizations, certainly for production employees but also for many white collar employees, was narrow, boring, un-involving and de-motivating. Since the seminal book *Man on the Assembly Line* by Robert Guest, much research has confirmed that rationalizing work in the manner espoused by Frederick Taylor has negative consequences for the human condition at work and often many unintended consequences. Alienation and ͡alth problems have been found on the human side and resistance to change as well as low ͡f innovation, quality and commitment contribute to the underperformance of the

͡ing, has changed in the last three decades? How sustainable were the change ͡nt factory example and the other organization development efforts at ͡ent levels carried out at Corning by my associates and me as well ͡ations in the United States and Europe?

͡t out, while rationalization of work is still a problem in

many blue and white collar jobs, an equally ominous force is creating new human problems at work. The rising power of capital markets, globalization of financial and product markets and rapid technological change are creating pressures for speed and high performance at the corporate and individual levels. This in turn is causing what authors in this volume call 'work intensity' – under-bounded jobs, pressure for results, long working hours and little time for reflection and personal development. These conditions are creating work–life balance problems of a different but equally difficult nature when compared to the narrow and boring work of the assembly line. In recent work I have been doing with a number of corporations, employees report that the organization and they are overloaded and out of capacity. There are too many initiatives coming from the top. Feeling the pressure for higher performance and a burgeoning business management literature, top managers are unleashing programme after programme in their effort to adapt their organizations to perceived competitive threats.

And what do we know about the sustainability of the many improvements in work systems made in the last four decades? Ten years after the Corning manufacturing experiment started few of the innovations made were still in place. Changes in business conditions, plant growth and rotation of managers had simply overwhelmed the innovative work system. Innovative work systems in other companies suffered the same fate. Changing the 'what' of job and organization design does not seem to change the 'how' of organizational adaptation. That is, improvements in work systems did not create an underlying capacity of organizations – managers and employees – to adapt to changing circumstances while remaining consistent with the values and principles that gave rise to the innovation in the first place. What organizations internalized was a new system of management. They did not internalize the skills, attitudes and behaviours needed to adapt work systems to new circumstances in a way that would preserve the inevitable balance that must be struck among all the stakeholders of a corporation – investors, customers, employees and community.

How organizations might create sustainable work systems is a practical matter worthy of organizational experimentation as well as conceptualization and theory development. In this volume practical scholars concerned with the human condition in organizations have come together to discuss their ideas about how work systems that meet the needs of multiple stakeholders can be sustained over time. In effect, they are searching for an understanding of how organizations might learn to adapt work systems to an ever-changing context while maintaining the delicate but necessary balance between economic goals and human development. This is not an easy problem. Nor is it one that can be solved by this volume alone. The contributors to this book have, however, made an important contribution to a much-needed debate.

Michael Beer,
Professor, Harvard School of Business
Cambridge, Massachusetts, January 2002

Acknowledgements

This book has been written within the international research project 'From Intensive to Sustainable Work Systems', a project initiated and financed by the Swedish SALTSA research programme on 'Working Life Developments in Europe from a Union Perspective'. This programme was launched in 1997 by the National Institute for Working Life, a government agency for the conduct of research, development and educational work on work–life issues, in co-operation with the three central union organizations in Sweden, the Swedish Trades Union Confederation (LO), the Swedish Confederation of Professional Employees (TCO) and the Swedish Confederation of Professional Associations (SACO). The 'Sustain' project group is a network of American and European researchers. The network has met roughly twice a year from 1998 to 2000. The authors would like to thank SALTSA for its support in financing the essential conditions for the network's work in producing the book, such as meetings, conference participation and the preparation of the book. The authors wish to thank the SALTSA Work Organization working group, P.O. Bergström, Monica Breidensjö, Peter Docherty, Mats Essemyr, Märeta Johnson, Charlotta Krafft, Magnus Rehn and Peder Rehnström for their active support and interest in the project.

The authors wish to thank Giusto Barisi, Jean Ramon Figuera, Philippe Lefebvre and Jack Nash, their colleagues in the network who participated in the work of the project, including the meetings, but who have not participated as authors in the book.

This project has been a part of the research co-operation between the programme for Organizational Development and Learning (OUL) at the National Institute for Working Life and the FENIX programme at the Stockholm School of Economics and the Chalmers University of Technology, as well as the Work Science group at the Institute for Industrial Economics and Management (INDEK) at the Royal Institute of Technology, Stockholm. Armand Hatchuel and Rami Shani participated from the international faculty of the FENIX programme and Jan Forslin and Mari Kira from INDEK. All have participated as authors in this book. We also wish to thank colleagues in the OUL programme and the publisher's four anonymous reviewers of our book proposal and sample chapters for their very constructive comments on our work.

We would also like to thank those whose professional efforts have resulted in the book manuscript being completed. Mari Kira acted as general assistant to the project group, carrying out the administration of the project, including taking minutes at all the meetings. Inger Lundqvist and Gerd Wallin from NIWL have taken care of the economic administration. Anita Söderberg-Carlsson, from IMIT and the Stockholm School of Economics, has been our copy editor, who in this project on 'sustainable work' has had to experience very 'intensive' work. Our warmest thanks to you all.

Every effort has been made to contact copyright holders for their permission to reprint material in this book. The publishers would be grateful to hear from any copyright holder who is not here acknowledged and will undertake to rectify any errors or omissions in future editions of this book.

Finally deepest thanks to our families, and especially our wives, Elisabeth, Elsa and Elaine, for understanding, if not quite accepting, that our work situation was, as ever, 'rather intensive just now'.

Peter Docherty, Jan Forslin and A.B. (Rami) Shani
Stockholm, December 2001

Part 1

Framing

The outline of the book

We have chosen to organize the book in four parts that we call *Framing*, *Perspectives*, *Illustrations* and *Attainment*.

There are a few important ideas that run throughout the book. All are based on a shared concern for the emerging patterns of intensive work systems; each chapter provides new insights into the intensity–sustainability dimension of work systems, whether they are theory or empirically based. Finally, the chapters represent diverse theoretical points of departure illustrated by different national contexts. The following is a review of our purpose for each part.

The purpose of the *Framing* section is to provide grounding in the key research issues and the historical evolutionary dimensions of work and work intensity.

Perspectives is intended to present a range of paradigms, concepts, conceptual frameworks, ideas and lenses to examine the emerging practice. Each chapter takes the concepts of work intensity and sustainable work and discusses them from a particular perspective, conceptually or empirically.

Illustrations is intended to provide some examples of work systems in different contexts, nationally and industrially. The examples are practices that emerged in the interplay between intensity and sustainable work and are examined to varied degrees from different theoretical frameworks. We look at intensive and sustainable work systems through different lenses to see as much as possible, very much like natural scientists describing our physical world look at cells through microscopes and stars through telescopes. The observation lenses are chosen to respond to and respect the characteristics of each system or analysis level in question. However, what unites our lenses is their focus towards work, towards individuals and towards organizations at work. Sustainability and competitiveness have often been recognized as essential goals of our society, but the discussion has stopped only at societal and ignored the organizational and individual levels.

The *Attainment* part attempts to suggest some roadmaps for solutions. What seems to be a common denominator in this section is the aim of participation and consciousness of all the relevant actors. Furthermore, sustainability is not a state, it is a process; and in order to attain and maintain these processes expertiocratic approaches have to be re-examined. Scientists, consultants and managers do have important roles also in the more sustainable futures, probably not as creators, but rather as facilitators. Their task is to initiate and support the process of sustainability and to facilitate the continuous common search for balance in working lives and firms' efficiency, effectiveness and competitiveness.

As the notion of sustainable work systems is quite recent, it can only be said to be emerging theoretically and empirically. This book is an attempt to question that past and provide a starting point for formulating something presumably entirely new. As researchers we are formed by our past experience, our idiosyncrasies and favourite modes for changing the world. As with any 'paradigmatic' change, the trick is to get rid of obsolete perceptions and wisdom, while not throwing out the baby with the bath water.

One has again to learn from praxis while at the same time creating a conceptual world. As there is little empirical work done from the point of view of a sustainable work system, the evidence we can offer here is gleaned from existing cases and selective pieces of information on interesting partial solutions.

At this phase of theory building an abductive approach is thus difficult to escape. Much of the assumed pre-understanding is in this case socio-technical as several of the authors have a long history of working with approaches connected to socio-technical systems theory. This has been seen as the major challenger to the Tayloristic practice. Now the challenger is questioned – if yet heedfully – and not from a neo-Tayloristic perspective, but in order to move forward. Whether this means a complete brake on or just further adjustments to and integration of existing elements remains to be seen.

Introduction to Part 1

Promoting competitive and sustainable growth is an issue throughout the OECD. While the need is well recognized and urgent, solutions are emerging and being disseminated slowly. Furthermore, many of the experimented remedies for lagging competitiveness have increased work intensity, but have not met the competitiveness requirements of even the immediate future. The increased intensity of work is not only claiming a human toll but is also having an adverse effect on the quality of operations and business. New work organizational approaches are obviously needed to save companies and jobs, and to enhance employees' well-being and employability.

We argue that ways must be found to reverse current trends through pursuit of an innovative form of work organization called sustainable work systems. Sustainable work systems are based on the idea of regeneration and development of human and social resources. In sustainable work systems resources are not consumed, but allowed to grow. Employees are not confined to an intensive and meaningless work reality, instead they are allowed to learn and develop, to use their intelligence and creativity, to collaborate and participate.

The first section of the book provides the objectives, motivations and framing for later chapters. The emerging context of work sets the stage for the two central concepts of our study, namely intensive and sustainable work. As such it provides the grounding in the key research issues, the economic profile of globalization and its impact, emerging working conditions, the historical evolutionary dimension of work and work intensity and key definitions of concepts.

Chapter 1, 'Emerging work systems: from intensive to sustainable', presents the key paradoxes and imbalances that have emerged to present many people with intensive work situations. The new economy with globalization and the spread of information and communication technology (ICT) is accompanied by a radical 'up speeding' working and business life. Conflicting trends are noted: the so-called high road vs. low road, neo-Taylorism vs. self-organizing teams, growth, development and connectivity vs. insecurity, ambiguity and isolation. Key elements in the vision of sustainability are also presented.

Chapter 2, '*O tempora, O mores!* Work intensity – why again an issue?', takes a broad look at the history of organizations from Taylor to present day management doctrines with a focus on work intensity. The conclusion is that work intensity has been and will remain a critical factor if not always recognized as such. It also functions as an 'ideological' background for the rest of the book.

1 Emerging work systems

From intensive to sustainable[1]

Peter Docherty, Jan Forslin, A.B. (Rami) Shani and Mari Kira

Introduction

The workplace is essential to our existence. Economic logic tells us that the more firms produce and the more efficient organizations are, the healthier and happier society will become. But this is not happening. In fact many have begun to argue, based on research findings, that during the last ten years we have witnessed increasing stress, burnout, turnover, absenteeism, injuries and heart diseases. The balance between work and life also emerged as a major concern for many. A conservative estimate of the costs amounts to some 20 billion Euros annually. Even more staggering is the human suffering of many millions of European workers. Workload in hours worked is steadily increasing, with varying signs between countries of the limit being reached. The typical American works 350 more hours a year than the typical European, more hours even than the industrious Japanese. Only 8 per cent of Americans are prepared to work fewer hours for less pay, compared to 30 per cent for Britain and Japan and 38 per cent for Germany (Reich 2000, p. 6).

Recent international statistics on stress, burnout and healthy work organizations have indicated that many modern work organizations are consuming, rather than regenerating, their human resources. The brave new world of work envisaged to emerge from the ashes of Taylorism has not, in many cases, arrived and, where it has arrived, it has not been what it was expected to be. We have witnessed the persistence of Tayloristic organizations (Schumann *et al.* 1995) and the emergence of neo-Tayloristic organizations (Babson 1995; Landsbergis *et al.* 1999; Taylor and Bain 1999). At the same time, the post-bureaucratic organizations have not automatically created possibilities for mature adults to grow and develop (Argyris 1964); and where bureaucratic structures and rules have disappeared, they have rather left the mature adult lost, lonely and increasingly stressed.

In this book, our aim is to shed light on the emerging work systems and to describe the existing problems and paradoxes. Based on a four year collaboration by nineteen researchers representing different academic disciplines from ten nationalities in the United States and the European Union, our goal was to illuminate the existing possibilities and emerging solutions and to explore some alternatives to intensive work systems. The two central concepts of our work are *intensive work systems* and *sustainable work systems*. Work intensity refers to the consumption of human resources – physical, cognitive, social and emotional – in work organizations, while the sustainable work systems concept presents a vision for the future competitive organizations in which human resources are regenerated and allowed to grow.

The emergence of intensive work systems

What went 'wrong' in the development of business and working life in the last two decades? Developments in business and working life in the 1990s are frequently referred to as the 'new economy'. The basics in the new economy are two broad trends that have been under way for several years. The first is the *globalization* of business. Simply put, capitalism is spreading around the world – at least in the introduction of market forces, freer trade and widespread deregulation. It means that international trade and investment play a much greater role in many economies. World trade is increasing much more rapidly than world production, indicating growing interdependency among countries (see Figure 1.1). Foreign direct investments are also increasing at a more rapid rate indicating closer ties in the production of goods and services among different countries. The development of the financial markets may be said to have exploded in the 1990s. The value of the daily trade in the markets for currency, shares, bonds, etc., is in the order of trillions of dollars. The turnover in these markets is very rapid; for new speculation products such as index options and futures, it is every few hours or days (Reich 1994)

The second trend is the revolution in *information technology*. Digitalization has revolutionized the storage and transmission of information in media and the Internet. New industries and companies are being created before our eyes. Information and communication technology (ICT) has replaced the building construction and car manufacturing industries as the main motor in the industrialized economies. It affects all other industries, boosting productivity, reducing costs, cutting inventories and facilitating electronic commerce. In short it is a transcendent technology – like railroads in the nineteenth century and cars in the twentieth. In the new economy speed is all-important. It is no longer the large that force out the small, it is the fast that force out the slow. Two clearly documented strategies for economic growth are referred to as the 'low road' and the 'high road'. The former is characterized by the use of a low skill labour force with little participation and cost competition, whereas the latter is based

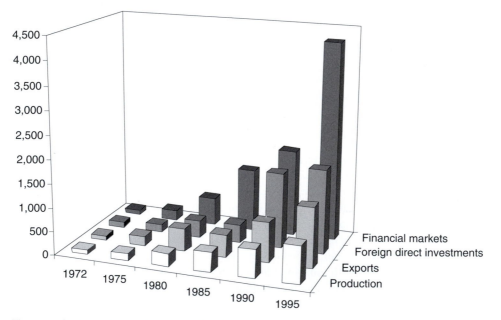

Figure 1.1 Globalization tendencies 1972–95 (1972 = 100).

Source: Wikman 2001, p. 3. Reprinted with permission.

on high skill and high participation and competition through quality and innovation. The pace of work is increasing and so is the pace of adaptation to new conditions, for example shorter learning times (Lundgren 1999).

The results of a number of European projects indicate that management is using ICT in very similar ways and with very similar consequences across sectors and countries (Wickham 2000). At its simplest, management appears increasingly driven by short-term goals of competitiveness. These short-term goals not only pay scant attention to any social issues, but may even be economically counter-productive in the long term. Individual national regulations have at most affected the pace of change, not the direction. Change is towards greater flexibility in the use of labour. The new flexible and ICT intensive workplace is profoundly ambiguous for the employees. Increased responsibility entails increased pressure. In addition such management practices as downsizing, outsourcing and temporary employment have led to a new insecurity which means the end of an essential prerequisite for high trust organizations – secure employment. Employees are required to be flexible and adaptable, both in terms of numbers and functions or skills, as well as not to expect secure employment.

As work intensity has grown, stress has become 'the kiss of death' or 'the spice of life' depending on specific conditions in the workplace. Work-related stress, its causes and consequences, are all very common in all the member states of the European Union. More than half of its 147 million workers report working at a very high speed, and to tight deadlines. More than one-third have no influence on task order, and more than one-quarter cannot influence their work rhythm. Up to 45 per cent report having monotonous tasks; 44 per cent no task rotation, 50 per cent short repetitive tasks. Such work-related 'stressors' are likely to have contributed to the present spectrum of ill-health: 13 per cent of the workforce complain of headache, 17 per cent of muscular pains, 20 per cent of fatigue, 28 per cent of 'stress' and 30 per cent of backache, and many other, even potentially life-threatening, diseases. Some European countries have even reported Karochi, the Japanese phenomenon of sudden heart failure at work.

A recent study found that workers in different countries rated *work–life balance* as one of their three key working priorities. This can be related to the concept 'social cohesion', though this is given different meanings. It is sometimes used to indicate 'low social inequality', sometimes to mean 'organic solidarity', the sense that all members of society have different roles, but share a common fate and mutual responsibility. There seems to be a widening inequality in society which was noticeable in the 1980s and became more marked in the 1990s. Now the richest 1 per cent of families (2.7 million people) in the USA have much more money to spend after tax than the bottom 100 million (Reich 2000). There has been a debate in Europe on how institutions in the welfare state, created to ensure cohesion, end up being run for the benefit of their employees rather than their clients. Especially in Scandinavia it has been argued that such institutions actually destroy social cohesion because they undermine the simple decencies of ordinary charity. The sufferings of our fellow citizens become the concern of the state, and nothing to do with us (Wickham 2000). Once the workplace becomes an entity that can be bought and sold, then 'shareholder value' replaces 'stakeholder value', further reinforcing employees' feelings of insecurity and eroding trust. So at the same time as one line of research is revealing the importance of trust and collective knowledge in organizations, another is documenting how these are being systematically undermined.

Time and workplace dynamics

The concept and meaning of time which emerged as a critical business dimension in the new economy is not new in the context of work. Yet, the socially constructed meaning and the role of time seem to be transforming. In the eighteenth century Benjamin Franklin coined a prophetic expression that would become the guiding principle to the industrial society then in being: 'time is money'. From being qualitative and cyclical in the agricultural economy, time now has become linear, clinical and without 'flavour'. The economic meaning of time has, however, changed during this period as shown in Figure 1.2.

In the cradle of industry Adam Smith and later Charles Babbage started the chase for reduced man-time in order to improve productivity. This line of development was completed by the contribution of Frederick Taylor and later time–motion studies of individual work. With mechanization and increasing fixed assets in machinery, however, the individual became less important from a cost perspective. It became more important to maintain maximum availability of the technical equipment. The group of operators turned out to be better equipped to handle larger sections of the production process taking care of tool changes, preventive maintenance and quality control – internal self-regulation. As the level of prefabrication and the cost of the now more advanced materials increased and there was a higher added value in the production process, it later became more important to reduce the capital tied up in stocks and buffer and thus to decrease the throughput time. Men and machines standing idle mattered less than that there was no waiting of goods in front of the machines. Money was earned not in the workshop, but in the warehouse with the help of Kan-Ban and just-in-time deliveries and it became important to co-ordinate various support functions in production including purchasing and logistics.

As customers required their deliveries just-in-time and as the product lifecycle time was in descent, lead time and delivery time became competitive weapons. In order to reduce time to market and the time from order to delivery, the perspective had to be enlarged, now encompassing whole business units or even enterprises integrating all business functions, not least product development, the strategic significance of which has increased dramatically. Finally, with the advent of virtual organizations and industrial networks the ability to activate the latent structure into an efficient concerted effort to satisfy a customer has again added to our time awareness (Forslin 2000).

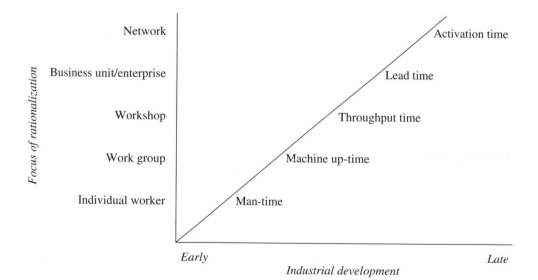

Figure 1.2 Shift in time focus of rationalization with industrial developement.

The historic character of the development hinted at here is partly misleading. Certainly the meaning of time has changed, but that does not mean that earlier perspectives have been discarded. They rather remain, affecting the operations simultaneously, peacefully coexisting or contradicting, causing often unique but always complex business situations – and highly intensive work systems.

The emerging demeaning work systems

An intensive work system has major consequences at individual, organizational and societal levels. At individual level, work intensity emerges from an imbalance between an individual's resources and work's demands, the individual's needs and work's opportunities and, eventually, leads to the consumption of psychological and physical resources, the potential to work and derive happiness from work. Maslach and Leiter (1997) state that such an imbalance between an individual and his/her work leads not only to tiredness or sadness, but also to 'erosion in values, dignity, spirit, and will – an erosion of the human soul' (p. 17).

Furthermore, the erosion is not a state, it is a process leading from the initial exhaustion to cynicism and detachment from work and, eventually, also to ineffectiveness. Consequently, the erosion of soul at individual level leads to serious negative consequences also at work group, organizational and societal levels. The negative consequences of work intensity at organizational level relate to both an individual's behaviour and actions deriving from his/her exhaustion and also to the collective downward spiral of a social system. Such a downward spiral starts when the consequences of work intensity at individual level cascade to problems at social level. As exhausted, disillusioned personnel interact, the whole work system may start to exhibit collective exhaustion and conflicts. Individual psychological defences transform into social defences (Hirschhorn 1988). There is a danger that work groups and organizations, rather than striving to fulfil their primary tasks and goals, turn inwards and concentrate on defences meant to contain collectively experienced anxieties. Productive and creative ways to operate are replaced by rituals and irrational norms. Hirschhorn perceives the current characteristics of working life leading to even higher risk of collective defensive behaviour.

Understanding the negative psychological consequences of work demands an understanding of the complex emotional and cognitive relations people have to their work and to each other at the workplace. Improving the situation and removing the imbalances between people and their work cannot obviously be done through either 'personal improvement' or 'organizational transformations'. If an imbalanced relation is to be resolved, both sides of the equation have to be looked at, simultaneously (Kompier and Cooper 1999).

Emerging trends: paradoxes and imbalances

As mentioned above, recent European statistics on health and safety at work are presenting a dire picture: many of Europe's citizens are not feeling well at work. For instance, both the Second and Third European Surveys on Working Conditions (from 1995 and 2000, respectively) indicate that 28 per cent of the employees in the European Union region are exposed to stress (Merllié and Paoli 2000; European Agency for Safety and Health at Work 2000). These figures are easy to understand in the light of the results from the Third European Survey on Working Conditions; 56 per cent of employees are exposed to high speed work, 67 per cent to work pace dictated by clients, and 40 per cent to monotonous work. The Third European Survey on Working Conditions by the European Foundation (Merllié and Paoli

2000) clearly indicates, furthermore, that working conditions are not improving and, in some cases, they are deteriorating.

The 'traditional' drudgeries of work, such as high physical and psychological load, physical health hazards and monotonous work, are still there. For instance, in the Third European Survey on Working Conditions, 47 per cent of employees interviewed reported working in painful or tiring positions and 37 per cent that they have to handle heavy loads. Both of these figures had increased (from 43 per cent and 31 per cent, respectively) when compared to year 1990 survey results, i.e. to the first wave of the European working condition surveys. Table 1.1 captures recent comparative statistics across fifteen European nations.

At the same time, new types of problem are emerging in the changing workplaces. People become consumed by work that was thought to be good for them; burnout and stress emerge also in the nice offices and jobs with extensive degrees of freedom and variety. The Second European Survey on Working Conditions reported that the occupation group most exposed to stress is 'professionals' with 39 per cent reporting being exposed to stress. Also in the new economy, work in the fast lane seems to be taking its toll in the stress statistics (see Chapter 4). This development, as we argue in sections of this book, necessitates develop- ment of the fundamental concepts in the occupational science, such as the concept of 'good work'. It seems that research has already revealed what good work is; much is known about employees' psychological needs at work (Thorsrud and Emery 1969; Murphy and Cooper 2000) and balanced work experiences (Karasek and Theorell 1990; Maslach and Leiter 1997), as well as work experiences that lead to personal development and growth (Antonovsky 1987). However, very little is known about how these principles of good, bal- anced work can be realized in the modern working life. Consequently, at the same time, we have to continue to improve work that is too limited for employees and begin to improve work that seems to be too much for them. Furthermore, we have to explore how this can be sustained.

The imbalances of modern work

Human resources consumption is always characterized by some kind of an imbalance between persons and their work. The imbalances of Tayloristic work are well known. As stated in several parts of this book (see Chapters 2 and 6), the bureaucratic solution does not work any more; rigid bureaucracies are not open or flexible enough to respond to the com- plex environment. At the individual level, the well-documented problem of the bureaucratic solution is, of course, the lack of opportunities at work. Burnout is not the question, but 'rust- out' is (Hobfoll 1998). Employees become consumed since they cannot use their potential and resources at work.

But why do people find themselves in imbalance with the modern, autonomous and ver- satile work? One reason for imbalance seems to be originating from the vanishing bureaucratic boundaries of work. Even though bureaucracy is consuming people by forcing them into tight rules and prohibitions, the situation without any boundaries around jobs and roles does not seem to work well either. In the modern work organizations, we find ourselves in the opposite situation to strict bureaucracies. In flexible, lateral organizations, where bureaucratic rules and structures are reduced, responsibilities and tasks become impossible to predefine. Autonomy means endless choices of where to go, what to do and whom to contact; the amount of possibilities in one's work is increasing, as are the things to care about. The need for personal judgements at work exposes employees more to social and performance demands. For instance Mohrman and Cohen (1995) state that both positive and negative

Table 1.1 Working conditions in Europe: some aspects

Percentage of workers whose . . .	A	B	DK	FIN	F	D	EL	NL	IRL	I	L	P	E	S	UK	Total
. . work causes stress problems.	27	23	25	34	24	24	50	38	12	41	38	26	22	38	27	28
. . job involves repetitive hand or arm movements all or almost all the time.	27	29	22	41	43	22	48	39	25	32	22	48	45	17	36	33
. . job involves painful and tiring positions all or almost all the time.	13	14	9	9	26	14	41	10	10	20	15	37	24	11	12	18
. . job involves working at very high speed all or almost all the time.	29	19	23	32	23	25	27	38	17	24	18	32	22	27	25	25
. . pace of work is dependent on direct demands from people such as customers, etc.	62	73	69	63	73	57	61	69	67	67	64	64	66	79	78	67
. . pace of work is dependent on automatic speed of machine.	19	16	14	20	22	20	26	21	23	22	25	24	24	12	25	22
. . job involves monotonous tasks.	29	36	39	47	48	32	59	32	43	41	36	43	61	27	67	45

A = Austria; B = Belgium; DK = Denmark; FIN = Finland; F = France; D = Germany; EL = Greece; NL = Netherlands; IRL = Ireland; I = Italy; L = Luxembourg; P = Portugal; E = Spain; S = Sweden; UK = United Kingdom.

Source: European Agency for Safety and Health at Work (2000). Original source: the Second European Survey on Working Conditions, 1995, by the European Foundation for the Improvement of Living and Working Conditions.

consequences may result when bureaucracy is reduced and 'people get out of the box': 'People have the opportunity for personal growth, skill development, and connectedness to others, but they also confront a lack of security, ambiguity, competing demands, and unrelenting work pressures' (p. 377). Similarly, when a central life interest shifts towards work, both family and community involvement seem to suffer.

As people get out of their boxes, they also often find the surroundings of the box drastically changed. What they consider to be the essence of their work is not that any more in the changed markets. For instance, many have received a professional education to become specialists in a narrow skill area, but now the modern organizations are desperately seeking generalist skills. A totally new kind of mindset is needed from employees to adjust to such a change. It seems, then, that in many organizations the old framework of organizational life and work is vanishing, but little has been built to replace it. Consequently, for employees it is increasingly difficult to comprehend and manage their work as they see the disappearing boundaries and outdated priorities without clear visions of what will be in the future.

A need to learn can also create imbalance at work. The boundaryless job roles and versatile, continuously changing job contents are creating continuous need for employees to learn; the need for life-long learning is growing. And as stated above, specialist skills and single-loop learning in which actions are modified to improve goal attainment have to be replaced by generalist skills and double-loop learning (entailing questioning the given context and arriving at new ways of doing things). Even though learning is an essential contributor for well-being, it can also become a source of stress. Learning is not easy; it is not only a question of motivation, but also of courage (Cell 1998). To be able to engage in continuous learning, employees have to have openness and courage to let go of their earlier level of knowledge and explore new opportunities (Shani and Mitki 2000). Also, they have not only to learn new things but also to be able to reflect on their own performance and ways of thinking. True learning means cognitive, and even in some cases affective, development which is possible only when people are aware of and critical about their existing cognitive patterns, their 'theory-in-use'. Very often defences to reduce anxiety get in the way of these profound learning processes. Rather than transforming their thinking, people build fortresses around it (Argyris 1991).

Another well-documented and studied imbalance between people and their work is the imbalance between work and private life, or actually between work and life, as it is often called. This problematic relationship between work and life can relate to two different processes: role conflict between work and private roles and the spillover of negative feelings from work to life (or vice versa) (Reich 2000; Kinman and Jones 2001). The stronger the involvement with a certain role, the more difficult it becomes to accommodate other roles. It seems safe to say that in modern working life, the demand for personal involvement and commitment to work can only increase the potential for conflict between roles in work and private life. Spillover takes place when stress at work spills over to private life; anxiety at work continues at home also. Research has also shown (Kinman and Jones 2001) that work activities (or in-activities) can spill over to private life; a person carrying out monotonous work may be more inclined to have simple rather than complex leisure experiences. Thus, the seemingly separate spheres of work and private life are in continuous interaction; our feelings, thoughts and behaviour carry messages from one to the other. Understanding the imbalances that plague the modern workplaces necessitates looking not only at work, but at whole life experience and its socio-cultural context (Antonovsky 1987; Hobfoll 1998).

All in all, trying to form a unified picture of the problems in modern jobs is difficult. What is the common denominator for all the imbalances discussed above? Is there such a common denominator? Why are the problems mounting? The immediate reasons for the imbalances seem to vary, but one pattern seems to bind them together. Namely, each potential source for imbalances is also a potential source for growth and well-being at work; the vanishing boundaries enable the versatile use of an individual's skills and give him or her a comprehensive view of the whole production/service processes, learning is the essence of healthy and meaningful adult life, and simultaneous existence of family and working spheres enriches one's life and self-image. However, all these possibilities may turn into imbalances, since they are not only possibilities but also challenges. One can argue that one of the main reasons for the mounting problems at work is that we have not created the new work organizational and social approaches and resources that would support the individuals dealing with the complex and rapidly changing world (Hage 1995). Organizations still rely on the old paradigm; yet, we abhor bureaucracy but cannot create the structures, processes and resources that could replace it. This book and its versatile contributions offer the resources and lenses that are needed in comprehending and managing the emerging world of work, as it is now, individually and collectively. This book and other contributions like it are needed if we are to bring out the positive possibilities of complex lives instead of falling under the mounting imbalances within and between different spheres of life and work.

The visions for sustainability

This book is about an exploration of a more sustainable world of work. The sustainable work systems concept presents a vision for future organizations in which human resources are regenerated and allowed to grow. The concept addresses four related fields and basic issues:

- *The regeneration and development of human resources.* The core concept of sustainable work systems is that the resources deployed are regenerated by the system. Human resources to be fostered include skills, knowledge, co-operation and trust, motivation, employability, constructive industrial relations, and also broader institutional/societal prerequisites, such as training systems.
- *The promotion of quality of working life and competitive performance.* Sustainable work systems pay equal attention to improving working conditions and organizational performance and effectiveness. Again their interdependencies require an integrated approach.
- *The nature of sustainable change processes for renewal and learning.* Sustainable work systems should not produce static conditions. Many processes of reorganization and re-engineering are failing or stalled: sustainability therefore has to include the question of how organizational change can be structured and guided. Put differently, since challenges and organizational environments are increasingly volatile, sustainability means creating 'liberating structures' and building up internal capabilities to carry through reorganizations and continuous change successfully and to facilitate learning.
- *The provision of employment.* Sustainable work systems provide a micro-economic context for increasing employment levels, as well as counteracting current tendencies of labour market segregation. Sustainable work systems could serve as paths of integration of unemployed people into the labour market by reversing processes of exclusion on the micro level.

Sustainable work systems is an important concept both at individual and organizational levels. At individual level, sustainability means possibilities for renewal and development. An old saying is 'experience makes us stronger', but experiences can also make us weaker. It is the quality of the experience that matters and, in this book, we present a foundation for the understanding of such work experiences that make us stronger. In contrast to the Taylorist view of working life there is an evolving trend which replaces predefined job descriptions. Organizational structures are replaced more and more by interaction, dialogue and negotiation. Answers are no longer given, but have to be created daily between people. As Hage states (1995, p. 487):

> in shifting from industrial to post-industrial society, people must learn to live in complex role-sets, each with a large number of role-relationships in which negotiations about role expectations or behavior become one of the major capacities for successful role behavior.

These new conditions, requiring new skills, vary themselves at the outset and constitute a risk for more intensity through, for example, self-exploitation. This may occur when commitment to organizational and customer goals and 'needs' overrides drawing limits or boundaries for personal efforts, in time and place: boundaries necessary for maintaining the health and well-being of the individual. Such self-generated intensity is a poorly recognized danger in today's working life.

At the organizational level, sustainability means potential for competitive existence. A sustainable organization is able to realize its potential and to generate value continuously for its stakeholders.

Sustainability – as we understand it – encompasses three levels: the individual, the organizational and the societal. Sustainability at one level cannot be built on the exploitation of the others. These levels are intimately related to the organization's key stakeholders: personnel, customers, owners and society. An organization cannot be sustainable by prioritizing the goals and needs of some stakeholders at the expense of others, for example, customers and owners at the expense of personnel (through their exploitation) or of society (through environmental neglect). Thus sustainability has a value basis in the due considerations and balancing of different stakeholders' legitimate needs and goals. A prerequisite for sustainability at the system level (individual, organizational or societal) is to achieve a balance between stakeholders' needs and goals at different levels simultaneously.

In producing this book we have aimed to practise what we preach: to be reflexive in our writing, to understand how our histories as researchers and persons influence our thinking. Not least the differences within our group, national and disciplinary, have helped us to see that such a complex concept as sustainability has no one truth. In the pages of this book we have allowed the diversity of our thinking to come through; there is no one unified message, but rather, different impressions on sustainability. In a sense, we respond to the recently more often heard call (e.g. Kompier and Cooper 1999) for an interdisciplinary, multi-perspective approach to studying why people become consumed at work and how better, healthier and more productive working lives could be achieved.

Note

1 In the context of this book, the concept of sustainability is limited to the discussion of people and the organization they work in. While we are aware of the great importance of the impact on the environment, this issue is only specifically dealt with in Chapter 18.

References

Antonovsky, A. (1987) *Unravelling the Mystery of Health. How People Manage Stress and Stay Well*, San Francisco: Jossey-Bass.

Argyris, C. (1964) *Integrating the Individual and the Organization*, New York: Wiley.

Argyris, C. (1991) 'Teaching smart people how to learn', *Harvard Business Review*, May–June.

Babson, S. (ed.) (1995) *Lean Work. Empowerment and Exploitation in the Global Auto Industry*, Detroit: Wayne State University Press.

Cell, E. (1998) *Organizational Life. Learning to Be Self-directed*, Lanham: University Press of America.

Emery, F. (1977) *Futures We Are In*, Leiden: Martinus Nijhoff Social Sciences Division.

European Agency for Safety and Health at Work (2000) *Monitoring the State of Occupational Safety and Health in the EU – Pilot Study*, Bilbao: European Agency for Safety and Health at Work.

Forslin, J. (1992) *Teknik och arbetsorganization* (Technology and Work Organization), Stockholm: NUTEK and Arbetsmiljöfonden. MDA-rapport 1992: 14.

Forslin, J. (2000) 'Regenerativt arbete' (Regenerative work), in S. Einarsen and A. Skogstad (eds) *Det gode arbeidsmiljø*, Bergen: Fagboksforlaget.

Hage, J. (1995) 'Post-industrial lives. New demands, new prescriptions', in A. Howard (ed.) *The Changing Nature of Work*, San Francisco: Jossey-Bass.

Hirschhorn, L. (1988) *The Workplace Within. Psychodynamics of Organizational Life*, Cambridge, MA: MIT Press.

Hobfoll, S. (1998) *Stress, Culture and Community. Psychology and Philosophy of Stress*, New York: Plenum Press.

Karasek, R. and Theorell, T. (1990) *Healthy Work. Stress, Productivity, and the Reconstruction of Working Life*, New York: Basic Books.

Kinman, G. and Jones, F. (2001) 'The home–work interface', in F. Jones and J. Bright (eds) *Stress. Myth, Theory and Research*, Harlow: Prentice-Hall.

Kompier, M. and Cooper, C. (1999) 'Introduction: improving work, health and productivity through stress prevention', in M. Kompier and C. Cooper (eds) *Preventing Stress, Improving Productivity. European Case Studies in the Workplace*, London: Routledge.

Landsbergis, P.A., Cahill, J. and Schnall, P. (1999) 'The impact of lean production and related new systems of work organization on worker health', *Journal of Occupational Health Psychology*, 4, 2, 108–30.

Lundgren, K. (1999) 'Kortare lärotider och ett nytt lärandesystem' (Shorter learning times and a new learning system), *Arbetsmarknad Arbetsliv*, 5, 4, 287–302.

Maslach, C. and Leiter, M.P. (1997) *The Truth about Burnout. How Organizations Cause Personal Stress and What to Do about It*, San Francisco: Jossey-Bass.

Merllié, D. and Paoli, P. (2000) *Ten Years of Working Conditions in the European Union. Summary*, Dublin: European Foundation for the Improvement of Living and Working Conditions.

Mohrman, S.A. and Cohen, S.G. (1995) 'When people get out of the box. New relationships, new systems', in A. Howard (ed.) *The Changing Nature of Work*, San Francisco: Jossey-Bass.

Murphy, R. and Cooper, C.L. (eds) (2000) *Healthy and Productive Work. An International Perspective*, London: Taylor & Francis.

Reich, R. (1994) *Arbetsmarknad inför 2000-talet* (The Labour Market in the Twenty-first Century), Stockholm: SNS.

Reich, R. (2000) *The Future of Success*, New York: Alfred E. Knopf.

Schumann, M., Baethge-Kinsky, V., Kuhlmann, M., Kurz, C. and Neumann, U. (1995) 'New production concepts and the restructuring of work', in W. Littek and T. Charles (eds) *The New Division of Labor. Emerging Forms of Work Organization in International Perspective*, Berlin: Walter de Gruyter.

Shani, A.B. (Rami) and Mitki, Y. (2000) 'Creating the learning organization. Beyond mechanisms', in R. Golembiewski (ed.) *Handbook of Organizational Consultation*, New York: Marcel Dekker, pp. 911–19.

Taylor, P. and Bain, P. (1999) 'An assembly line in the head. Work and employee relations in the call centre', *Industrial Relations Journal*, 30, 2, 101–17.

Thorsrud, E. and Emery, F.E. (1969) *Medinflyttande och engagemang i arbete. Norsk försök med självstyrande grupper* (Participation and Engagement at Work. Norwegian Experiments with Semi-Autonomous Groups), Stockholm: Utvecklingsrådet för Samarbetsfrågor.

Wickham, J. (2000) 'Organizational change, work and ICTs', paper presented at the conference 'Towards a Learning Society', Lisbon.

Wikman, A. (2001) *Internationalisering, flexibilitet och förändrade företagsformer* (Internationalization, Flexibility and Changes in Company Structure), Stockholm: National Institute for Working Life; report series: Work Life in Transition 2001: 8.

2 *O tempora, O mores!*[1]

Work intensity – why again an issue?

Peter Brödner and Jan Forslin

Innovation and time saving

Technical artefacts have always been humankind's companions in work. For better or worse this dependency on technology is profound. Human ingenuity has helped ease the burden of work, made possible extraordinary achievements, where people surpass themselves – and saved time, which turned out to be a problematic aspect. Technology is a three-sided coin, as it contributes not only to intended problem solving but also to negative not intended social effects. The third side has to do with its potential for other benefits than those it was intended for. The outcome depends on values and creativity in the technical application, e.g. in terms of design of the work organization – there are always human choices. In that choice human rationality unfortunately tends to disregard human needs.

Hence there seem to be limitations in people's ability fully to utilize technical improvements to their own benefit. Increased productivity and implied time saving do not mean that the time pressure is reduced – rather the opposite. Let us take an obvious example. Crossing the Atlantic by steamboat took seven days, before the aeroplanes took over. The trip involved a comfortable life away from duties, time to relax and reflect and maybe some dancing and flirting – unless you were seasick. With a modern jet the travelling time has decreased by a factor of 24, but not to the benefit of the congested traveller. Business travellers seldom get an extra hour for themselves, but must utilize the time abroad effectively and hurry back home. They are not only even more harried than before, but also have to cope with jet lag, while carrying out a demanding job in a new environment. And back in the office a backlog is piling up with an e-mailbox beyond rescue. Something has gone very wrong!

A rediscovered problem

If one is to believe history, intensity of work has been a central issue in management science ever since the start of industrialization and a problematic one at that, as it captures the essence of the antagonism between the person who does the work and the person who wants it done; sometimes formulated as a conflict between capital and labour, inherent in the capitalistic industrial system. This perspective does not indicate many remedies apart from a proletarian revolution – still there would be conflicting interest. It is thus indicative that in Sweden problems related to work intensity are greatest in the tax financed public sector.

Intensity is becoming an ubiquitous phenomenon again and is now hitting new categories of employee. The actual working hours of highly qualified employees are increasing in many countries and there are innumerable reports on health risks and hazards due to stress and overload. In particular this is true for knowledge workers, who normally have a high degree of work autonomy. They form the fastest growing category of worker in modern economies. Work intensity is hazardous not only to the individual. It also has negative impacts on the performance of organizations and costs due to loss of knowledge, increased health care and early retirements.

The course of industrialization has experienced radical changes in the way work is designed and organized – from marked division of labour with bureaucratic co-ordination to decentralized organizations with widely autonomous units. Interestingly, these two ideal-types still coexist and compete even within the same technology, as reflected in the discussion on new craftsmanship and neo-Taylorism. With self-controlled jobs in decentralized organizations, where the buffer effect of management layers is reduced and market requirements almost directly hit the workers, slack tends to be diminished and work intensity to increase. Is intensity the price for autonomy?

Scientific management: controlling work intensity

Higher output in work processes can be achieved by either raised productivity or intensification of work. These two approaches are entirely different. Increasing productivity by implementing new, more efficient working methods and technical support means 'working smarter', whereas increased intensity means 'working harder' on the basis of the same operational procedures. Productivity is based on process innovations, while intensity merely heightens workforce utilization – again typical of the low-mechanized public sector and some white collar work.

The dynamics of industrial development started with the introduction of the horizontal division of labour according to the thinking of Adam Smith. The whole work process was split into a sequence of functionally specialized operations, to which specialized workers were allocated. This 'smarter' working proved to achieve a dramatic increase of productivity – as predicted – and also reduced the need for training. Moreover, the division of labour permitted extracting and refining knowledge on production processes and work operations that then could be externalized and objectified in production machinery. Charles Babbage applied the principles of the horizontal division of labour also to mental work – an almost unthinkable endeavour in his time, which led him to the invention of the basic computer architecture (Babbage 1835; Brödner 1990).

For the founding father of modern work management, Frederick W. Taylor, the intensity problem stood in the forefront. Believing in human rationality, he developed a systematic approach for studying and designing work – *scientific management*. This approach would meet the requirements of both management and workers, as it increased the productivity of the individual and at the same time protected him or her from being overworked (Taylor 1911). Ironically, these two issues have remained central in later applications of the ideas of scientific management. As Taylor later became the favourite scapegoat for industrial misery, there has been little interest in his pronounced concern for the workers: the control of work intensity.

The principles of scientific management promoted a vertical division of labour that formed a central column of the work design tradition. Taylor's approach was to separate conceptual from manual, to derive prescriptions of how to produce and of how long it should take. This separation of thinking from doing also created new forms of direct management control of work, the basis for the bureaucratic control typical of mass production – bureaucracy literally meaning that the power is with the office.

With his conception of the scientifically determined 'one best way' to work and produce, Taylor was rooted in the rationalistic tradition of the West. This tradition is built on the far reaching assumption that the world is fully comprehensible in objective terms and accordingly human behaviour can be explained by the functioning of machines. In the 1980s, the ambition of replacing humans by machines also in intellectual work culminated (so far) with computer integrated manufacturing systems (CIM), designed to eliminate the 'human error' factor – but also learning and experience – by computers.

Taylor's approach was, indisputably, extremely successful, but under specific historical circumstances. In stable markets for mass products, and products with simple production processes with few changes over time, the potential in the Tayloristic system can be exploited to a large extent. However, the advantage of stability became a drawback of rigidity, when market conditions required flexibility. In a highly dynamic environment difficult to grasp, with increasing complexity and rapid changes, only learning systems survive. These are dependent on human skills, experience and knowledge, in particular on the ability to learn and to act under uncertainty.

Conventional organizational structures based on division of labour are often found to be inappropriate to develop and fully use such skills. The Taylor model was based on simple tasks tied together and made effective by a complex organization. Growing flexibility requirements from a changing environment and more demanding functional specifications led to further differentiation and more co-ordinating efforts, resulting in an even more complex and rigid organization. This trend could only be broken by a fundamental shift of perspective – complex tasks in simple organizations.

Nevertheless, from Taylor's principles, a whole system of methods and procedures has developed to design work such that an average working person could perform it throughout his/her working life without health impairments. Even the unions accepted the model, despite opposition of workers against the harsh control, and learnt to use it as an instrument for controlling conditions of work – including work intensity. This was actually in line with Taylor's intentions.

The main concern was the quantitative aspect of work intensity, i.e. the amount of work to be performed per unit of time – pace and load of work. That work overload and health risks still can be found in Tayloristic work systems may be a consequence of insufficient knowledge and poor management rather than a system deficiency, not to be confused with its basic orientation.

The principal deficiencies of Taylorism showed up elsewhere. Standard operating procedures, at least in mass production, reduced human work to pure sensorimotor functions, deprived of any intellectual activities. In the long run, this one-sidedness had, counter to the original intentions, negative effects on the workers' skills and frequently led to psychosomatic reactions. Above all, this type of work stood in sharp contrast to the humanistic image of human beings and the quest for personal development. These were the essential reasons for the prolonged resistance of workers and for the emergence of the *socio-technical* approach as a more holistic alternative in the design tradition.

Socio-technical systems: self-managed intensity

Experiments with work intensity in Taylor's tradition during the 1920s and 1930s at Western Electric became unintentionally the point of departure for a direction that later would challenge, or rather supplement, Taylorism – the *human relations* school. More or less accidentally an understanding of the importance of the psychological needs of the employees, the informal organization and a human oriented leadership emerged from these initially strictly Tayloristic experiments. The platform was laid for modern personnel management.[2] Also, one important element for new work design was in place: the social psychological under-standing of work.[3]

As claimed by its proponents at the Tavistock Institute in London, the *socio-technical systems* school of organization (STS) aspired to merging Taylorism and human relations, neither of which single-handedly offered an alternative after the Second World War in a business world that demanded both efficiency in a turbulent environment and – in the light of an increasingly scarce and volatile labour force – decent working conditions. In particular the latter compon-ent was a determining motive for a large-scale application in Scandinavia of STS ideas from the 1960s (Forslin 1990).[4]

Reviews have frequently documented the success of organizations designed according to STS principles (e.g. Cummings and Shrivastra 1977; Pasmore *et al.* 1982; Kolodny and Stjernberg 1986; Shani and Elliot 1989; Forslin 1990; Taylor and Felten 1993). The design of work and technology in the STS tradition led to enlargement and enrichment of working tasks by reintegration of functions into complete tasks. These comprehensive tasks with a wide scope of action were accomplished by self-managing teams with specific production goals (e.g. Ulich 1994). The autonomous working group, implying empowerment and an end to job dequalification, was in ideological accord, albeit disputed, with the ideas of a more demo-cratic working life in the welfare state. The group became an often unreflected panacea for all, but most frequently social, illnesses.

Self-management encompassed organization of work by the teams, control over pace and planning, i.e. fundamental aspects of work intensity. Apart from vague assumptions that a well-treated and motivated workforce would work 'better', work intensity was, however, ini-tially seldom central in most applications of STS thinking. In the design of Volvo's Kalmar factory in the early 1970s, top management economic requirements were restricted to 'at least maintained' level of productivity (AB Volvo, pers. com.). However, a closer look at the sup-posedly highly productive assembly line had also shown that the time waste was substantial, when taking the whole system into consideration (Wild 1975). There was a quest for increased productivity, but with a smarter working than Taylor's approach (Swedish Employers' Confederation, pers. com.).

However, enlarged work cycles for increased work content reduced the small involuntary pauses from waiting times and intensity of work increased. Delegation of indirect tasks to the group added to the workload. In addition the increased discretion over work pace often resulted in forced work, self-induced or from group pressure, during most of the shift and then idle waiting the last one and a half hours. It is appropriate here to remember Taylor's exam-ple of Schmidt carrying pig iron. His vastly increased productivity was achieved only by compulsory rest pauses.

An important factor for the socio-technical development was the interest in human work motivation triggered by the human relations movement. In pace with its diminishing explana-tory value, the notion of 'economic man' (Drucker 1939) was supplemented by psychological theories on human nature. One criticism against Taylorism was that it systematically frus-trated work-related psychological needs. The implication was that there was a potential for improved performance, if only workers were given a chance. As Douglas McGregor (1960) once claimed, work is natural to all men – if intrinsically motivating. There was a strong emancipatory streak in the search for a new work organization.

In the 1950s a number of authors such as Abraham Maslow (1957) and Fredrick Herzberg (Herzberg *et al.* 1959; Herzberg 1966) published theories on what motivates people to work – apart from money. These theories, emphasising the intrinsic motivation of work, had an important impact on STS thinking, and Fred Emery and Einar Thorsrud (Emery and

Thorsrud 1969) formulated six psychological job demands. These criteria gave the engineers guidance on the social system for their work design in addition to the technical and economical requirements. What was not seen in the discussion on work motivation and new work design was the health risk to the over-motivated and highly committed worker.

Economic and human values

Without economic demands, work intensity would hardly be a problem. The trick is to please both the need for productivity and human welfare, which the STS approach regarded as compatible in an appropriate work organization. Historically the issue had actually been present to the major thinkers, although the assumptions about values and the view on efficiency vary over time, tentatively summarized in Table 2.1.

Table 2.1 Economy and welfare

	Economic objectives	Social values
Adam Smith	Productivity by horizontal division of labour	Subsistence
Scientific management	Rationalization of work Reduced strife	Material welfare Reduced human wear
Human relations	Productivity by social consideration	Fulfilling social needs
Socio-technical systems	External efficiency Internal self-regulation	Fulfilling psychological job demands
Sustainable work systems	Competitiveness	Generative use of human and social resources

In Maslowian terms the development can be seen as a journey from satisfaction of basic physiological needs to intrinsic motivation and a need for self-actualization. The impression today is that at least some segments of the economy might have managed too well in creating stimulating work, which makes intensive work systems partly an issue of over-motivated participants or self-generated intensity. A recent survey in Sweden shows that 46 per cent of employees in the IT sector experience stress due to their own demands, while only 4 per cent are stressed by direct employer demands (*Computer Sweden* 21 2001). According to another survey one-third have daily contact with the workplace even during vacation time, checking email and wanting to know what is going on (*Metro* 36 2001). Self-induced stress is probably a real issue in many qualified jobs. The ambition here is to formulate models of sustainable work systems, which then would add the final lines to Table 2.1. This ambition raises the profound question of what – if any – psycho-biological processes are regenerative to human energy and how should work then be designed, organized and managed in order to promote these processes and still or because of that stay competitive.

Internalization of the markets as intensity risk

Dramatic changes during the last decades have forced companies to review their organizational structures and procedures. Markets have undergone turbulent movements with enforced competition in the wake of deregulation. New business opportunities develop, in particular in the field of ICT technologies, and with globalization new competitors are stepping on stage even in traditional businesses. Moreover, knowledge usable for new products, services and processes is expanding, although it is also getting more and more fragmented into different knowledge domains, disciplines and professional communities. This adds up to widely increased complexity in markets, products and processes that causes high levels of uncertainty in work and leads to a growing number of contingent and conflicting requirements.

As a response, a whole set of management doctrines has appeared in public discourse: e.g. 'lean production', 'business process re-engineering', 'total quality management', 'agile manufacturing'. More than thirty such doctrines compete for management's attention by presenting themselves as radical and necessary alternatives in the new world of business. In this confusing 'sloganeering' most managers have already lost overview and orientation. The concepts labelled in this diversity often lack theoretical foundation or merely present well-known organizational principles with new labels. There are only a few serious efforts to systematically analyse and compare the diverse conceptions and strategies.

Proponents of these doctrines claim that the leap from Taylorism and mass production is big and difficult – although some cases appear as mere extensions of Tayloristic thinking. However, at a closer look many of the original STS ideas can be recognized in these doctrines, such as team-based work with emphasis on flexibility, skill formation and problem solving directly on the operational level. Many of the doctrines share the idea of *process management* focusing on work activities – as Taylor once did – and creating value for customers. The latter is a contribution from the *quality movement* as developed by Juran (e.g. 1989) and Deming (e.g. 1986), whose success with Japanese industry by focusing on the customer and involving workers in continuous improvements initially stunned Western managers (e.g. Axelsson and Bergman 1999). These ideas would be copied and transformed into the new management approaches. Sweden, like many Western countries, had been dominated by the rationalization movement and would only during the 1980s hesitantly detect the customer. Interestingly, out of the Japanese experiences the doctrine of *lean production* developed (Womack, Jones and Roos 1990), which in many cases has been associated with intensive work (e.g. Sandberg 1995).

However, at least in a minority of organizations on the 'high road' of innovation (Brödner *et al.* 1998), new forms of work organization are presently practised in a more sophisticated way, corresponding to the design criteria of the socio-technical approach. However, as mentioned, the price for autonomy is often intensity. With highly autonomous units and the striving for integration, important management functions now disappear as separate activities. In the hierarchical and functionally divided organization, these functions served as a filter between the competitive and market requirements and the actual work processes. With the new organizational forms this buffering is removed. Accordingly, workers find themselves under pressure and heavy workload, coping with quality problems and process disturbances, in meeting delivery dates or in dealing with conflicts and customer complaints.

This workload and situated stress imposed from outside are frequently further increased by self-induced workload and stress on the part of the (knowledge) workers. Staff functions are bifurcated into decentralization of functions close to the workflow, while also strengthening the advanced specialist knowledge. In addition, there is a movement to counter the effects of functional specialization by integrating contributions from various areas such as design and production (Andreasen and Hein 1986; Wheelwright and Clark 1992). Integration and concurrency in processes like product development with simultaneous rather than sequential steps increase intensity in engineering work.

This development towards 'internalization of the market' (Moldaschl and Sauer 2000) turns out to be an important source of intensity. With good intentions and the ambition to provide more challenging work, while also meeting a turbulent environment and optimizing in a complex business situation, conditions are moving towards unacceptable work intensity. Newspapers are full of complaints not only about burnouts and early retirements among high performance workers, but also about mistakes, failures and poor quality in products and services. It seems as if productivity is maintained at a high price.

A new world of work: from intensive to sustainable work systems?

Various expressions of growing intensity associated with new forms of work organization can partly be traced to a common cause: the relaxation of the delimitation of work processes of the Tayloristic world. The new management doctrines are shedding 'confinements'. Many tasks have high prescriptions, but low limitation and only limited design, in order to ensure flexibility. Strict time regulations are no longer possible and work processes can no more be prescribed in detail. In addition, a complex and non-transparent technology raises uncertainty and surplus effort in use. This complex and unpredictable situation undermines the traditional basis for controlling intensity and balancing workload with available resources.

The 'lean nineties' meant cutting resources – human and other – by slimming, outsourcing, and increasing time pressures. The intended effect was to do more with the same time resources, including more simultaneous handling of several tasks. Work roles are made more flexible, but also more ambiguous and with conflicting demands. Partly due to reduced resources and haste, but also because of premature releases and insufficient implementation time, a low-transparent ICT technology often contains flaws. This has marked negative consequences for quality, causing delays, delivery problems, time pressure and overtime in the operations the nationalization techniques and poorly tested ICT applications are designed to facilitate, with aggravated effects due to intolerance for delays under just-in-time requirements.

Teamwork means sharing workload and reduced stress, but is also a source of harassment and conflict. Group pressures demand considerable social competence. Mental overload easily causes frictions with colleagues and impairs the ability for co-operation and collective learning requiring trust. Social tensions reduce efficiency, slow down work, enlarge the risk of errors and ultimately increase costs. In cases of burnout and early retirement, the organization suffers from losses of experience and expertise difficult to replace.

In the project organization the individual is subject to simultaneous and independent demands from several internal or external clients. Work entails running between meetings, each triggering high commitment and resulting in additional tasks and pledges. Over the day this process accumulates and unfulfilled promises bring the level of unrelieved arousal beyond natural recovery.

Learning and continuous improvement are demands on top of productive work. Competence development outside working hours is expected. Organizations are in a continuous flux entailing instability and uncertainty. In addition, employees experience discontinuity and unpredictability induced by frequent changes in policy and management philosophy.

Intensification of work is generated partly by its social environment, partly by the work process itself. Human and social resources in the workplace are being depleted, impairing the ability of the social system to maintain – let alone regenerate – its productive forces to cope with the demands imposed on work. A mismatch between job requirements and available resources creates severe health risks and negative socio-economic consequences.

On the human side, these conditions lead to dissatisfaction, feelings of inadequacy, poor climate and conflicts, low tolerance for mistakes, lowered capacity and absenteeism. Health problems such as physical strain and wear, psychosomatic illnesses and stress cause exhaustion, disablement, chronic tiredness and in severe cases burnout.

Social relations outside work deteriorate (Sennett 1998). Tiredness, absence through overtime, working at home and difficulty in relaxing infringe the climate at home. The prime resource for support and recovery turns into a source of frustration and an impaired quality of family life may lead to unforeseeable risks for the well-being of the children. All in all, the space and ability for *savoir vivre* become seriously reduced, as Burenstam Linder (1970) was already warning in the 1970s. Today's detailed and complete time orientation was entirely unknown in the ancient world. To be in a hurry was as alien to the ideals of the citizen in Athens as it was to the dignity of the Roman. A free man did not hasten from place to place; there was something slavish about rushing (Eriksen 2000).

Regeneration of resources

There are thus strong reasons for us free citizens to look for a remedy in alternative ways of organizing and re-regulating work, so that human and social resources are maintained or even regenerated in work. Accordingly, the very first issue is whether work has inevitably to be consuming; or rather, to identify social and psycho-biological processes that regenerate human energy – at least in the long run. It is all right to be exhausted after work; a powerful push at work may make a person feel stronger, healthier, more energetic and more complete as a human being, provided that it is limited in time and there is room for recovery. For the same reason being entirely immersed in a challenging and creative work process can be exhausting and invigorating at the same time. With some optimism it can be assumed that humans are designed for work, profoundly productive and creative and that favourable social relations foster personal growth. Work should then not only be satisfactory, but invigorating and salutary (Kira 2000).

Since research on sensory deprivation started in the 1950s (e.g. Zubeck 1969), 'optimal level of stimulation' has become a crucial notion in the area of stress research. There is a craving for stimulation and when deprived, higher mental functions do not develop or even deteriorate, emotionally accompanied by depression similar to the anaclitic depression in neglected infants (Spitz 1946). In the world of work more challenging tasks for the sensory deprived on the assembly line has been a staple for reforms. However, as pointed out, the negative consequences of over-stimulation due to mental work overload are an increasing problem. What is 'optimal' varies among individuals and is also affected by learning and competence development, as addressed in later stress research (Karasek and Theorell 1990; Karasek 1997). Growth of knowledge and personal mastery help in coping with stress, as they raise the stress threshold and provide a sense of control.

There is also something about goal directedness driving us humans. To accomplish what one has intended is intrinsically rewarding. Being productive is in a psychological sense to utilize one's resources in a meaningful and successful way (e.g. Meissner 1997). Unfortunately work today is often characterized by constant side-tracking and distractions from the main goals. Completion, goal realization and finalizing have to be postponed again and again, an uneconomical process, that requires repeated and psychologically draining restarts. The psychologist Zeigarnik (1927) once demonstrated that uncompleted tasks stay with us, preoccupying memory and attention, while completed ones, having a *Gestalt*, are dumped and do not bother us any more. It is less the victories and more the defeats that we remember. A healthy work situation should let us concentrate on fewer things and allow the pleasure of having completed some – to be victorious.

A concept connecting to optimal stimulation, but also bearing on splitting of attention, is 'flow experience'. Csikszentmihalyi (1990) defined this as enjoyment growing from the continuous mastery over what happens in one's consciousness. A way of handling over-exposure to external stimuli is selection, a foundation for mastery of the consciousness and possibly the enjoyment in any situation (Kira 2000 and Chapter 5). Some elements of a flow experience are identified: first, a clear focus on a challenging task that requires skills, while action and awareness are emerging: second, having clear goals and receiving feed-back, concentrating on the task at hand. The third is a special feeling of control, with a loss of self-consciousness and the linear meaning of time. Csikszentmihalyi maintains that flow can be experienced in work either through the character of work itself or by learning to create a flow experience.

'Shared burden is half burden, shared joy is double joy', as the Nordic Havamal so tersely puts it. Humans are gregarious. Sympathetic and rewarding relations to colleagues and friends are central to well-being. Social support is essential to reduced stress, learning from others an opportunity, and help from others an indispensable asset, provided that work leaves enough room for developing good social relations. As groups and teams are presently evolv-ing in most businesses and on all organizational levels, this can be turned into a productive source for recovery.

Based on this reasoning, the nature of *sustainable work systems* (SWS) can, in contrast to inten-sive work, be characterized as allowing the workers involved to maintain health and to regenerate their human and social resources while utilizing them. This means that work processes allow development of personal skills and competence as well as collective expertise in 'communities of practice', to recover from tiring workload, to develop sound relations to colleagues as a 'culture of dialogue', and to stay open for other experiences of life outside work.

The transition towards sustainable work systems may require a resource-centred perspec-tive of work; see Chapter 5. Since the consumption or regeneration of human and social resources are regarded as a central issue in discriminating intensive from sustainable work sys-tems, the conditions under which they may develop or else rather degenerate are crucial for the transition. In terms of the structuration theory approach (Giddens 1984), intensity is basi-cally caused by a misfit or imbalance of high demands and prescriptions of work on one hand and inadequately developed rules and resources in the collective acting of the working on the other. This imbalance is experienced as loss of control and leads to consumption of individ-ual and social resources that could otherwise be re-created. The point of intervention, therefore, must be a review and redesign of work processes with new rules and resources.

According to this wider perspective on what may be called *salutary work*, three levels of social sustainability should be considered in conceptualizing and designing sustainable work systems. Resources need to be regenerated:

*   at the personal level, e.g. knowledge, skills and competence, health and well-being (worker perspective);
*   at the organizational level, e.g. trust relations allowing for co-operation, collective exper-tise and learning allowing for innovation, and social recognition (enterprise perspective);
*   at the societal level, encompassing the interplay between work systems and social envir-onment with its institutions (societal perspective).

In order to achieve the characteristics of sustainable work systems, a new balance of reasonable demands and available resources has to be found by reconfining work on a higher level (see Chapter 5). This requires, since all changes of work inevitably produce unintended side effects, a reflexive approach to the development of new rules and resources (see Chapter 15). As pointed out in sketching the general lines of development in production systems, delimitation of work is presently, in spite of all institutional differences, to some degree an inescapable course of future growth, in particular in the enterprise perspective. Market forces call for more flexibility and faster responses to external events. Regression into old institutional arrangements and organizational schemes, therefore, is no bearable solution. What is needed then is a reflexive work design and institutional rearrangement that allows for confinement at higher levels and, thus, forms a sound basis for establishing sustainable work systems. The rapidly growing economic and social costs of intensity might foster this new orientation.

Notes

1 'O times, o morals!' From Cicero, then concerned about contemporary moral decline.
2 See Gillespie (1991) for a review of the Western Electric experiments and the origins of innovations in the wake of human relations.
3 It is both an encouraging and a depressing observation that a work from 1950 on modern industrial organization based on human relations thinking, *Are Workers Human?* by Gordon Rattway Taylor, still appears so modern.
4 The development in Sweden is analysed for example in Sandberg (1982) and Bäckström (1999). For an overview of concepts and developments within STS see van Eijnatten (1993) and for some of the classic articles see Pasmore and Sherwood (1978). Basic STS design principles are found in an article by Cherns (1987).

References

Andreasen, M.M. and Hein, L. (1986) *Integrert produktutvikling* (Integrated Product Development), Drammen: Tangen-Trykk A/S.
Axelsson, J.R.C. and Bergman, B. (1999) 'Att bygga och riva pyramider – offensiv kvalitets- och arbetsutveckling' (To build and pull down pyramids – active development of quality and work), in T. Nilson (ed.) *Ständig Förbättring – om utveckling av arbete och kvalitet* (Continous Improvement), Solna: Arbetslivsinstitutet.
Babbage, C. (1835) *On the Economy of Machinery and Manufactures*, London: Knight. Reprint New York: Kelley, 1971.
Bäckström, H. (1999) 'Den krattade manegen – svensk arbetsorganisatorisk utveckling under tre decennier' (The Prepared Manege: Swedish Development in Work Organization over Three Decades), doctoral thesis no. 79, Uppsala: Department of Business Studies, Uppsala University.
Brödner, P. (1990) *The Shape of Future Technology. The Anthropocentric Alternative*, London: Springer.
Brödner, P., Garibaldo, F., Oehlke, P. and Pekruhl, U. (1998) *Work Organisation and Employment. The Crucial Role of Innovation Strategies*, Project Report 1998–2005. Gelsenkirchen: IAT.
Burenstam Linder, S. (1970) *The Harried Leisure Class*, New York: Columbia University Press.
Cherns, A. (1987) 'Principles of sociotechnical design revisited', *Human Relations*, 40, 3, 153–62.
Computer Sweden, 21, 2001.
Csikszentmihalyi, M. (1990) *Flow. The Psychology of Optimal Experience*, New York: Harper & Row.
Cummings, T.G. and Shrivastra, S. (1977) *Management of Work. A Socio-technical Approach*, Kent, OH: Kent State University Press.
Deming, W.E. (1986) *Out of the Crisis*, Cambridge: Cambridge University Press.
Drucker, P. (1939) *The End of Economic Man*, London: Heinemann.

Emery, F.E. and Thorsrud, E. (1969) *Form and Content in Industrial Democracy*, London: Tavistock.

Emery, F.E. and Trist, E. (1969) 'Socio-technical systems', in F. Emery (ed.) *Systems Thinking*, Hammondsworth: Penguin.

Eijnatten, F.M. van (1993) *The Paradigm that Changed the Work Place*, Stockholm: Arbetslivscentrum.

Eriksen, T.B. (2000) *Tidens historia* (History of Time), Stockholm: Atlantis.

Forslin, J. (1990) *Det klippta bandet. En Volvo-industri byter kultur* (The Cut Line. A Volvo Industry Changes Culture), Stockholm: Norstedts.

Giddens, A. (1984) *The Constitution of Society. Outline of the Theory of Structuration*, Cambridge: Polity Press.

Gillespie, R. (1991) *Manufacturing Knowledge. A History of the Hawthorne Experiments*, Cambridge: Cambridge University Press.

Herzberg, F. (1966) *Work and Nature of Man*, Cleveland and New York: World Publ. Co.

Herzberg, F., Mausner, B. and Snyderman, B. (1959) *Motivation to Work*, New York: Wiley.

Juran, J.M. (1989) *Juran on Leadership for Quality. An Executive Handbook*, New York: Free Press.

Karasek, R. (1997) 'Demand/control model. A social, emotional, and psychological approach to stress risk and active behavior development', in J.M. Stellman (ed.) *Encyclopaedia of Occupational Health and Safety*, 4th edn, Geneva: International Labour Organization.

Karasek, R. and Theorell, T. (1990) *Healthy Work. Stress, Productivity, and the Reconstruction of Working Life*, New York: Basic Books.

Kira, M. (2000) *From Intensive Work Systems to Sustainable. A Literature Review*, Stockholm: Department of Industrial Economics and Management, Royal Institute of Technology.

Kolodny, H. and Stjernberg, T. (1986) 'The change process of innovative work designs. New design and redesign in Sweden, Canada and the US', *Journal of Applied Behavioral Science*, 22, 287–301.

McGregor, D. (1960) *The Human Side of the Enterprise*, New York: McGraw-Hill.

Maslow, A. (1957) *Motivation and Personality*, New York: Harper.

Meissner, W.W. (1997) 'The self and the principle of work', in C.W. Socarides and S. Kramer (eds) *Work and its Inhibitions. Psychoanalytic Essays*, Madison, CT: International University Press.

Metro, 36, 2001.

Moldaschl, M. and Sauer, D. (2000) 'Internalisierung des Marktes – Zur neuen Dialektik von Kooperation und Herrschaft', in H. Minssen (ed.) *Begrenzte Entgrenzungen. Wandlungen von Organisation und Arbeit* (Limited Limitations. Changes in Organization and Work), Berlin: Edition Sigma.

Pasmore, W.A. (1988) *Designing Effective Organisations. The Socio-Technical Systems Perspective*, Chichester: Wiley.

Pasmore, W.A., Francis, C. and Shani, A.B. (1982) 'Socio-technical systems', *Human Relations*, 35, 1179–204.

Pasmore, W.A. and Sherwood, J.J. (eds) (1978) *Sociotechnical System. A Sourcebook*, La Jolla, CA: University Associates.

Reich, R.B. (1991) *The Work of Nations*, New York: Knopf.

Sandberg, Å. (ed.) (1995) *Enriching Production. Perspectives on Volvo's Uddevalla Plant as an Alternative to Lean Production*, Aldershot: Avebury.

Sandberg, T. (1982) *Work Organization and Autonomous Groups*, Lund: Liber Förlag.

Sekaran, U. (1986) *Dual-Career Families. Contemporary Organizational and Counseling Issues*, San Francisco: Jossey-Bass.

Sennett, R. (1998) *The Corrosion of Character*, New York: Norton.

Shani, A.B. and Elliot, O. (1989) 'Sociotechnical system design in transition', in W. Sikes, A.B. Drexler and J. Grant (eds) *The Emerging Practice of Organization Development*, La Jolla, CA: University Associates, pp. 187–98.

Spitz, R.A. (1946) 'Anaclitic depression', *Psychoanalytic Study of the Child*, 2, 313–42.

Taylor, F.W. (1911) *The Principles of Scientific Management*, New York: Harper & Brothers.

Taylor, G.R. (1950) *Are Workers Human?* London: Falcon Press.

Taylor, J.C. and Felten, D.F. (1993) *Performance by Design. Sociotechnical Systems in North America*, Englewood Cliffs, NJ: Prentice-Hall.

Ulich, E. (1994) *Arbeitspsychologie* (Work Psychology), 3rd edn, Stuttgart: Poeschel and Zürich: vdf.

Watzlawick, P., Weakland, J. and Fish, R. (1974) *Principles of Problem Formation and Problem Resolution*, London: Norton.

Wheelwright, S.C. and Clark, B. (1992) *Revolutionizing Product Development*, New York: Free Press.

Wikström, S., Normann, R., Anell, B., Ekvall, G., Forslin, J. and Skärvad, P.-H. (1994) *Knowledge and Value. A New Perspective on Corporate Transformation*, London: Routledge.

Wild, R. (1975) *Work Organization. A Study of Manual Work and Mass Production*, London: Wiley.

Womack, J.P., Jones, D.T. and Roos, D. (1990) *The Machine that Changed the World. The Story of Lean Production*, New York: Macmillan.

Zeigarnik, B. (1927) 'Über das Behalten von erledigten und unerledigten Handlungen' (On the retention of completed and non-completed actions), *Psychol. Forsch.*, 9, 1–85.

Zubeck, J.P. (ed.) (1969) *Sensory Deprivation. Fifteen Years of Research*, New York: Appleton-Century-Crofts.

Part 2

Perspectives

Alternative disciplinary lenses

Part 1 provided the objectives, motivations and framing for this book. The argument was advanced that the emerging context of work sets the stage for the two central concepts of our study, namely intensive and sustainable work. As such it provided the grounding in the key research issues, the economic profile of globalization and its impact, emerging working conditions, the historical evolutionary dimension of work and work intensity and key definitions of concepts.

This section of the book – *Perspectives* – is intended to present five different disciplinary lenses: individual-focused perspective, work organization-based perspective, resources-based perspective, complexity-based perspective and institution-based perspective. Each chapter, being anchored in a different discipline, provides theoretical grounding, a view on intensive and sustainable work systems and identification and definition of key concepts. As such, a wide range of conceptual frameworks, ideas and lenses are presented.

Chapter 3, 'Moving from consuming to regenerative', provides an individual-focused perspective. This chapter discusses how work intensity leads to the consumption of human resources, while in a sustainable work system (SWS) human resources are allowed to grow and develop. SWS are, consequently, characterized by regenerative work, that contains possibilities for current moments of enjoyment, but also supports and creates individual potential for future coping with the challenges of work. The sense of coherence concept provides an example of psychological resources underlying coping and the flow concept explains enjoyment at work.

Chapter 4, 'Sources of intensity in work organizations', provides a work organization-based perspective. In this chapter 'intensity' at work is defined as a potential logic of 'unconfined' jobs. Job 'confinement' is the process (rules, techniques, interactions) by which organizations limit the cognitive and social needs of work. Hence, 'unconfined' jobs tend to require broad cognitive abilities (making personal inferences and re-combining existing means of action) which are difficult to learn and assess. They will also imply the instability of interpersonal and professional work relations. Therefore typical good symptoms of 'intensity' are a permanent need for re-learning and re-socializing. The expansion of unconfined jobs is clearly a deeply rooted trend in contemporary socio-economic contexts. This means that the main source of intensity at work is not some new psychic attachment to the organization. Intensity is a consequence and an indicator of deep changes in the nature of work definition itself. These ideas are illustrated using the concept of *self-management* defined as the process through which these workers elaborate the artefactual definition and boundaries of their job. One of the advantages of this conceptual framework is that it clarifies the need for collective or personal 'reconfining' policies to reduce intensity while maintaining work performance. Such policies are a first step towards a more general approach of SWS.

Chapter 5 provides a resource-based perspective. This chapter presents a resource-centred theoretical perspective on the utilization of the workforce and challenges well-known models of human-centred organization and design. It argues that the concepts proposed for decades to overcome the logic and the problems of Taylorism and Fordism had turned into a major source of workforce problems themselves. An alternative analytical perspective is presented describing how to evaluate the sustainability of organizational practices for the workforce, the organization itself and the institutional and social context in terms of human, social and cultural resources.

Chapter 6, 'A complexity perspective', discusses sustainable work systems using the metaphor of complexity, using a holistic way of looking at reality, in which the object of study is not divided into parts, but is left completely intact. An SWS strives towards development at different levels, and is a system constantly 'on the move'. These two features explain why the lens of complexity is viable when discussing sustainability. It enables simultaneous inclusion of all different system levels and focuses on the dynamics of the system. Three central features of SWS, seen as holons, are described: alignment of individuals, coping with environmental change and fitness development for competitiveness.

Chapter 7, 'The institutional contexts', presents an institution-based perspective. This chapter discusses the influence of institutional frameworks on work intensity and sustainability. It tries to make sense of the general observation among students of work that, despite decades of internationalization and the transfer of 'best practices' in organization, different countries keep on exhibiting marked variation in work organization and job contents. In order to do so, the chapter combines neo-institutional and neo-contingent insights to produce a political economy of work organization (i.e. labour market legislation, unionization and industrial relations).

3 Moving from consuming to regenerative work

Mari Kira[1]

Introduction

During the past decades, we have witnessed profound changes in economy, technology, society and, consequently, at work. New kinds of jobs are created and traditional occupations are transformed. In Sweden, the developments in the so-called new economy and the 'old' economy are widely discussed, and what seem to cause astonishment are the effects the developments have on people as employees. Both stress statistics (e.g. Wingborg 2000) and public discussion reveal an almost epidemic stress phenomenon. It seems that we are creating a world where quite a few of us will not be able to live happy, productive lives.

This chapter discusses consuming and regenerative work. The focal question is how to create work that regenerates, rather than consumes, employees' resources in the contemporary working life? Regenerative work at the individual level of sustainable work systems is important, since the other levels of sustainability are founded on individuals' sustainable development. Long-term sustainability at group, organizational and societal levels builds on the well-being and development of individuals and their continuous ability to face new challenges and deal with them alone and collectively. Furthermore, sustainability at individual level – the regeneration of invested personal resources – is simply a human right. Work should lead to the growth rather than to the consumption of psychological resources. Sustainable work systems, by definition, do not make trade-offs between organizational results and people. They differ from non-sustainable systems by the holistic aim for concurrent development and growth at all system levels (see Chapter 6 below).

Reasons for human resources consumption

Based on a literature review reported and an ongoing study, Kira (2000, 2001) concluded that human resources seem to be consumed in the contemporary working life – rather than regenerated. Consumption takes place at psychological, physical and emotional levels, and leads to experienced stress and exhaustion. The reasons for the human resources consumption are varied. Some of the most profound reasons are captured in Figure 3.1.

First, human resources become consumed when too few resources are allocated for the job to be done. See e.g. Delbridge (1998), O'Donnell *et al.* (1998) and Landsbergis *et al.* (1999) on incidences in different sectors. Hobfoll (1998) categorizes possible resources in four groups: object, personal, condition and energy resources. For instance, when too few people are assigned to take care of a certain work process, they may initially seem to be able to handle the situation. People have the ability to stretch, to accommodate the situation. The problems show, however, in the long term in terms of exhaustion. The invested resources have become

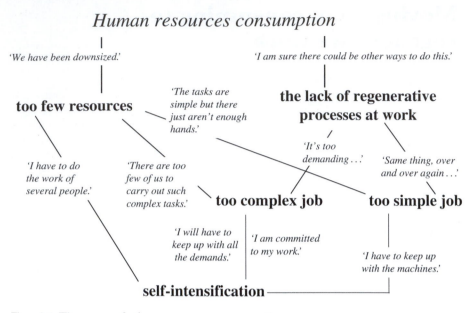

Figure 3.1 The reasons for human resources consumption.

consumed. For an organization, providing adequate human resources for each task is maybe the most basic way to support employees in their work. The problem, of course, is to determine what 'adequate human resources' means in the 'boundaryless' jobs that are not delimited by time and space or by traditional bureaucratic structures, rules and boundaries – the situation one often encounters in jellyfish-like IT companies (Kira 2001; Chapters 4 and 6 below).

The lack of regenerative processes at work also leads to human resources consumption. Work may be designed in a way that does not allow an employee to learn and develop, or 'reload' and recuperate at work. Earlier, work science emphasized autonomy as the key element of good work (e.g. Thorsrud and Emery 1969; Lindström 1994; Vartiainen 1994). The opportunity to use different kinds of skills according to one's discretion as well as an opportunity to decide how and when to work were perceived to lead to balanced, versatile jobs in which employees are able to develop. The recent changes in working life have left us wondering, however, whether intensity is the price for autonomy. Even in a boundaryless and autonomous work, business imperatives and external demands may allow only for certain types of individually consuming choices (i.e. self-intensification in the context of too complex jobs). Finally, the problems with work design do not only relate to excessive complexity of jobs; there still are jobs that are standardized, simple and repetitive. Instead of burnout – the overtax on individuals' resources – we witness 'rust-out', the consequence of undertax (see Hobfoll 1998). Empirical research in Europe (e.g. Schumann *et al.* 1995; Huys *et al.* 1999) indicates that Taylorism is still alive with its negative consequences on employees.

All in all, consuming work can be understood as work that is not in balance with the person carrying out that work. Above, imbalance has been discussed in terms of needed resources and available resources as well as the challenges of work and need to learn, develop and recuperate. Maslach and Leiter (1997) note that burnout (as a severe case of human resources consumption – the erosion of soul, as they call it) is more likely when there is an imbalance between, for instance, an employee's resources and workload; an employee's need for control and available possibilities for choices, decisions, innovativeness, etc.; work effort and rewards; an employee's need for positive social contacts and possibility for living in a true community; the right to be treated fairly within the workplace; as well as accord between an employee's values and the company's values.

It is, thus, clear that the unsustainable situation of human resources consumption has several sources and these sources differ from one work situation to another. There cannot be, consequently, any 'best practice' solution to the problem. It is necessary to start from the basics and see why human resources are consumed in a particular work system and how regenerative processes could replace the consumption. Prescriptions and paradigms for organizational structures must make way for the understanding of the different processes at individual, group, organization and community levels that contribute to the human resources regeneration.

Regenerative work – coping with challenges and enjoyment at work

In this chapter, the aim is to see how work can offer opportunities for well-being and enjoyment and, above all, for the creation of individual resources enabling coping with the challenges of working life. The underlying idea of our approach to the regenerative work is that life always contains a potential for stress and resources consumption. The negative aspects of life are not only unavoidable, but also vital: potential for growth lies in demanding situations, not when we are muffled in a daydream-like reality. Consequently, as negative experiences cannot and *should* not be avoided, our personal and collective resources that enable dealing with potentially negative situations become invaluable. Happiness and growth emerge not only from what the world is like, but also from how we deal with it, individually and collectively.

Truly good work enables not only positive experiences now, but also the development and growth of such psychological resources that make dealing with the world possible in future. In other words, whether work is good or not from an individual's point of view does not only depend on the qualities of the situation in question. Important also is what kind of a long-term effect work experiences have on an employee. The idea that good, regenerative work contributes to the growth of employees' personal resources has been present already in the traditional definitions of good work (e.g. good work should lead to professional development), but has been contradicted by the prescriptive tone in the applications of these definitions. For instance, the socio-technical systems tradition held autonomy as an essential element of good work. However, as the discussion in Chapters 4 and 5 indicates, autonomy does not directly equate to good work, but can also lead to stress and burnout. Consequently, good work cannot be defined simply as certain universal parameters of work, but rather each situation has to be considered separately and essential criteria for the quality of work are the long-term consequences of the situation in question. Autonomy, for example, is good only when it allows an individual to grow and develop in his/her work as well as creates such resources that the individual can use in the future when facing a demanding situation. Autonomy turns into a problem when its long-term consequence is a consumed employee.

In this chapter, we shall look at the interaction between an individual and his/her work in order to see how work experiences can support the development of psychological resources that underlie coping. As an example of such a resource, we shall discuss a person's world-image. Furthermore, we shall go a step beyond coping and explore a theory that discusses enjoyment at work.

The world-image and coping with work

A person's understanding of the world and his/her relation to the world have been distinguished as important psychological resources for coping with the world (see e.g. Murphy and Hurrell 1997; Ouellette 1997). The way a person perceives him/herself to be as well as the way he/she perceives the world to be (i.e. the world-image including self-image) affect the way the person is able to deal with the world. Below, we shall present some ideas about a world-image related coping. We shall also formulate some hypotheses on how work and work organization can support the development of such world-images that create potential for successful coping.

An interesting concept when considering world-image related coping is Antonovsky's (1979, 1987a, 1987b) *sense of coherence*. An individual's sense of coherence can be understood as a dispositional orientation, as a characteristic way to perceive the world (at least to some degree) as a comprehensible, manageable and meaningful place. Studies (see e.g. Antonovsky 1987a; Kalimo and Vuori 1990; Johansson Hanse and Engström 1999) indicate clearly that a higher sense of coherence, as a personal resource, increases the potential for health; people with a higher sense of coherence seem to move along the disease–health continuum towards the health end.

According to Antonovsky, the development of sense of coherence depends on the availability of different kinds of individual, material, social and cultural resources, in other words, *generalized resistance resources*. The availability of generalized resistance resources enables a person to make sense of the world. While potentially negative factors in the environment increase the disorder in a person's existence, generalized resistance resources make it instead possible for a person to try and create order in a seemingly disordered situation. The world starts to seem more and more understandable and manageable; the sense of meaningfulness of one's efforts in relation to the world increases. This process, little by little, creates sense of coherence. A person with a high sense of coherence is able to mobilize different generalized resistance resources as needed and is able to experience something comprehensible, manageable and meaningful in each new situation. In a way, sense of coherence can also be understood in the context of sense-making processes (see e.g. Weick 1995; Chapter 16 this volume). Sense of coherence is both a psychological resource that supports an individual when entering and engaging in (often complex and socially demanding) sense-making processes (as Antonovsky notes – sense of coherence supports an individual to make sense of the world) as well as a psychological outcome from the sense-making process – a more coherent, more sensible and meaningful understanding of the world starts to emerge.

Sense of coherence is a dispositional orientation; a person's quite stable, but nevertheless flexible, way to see the world. Thus, development is possible; experiences and reflections enable an individual to learn to know him/herself and, eventually, to change and develop. As Fontana (2000, p. 14) writes: 'The capacity to change during adult life seems to depend a great deal on the conscious effort we make to work on ourselves.'

Sense of coherence is an existing psychological resource, but also a resource that may grow and develop during the adult life through experience and reflection – through learning. This provides the grounds for the usefulness of sense of coherence concepts. The patterns of our experiences – whether characterized by lack or plentifulness of resources, coherence or incoherence – may in the long term lead to gradual personal growth or deterioration.

Furthermore, the possibility to reflect on the experiences, to learn from them is important. Also, Antonovsky encourages research on working conditions' influence on employees' sense of coherence (1987b, p. 159): 'By asking an individual worker [. . .] how working conditions contribute to their feelings in regard to comprehensibility, manageability, and meaningfulness, a better understanding can be gained of the health consequences of work'.

In Figure 3.2 we suggest a hypothesis on how an organization can support the development of its employees' sense of coherence and how sense of coherence supports an individual's coping. First, an organization can provide material, cultural and social resources to its employees – in other words, 'objective' generalized resistance resources that employees may benefit from in their work. An organization may also consciously aim to create work experiences characterized by comprehensibility, manageability and meaningfulness to support employees' coherent experiences. The 'objective' resources also contribute to the comprehensibility, manageability and meaningfulness of work. All this may support employees' sense of coherence. High sense of coherence, in its turn, enables the employees to perceive and mobilize existing resources. Similarly, high sense of coherence enables the employees to see comprehensibility, manageability and meaningfulness even in a difficult work situation. Finally, if an employee is able to perceive his/her work as comprehensible, manageable and meaningful, he/she is also very likely to be able to cope with it. The challenges of work are faced with successful tension management.

Consequently, an organization providing its employees with resources corresponding to the demands of work (cf. Karasek and Theorell 1990) and the needs of employees (cf. Thorsrud and Emery 1969), as well as aiming to create comprehensible, manageable and meaningful work experiences, supports its employees. This kind of support relates to the work situation at hand, but expands also to the future. Resources and 'coherent' work experiences, in the long term, contribute to the development of sense of coherence. The hypothesis presented indicates several interesting research questions. First, how is it possible for an organization to

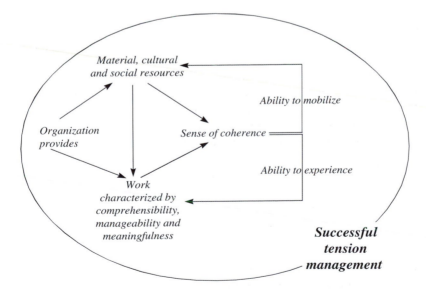

Figure 3.2 An organization supporting its employees' sense of coherence and coping – successful tension management (see also Antonovsky 1979, 1987b).

provide its employees with necessary resources? How are the resource needs of employees identified and what is the process for providing them with, often scarce, resources? Furthermore, how is it possible to ensure employees' possibility to effectively use the resources they have at their disposal (Hobfoll 1998)? These questions are also raised elsewhere in this book, in Chapter 5. A second important question relates to the comprehensibility, manageability and meaningfulness of work – what does comprehensible, manageable and meaningful work mean and how can it be created?

In a comprehensible situation employees perceive that they receive ordered, consistent, structured and clear information on the work situation and, consequently, can predict the way things proceed (Antonovsky 1987a, 1987b). When a work situation is comprehensible, it makes sense both emotionally and cognitively, and an employee understands the connections of his/her work to the whole work process. In other words, employees receive enough information on the work situation to understand their role in it as well as to understand the context of their work and relationships between their work and the work of others.

Manageability relates to the resources available for coping with work situations (Antonovsky 1987a, 1987b). The resources available for employees should be in balance with the demands set by the situation: both overload and 'underload' of resources are bad. The overload on personal resources, for instance, decreases employees' belief that they can manage in the situation. Underload also creates feelings of low manageability. Employees with monotonous jobs start over time to feel that they will not be able to manage disruptions of even the most basic kind. Continuous underload thus causes a sort of mental paralysis in which employees' potential for complex task performance has been lost. Also formal and informal social structures at workplaces relate to the manageability of a situation. Employees should be able to trust that the formal social structure provides them with an appropriate environment and equipment to carry out their work well. For instance, the knowledge that other employees are also doing their work well creates a necessary condition for individual manageability. Furthermore, it is important for the employees to know that the informal social structure supports them when something goes wrong, that there is help available.

When an individual finds the work situation meaningful, he/she feels that demands encountered are worth an investment in energy, commitment and engagement, and as a consequence, will exert an effort to carry out his/her work (Antonovsky 1987a, 1987b). Sense of meaningfulness requires also that an employee can perceive the whole work process and his/her connections to it as meaningful. Furthermore, meaningfulness relates to the feelings of joy and pride at work. Joy and pride at work depend on the employees' own valuations of work, but also on the way society in general evaluates their work and work organization (cf. Hirschhorn 1988). Also both intrinsic and instrumental gratifications from work (e.g. internal work motivation and monetary rewards) increase the joy, pride and meaningfulness of work.

When we look at the comprehensibility, manageability and meaningfulness of work, it becomes obvious that resources provided by an organization contribute directly to all of them. The question is not, however, only about organizational resources but also about something else; for instance, about organizational values. To put it crudely, an organization cannot create comprehensible, manageable and meaningful work if it does not put these things on its agenda (of course, such values can also be understood as resources, as cultural resources). Furthermore, it seems that comprehensibility, manageability and meaningfulness cannot only be defined at organizational level, but also local self-design through dialogue (see Chapter 8) is needed. Understanding one's role in the organization as well as the organization's overarching goals (i.e. sense of comprehensibility) necessitates that these issues are continuously a subject of dialogue within work groups and between supervisors and employees. This is the case especially in the contemporary working life. Roles and jobs cannot be predetermined in changing organizations operating in rapidly changing environments; precise job descriptions cannot be written any more in boundaryless jobs that are formed by the choices of employees. What can be done, however, is to define the roles, goals and task priorities through continuous dialogue among the individuals of an organization (on approaches to dialogue, see e.g. Senge 1990; Bohm *et al.* 1991; Heckscher *et al.* 1994; Chapters 6 and 16 this volume). Furthermore, for each individual it becomes more important to understand him/herself as a person and as an employee. In order to engage in the local processes of defining roles, goals and priorities at work, an employee has to be aware of his/her strengths and weaknesses as well as needs and dislikes. It can be said that in contemporary working life, it is important that while working, an employee also has opportunities to learn to know him/herself.

Similarly, sense of manageability relates to self-design. Many of the emerging jobs cannot be predefined; they are boundaryless and highly dependent on the individual choices of employees. How would it then be possible to define necessary resources beforehand and 'from above'? Probably that is not possible, but employees and their supervisors have to engage in continuous processes of redefining resources needed at work. Also this can only be done at the local (in contrast to organizational) level. Finally, the social connections – so vital for both sense of manageability and meaningfulness – cannot by definition be predetermined in rigid organizational charts, but have to be built both on the official needs of an organization and also on free collaboration among the people within and around the organization.

In summary, sense of coherence stands for an employee's ability to find something comprehensible, manageable and meaningful in any situation and consequently, to cope with the situation. To put it in another way, sense of coherence is like a psychological equivalent for Ariadne's thread – it can provide the guidance through the complex and dangerous labyrinths of our lives. Above, we noted that work can support the development of sense of coherence and the growth of an employee. Work experiences, corresponding to the discussion above, are thus regenerative and increase the sustainability of individual resources.

The enjoyment of work

Being able to cope with emerging, potentially negative, situations is undeniably important but, nevertheless, presents quite a negative perspective to the interaction between work and an individual. This interaction should be much more than a battlefield of challenges and coping efforts. It should also, as an important factor influencing our lives, provide enjoyment, even happiness. We are faced by yet another question: how to create enjoyable work? Csikszentmihalyi (1990) has provided one answer to this question with his studies on the experiences that provide enjoyment in life. He has been able to pin down the optimal, enjoyable experience in his concept of *flow*. Below, we shall discuss flow in connection to work. The idea of flow also complements the discussion above on sense of coherence since sense of coherence addresses psychological resources enabling coping with work, while flow addresses actual action processes at work that lead to enjoyment and coping. Furthermore, sense of coherence and flow do share a common thread; both concepts discuss experiences that are regenerative in the sense that they build psychological resources that can be relied upon when encountering potential stressors.

Csikszentmihalyi states that the quality of an experience depends on an individual's mastery of his/her consciousness. Often, numerous and simultaneous stimuli from the environment lead to a situation where, rather than concentrating on those issues that at the time are important to us, consciousness is filled with unrelated, threatening thoughts. Instead, a person who is in control of his/her consciousness has the ability to focus it at will. The person's attention is not diffused into following contradictory and chaotic stimuli, but instead he/she can intentionally allocate attention to those stimuli that are relevant for him/her. Thus, the mastery of consciousness enables a person to concentrate, rather than consume psychological resources in dealing with the entropic reality of life. Csikszentmihalyi calls these moments of optimal experience and concentration 'flow'.

In short, then, flow stands for a state where a person is able to invest all his/her attention in his/her immediate goals and is thus free from disturbing thoughts. The ability to organize consciousness this way and, thus, ability to experience flow as often as possible improve the quality of life through two different paths. First, flow – the state of total concentration, order, and the absence of disturbing thoughts – is an enjoyable experience. Second, these moments of mental harmony and concentration lead to the development of the *self*. On the one hand, the self becomes more differentiated since flow allows experiences of being capable and skilful. A person's self becomes more unique after each flow experience. On the other hand, in the state of flow, consciousness becomes more ordered and internal harmony in a person grows. In this sense, the integration of the self takes place. Flow can thus be understood as a regenerative experience increasing individual sustainability.

Csikszentmihalyi writes that the state of flow is often achieved when engaging in hobbies. Activities like mountain climbing may lead to flow; to order in consciousness and enjoyable concentration in the activity. However, work also can be a source of flow experiences. According to Csikszentmihalyi, work that is like a game – variable, clear and goal oriented – is experienced as enjoyable. Another important characteristic of a flow activity is the balance between the demands of the situation and the person's resources. Thus, Csikszentmihalyi's 'receipt' for regenerative work leading to the growth of the self is variable, clear and goal-oriented work that, furthermore, is in balance with an employee's resources.

When studying experiences of people at work and at leisure, Csikszentmihalyi distinguished a paradox in the way people relate to their work. People tend to report relatively more flow experiences when they are working than when they are doing other things. When work is at its best, people feel skilful and challenged and, consequently, happier and more satisfied. They focus and concentrate. During free time, challenges are fewer and skills are not used. There are feelings of sadness, weakness and dissatisfaction. Despite the difference of the quality of experience at work and during free time, working people reported that they would rather not be working. Also most would like to have more free time, even though it contains such negative feelings.

According to Csikszentmihalyi, one reason for this paradox may be that people disregard their immediate experiences and, instead, perceive work situations based on the stereotypical images of work. Consequently, work is perceived as 'have to', a constraint of freedom and not related to the overall goals of life. Instead of reaching for their own goals, employees have to toil to make somebody else's goals come true. When the goals at work do not relate to employees' personal goals, employees tend to disregard their moments of flow at work, the optimal experiences. Consequently, enjoyment at work and the development of the self seem to be closely connected to the relation between personal and work goals.

Work experiences as a forum for growth and competitiveness

In this chapter, we have discussed sustainable work systems from an individual's point of view. The goal has been to increase the understanding of work intensity leading to human resources

consumption. Furthermore, possibilities for sustainable personal and professional development at work have been explored through the idea of regenerative work.

Regenerative work is a hallmark of a sustainable work system. Such work contains possibilities both for the current moments of enjoyment at work and also for supporting and
creating individual potential for future coping with the challenges of work. The problems of
contemporary working life have demonstrated that 'good work' cannot only be defined as
parameters of jobs and work organizations but, rather, good and regenerative work is defined
by its long-term consequences. Therefore, more needs to be known about an individual's psychological (cognitive and emotional) development at work; we need to learn what kinds of
work experiences enable personal growth and create psychological resources. In this chapter,
we have discussed sense of coherence and flow as ways to approach the interaction between
an individual and work from this perspective. Both of these concepts seem to indicate a need
for local self-design processes at work in which employees have possibilities to find a unique
balance between themselves and their work. This balance should exist in various dimensions
and address such issues as

- resources at work;
- comprehensibility, manageability and meaningfulness of work; and
- the integration of personal and work goals.

Sustainable, regenerative work is a challenging research subject, since it can neither be
defined in an expertocratic fashion nor can it be defined as a paradigm, as an organizational
prototype. Instead, the search for sustainability is a search for local values, practices and
processes; ways for people and work to interact with regenerative consequences. Furthermore,
the search for sustainability has to be a collective effort bringing together not only researchers
and experts, but also the people and work groups who currently are struggling with expanding, complex work realities while striving to envisage and realize meaningful work and
possibilities to develop at work.

The search for regenerative work also necessitates quite a complex view of work experiences.
It is not enough to develop organizations to be free from stressors or to nurture employees' psychological resources and coping strategies that should enable them to deal with any kind of
situation. On the one hand, the work and work environment will always contain stressors. On
the other hand, it is not humane to expect that the psychological resources of an individual and
his/her strategies could help him/her survive mentally or develop in any given situation.
Sustainable work systems with regenerative work are based on both thinking patterns. First,
organizations should be developed continuously to remove stressors and, furthermore, to contain elements that contribute to the regeneration of psychological resources and enjoyable
experiences at work. Second, employees should be supported to renew their psychological
resources, to grow as people in their work. And as can be deduced from the discussion in this
chapter, these lines of thinking are, in no sense, excluding one another – they probably are
mutually reinforcing. Developing work and organizations based on sense of coherence and flow
concepts directly creates possibilities for the growth and development of the psychological
resources of employees and enables successful coping in the future.

As noted in Chapter 1, sustainable work systems aim to achieve employees' growth and
well-being at the same time as organizational competitiveness. How then does work allowing
personal and professional growth, even enjoyment, as discussed in this chapter, contribute to
organizational competitiveness? To be quite frank, it does not necessarily. Organizational
competitiveness is not only the sum of the potential of its members; there are simply too many

intervening factors. The best efforts within organizations can be undermined by one mistake in the stock or product markets or simply by an economic recession. The potential from the growth and development of a thousand employees may not be translated into organizational success, but rather be undermined by one erratic investment decision or a failed business deal. The concepts of good work and organizational competitiveness move at different levels and creating a force for sustainability at both levels is one of the aims of sustainable work systems. Well-being and competitiveness, however, cannot be equated to each other; they can exist at the same time, but may not necessarily be created by the same organizational measures.

Nevertheless, we think it is justifiable to demand that regenerative work has a positive effect on the productivity or competitiveness at local level, in the context that is directly affected by the employees and work groups 'enjoying' the good, regenerative work. Through an individual's behaviour, what is 'individual' rises on the social level; individual ideas become shared and individual emotions become commonly experienced (see also Maslach and Leiter 1997). It was stated above that through dialogue individuals may gain resources and coherent, enjoyable work experiences. Similarly, through dialogue individual potential can become organizational potential (e.g. Senge 1990). The challenge for organizations is to create opportunities for dialogue in its real sense; a dialogue that raises individual potential to social level and vice versa, a dialogue that can survive conflicts and is not easy but – nevertheless – possible. This challenge to create dialogue becomes even more important as the traditional ways to structure work and make sense of it do not seem to succeed any more. Bureaucratic rules and structures are not flexible, changeable and open enough to deal with the existing context of work, the market conditions and customer demands. Organizations have, consequently, to combine the drive for individual and organizational sustainability; to develop resources and dialogue opportunities that both create good – comprehensible, manageable and meaningful – work and make sustainable performance possible at each and every local level possible.

Notes

1 I wish to acknowledge financial support from the Swedish Council for Work Life Research.
2 When considering the ways for an organization to support its employees' sense of coherence, two issues of caution are in order. First, an individual's sense of coherence is quite stable. An organization cannot 'improve' its employees or donate them a better sense of coherence, but work can support the existing sense of coherence and – in the long term – also contribute in either positive or negative shifts in it. Second, employees are not only employees, but individuals who are affected both by their private lives and socio-cultural situation in which they live. Work is not the only determinant of an individual's development, but we consider it of utmost importance both because of the amount of time we spend working as well as because of the importance of the experiences work provides (e.g. belonging to a community; being productive, needed and useful).

References

Antonovsky, A. (1979) *Health, Stress and Coping. New Perspectives on Mental and Physical Well-Being*, San Francisco: Jossey-Bass.

Antonovsky, A. (1987a) *Unravelling the Mystery of Health. How People Manage Stress and Stay Well*, San Francisco: Jossey-Bass.

Antonovsky, A. (1987b) 'Health promoting factors at work. The sense of coherence', in R. Kalimo, M.A. El-Batawi and C.L. Cooper (eds) *Psychosocial Factors at Work and Their Relation to Health*, Geneva: World Health Organization.

Bohm, D., Factor, D. and Garett, P. (1991) *Dialogue. A Proposal*. Online. Available http://www.muc.de/~heuvel/dialogue/dialogue_proposal.html

Csikszentmihalyi, M. (1990) *Flow. The Psychology of Optimal Experience*, New York: Harper Perennial.

Delbridge, R. (1998) *Life on the Line in Contemporary Manufacturing. The Workplace Experiences of Lean Production and the 'Japanese' Model*, Oxford: Oxford University Press.

Fontana, D. (2000) *Personality in the Workplace*, Basingstoke: Macmillan.

Heckscher, C., Eisenstat, R.A. and Rice, T.J. (1994) 'Transformational processes', in C. Heckscher and L.M. Applegate (eds) *The Post-Bureaucratic Organization. New Perspectives on Organizational Change*, Thousand Oaks, CA: Sage.

Hirschhorn, L. (1988) *The Workplace Within. Psychodynamics of Organizational Life*, Cambridge, MA: MIT Press.

Hobfoll, S. (1998) *Stress, Culture and Community. Psychology and Philosophy of Stress*, New York: Plenum Press.

Huys, R., Sels, L., van Hootegem, G., Bundervoet, J. and Henderickx, E. (1999) 'Toward less division of labor? New production concepts in automotive, chemical, clothing and machine tool industries', *Human Resources*, 52, 1, 67.

Johansson Hanse, J. and Engström, T. (1999) 'Sense of coherence and ill health among the unemployed and re-employed after closure of an assembly plant', *Work & Stress*, 13, 3, 204–22.

Kalimo, R. and Vuori, J. (1990) 'Work and sense of coherence. Resources for competence and life satisfaction', *Behavioral Medicine*, 18, 76–89.

Karasek, R. and Theorell, T. (1990) *Healthy Work. Stress, Productivity, and the Reconstruction of Working Life*, New York: Basic Books.

Kira, M. (2000) *From Intensive Work Systems to Sustainable. A Literature Review*, Stockholm, Royal Institute of Technology: TRITA report.

Kira, M. (2001) 'Post-industrial work and its consequences on employees. Comprehending incomprehensible work'. A paper presented at the First Annual Meeting of the Sustain Network 'Dilemmas of Autonomy and Responsibility', Eindhoven, The Netherlands, September 7–8, 2001.

Landsbergis, P.A., Cahill, J. and Schnall, P. (1999) 'The impact of lean production and related new systems of work organisation on worker health', *Journal of Occupational Health Psychology*, 4, 2, 108–30.

Lindström, K. (1994) 'Psychosocial criteria for good work organization', *Scandinavian Journal of Work, Environment and Health*, 20, Special Issue, 123–133.

Maslach, C. and Leiter, M.P. (1997) *The Truth about Burnout. How Organizations Cause Personal Stress and What to Do about It*, San Francisco: Jossey-Bass.

Murphy, L.R. and Hurrell, J.J. Jr (1997) 'Locus of control', in J.M. Stellman (ed.) *Encyclopaedia of Occupational Health and Safety*, 4th edn, Geneva: International Labour Organization.

Newton, T. (1995) *'Managing' Stress. Emotions and Power at Work*, London: Sage.

O'Donnell, M., Peetz, D. and Allan, C. (1998) *What's Happening at Work? More Tasks, Less Job Security and Work Intensification*, University of New South Wales, School of Industrial Relations and Organisational Behaviour, Working Paper Series, no. 124.

Ouellette, S. (1997) 'Hardiness', in J.M. Stellman (ed.) *Encyclopaedia of Occupational Health and Safety*, 4th edn, Geneva: International Labour Organization.

Schumann, M., Baethge-Kinsky, V., Kuhlmann, M., Kurz, C. and Neumann, U. (1995) 'New production concepts and the restructuring of work', in W. Littek and T. Charles (eds) *The New Division of Labor. Emerging Forms of Work Organisation in International Perspective*, Berlin: Walter de Gruyter.

Senge, P. (1990) *The Fifth Discipline. The Art and Practice of the Learning Organization*, New York: Doubleday Currency.

Thorsrud, E. and Emery, F.E. (1969) *Medinflytande och engagemang i arbetet. Norska försök med självstyrande grupper* (Participation and Commitment at Work. Norwegian Experiments with Semi-Autonomous Groups), Stockholm: Utvecklingsrådet för Samarbetsfrågor.

Vartiainen, M. (1994) *Työn Muutoksen Työväineet. Muutoksen Hallinnan Sosiotekniset Menetelmät* (The Tools for Work Transformation. The Socio-Technical Methods in Mastering Change), Espoo: Otatieto.

Weick, K.E. (1995) *Sensemaking in Organizations*, Thousand Oaks, CA: Sage.

Wingborg, M. (2000) *En vårflod av stresslarm. En sammanställning av aktuell forskning om ohälsan i arbetslivet* (A Spring Flood of Stress Alarms. A Summary on the Contemporary Research on Health Problems in Working Life), Stockholm: TCO.

4 Sources of intensity in work organizations

Armand Hatchuel

The theoretical problems of work intensity

Several observations support the idea of increased work intensity in many work sectors. However, the definition of intensity is not established in the organizational literature. The term is not even mentioned in a recent handbook on organizational behaviour (Sorge and Warner 1998). Most empirical observations of intensity at work come from psychologists and industrial physicians, who usually refer to excessive work and stress as major issues of contemporary work life (Dejours 1999).

If intensity is better known by its physical and mental symptoms than by its content, organization scientists are left with the option to analyse intensity indirectly. A recent study of internal consultants' teams in a large corporation describes unreserved commitment (Deetz 1998). The commitment was expressed in relation to satisfaction derived from putting a lot of effort into the mission, despite the sacrifices in the private sphere. 'Is this the best or the worst work place?' the author wonders. He also remarks that the consultants' ideology impregnates both practices of the team and the justifications put forward to explain their satisfaction. Such ideology had no boundaries and for the author nothing could limit it, except the surprising fact that in spite of their intense work the consultants seemed economically inefficient.

This example is a good introduction to the theoretical problems met by the organization scholar attempting a definition of work intensity. The classical views of job satisfaction, quality of work life, job enrichment and empowerment that for long were the symbols of social progress could now appear as vectors of work intensity. Thus, the task of proposing a new concept of 'good life' at work would lie ahead of us. What can management and organizational scientists add to the study of intensity at work?

Intensity at work and management trends

Some authors consider intensity as the result of new forms of management (Karasek and Theorell 1990; Aubert and de Gaulejac 1991; McKinlay and Taylor 1998). The core idea is the following: contemporary management does not look any more for conformity or obedience at work, instead it fosters a strong commitment of the employees to the values and goals of the company. Therefore, new management techniques are mainly designed to align all energy and the whole personality of the employees towards their jobs, thus creating intensity at work. In this literature, intensity becomes the baseline of a new management critique that tends to replace the classical arguments of labour process theory (Smith 1998).

In this chapter, we do not reject the empirical facts that support the idea of increased stress and mental pressure at work; yet, we consider that such a point of view suffers from the classical bias of systematic critical trends in social sciences. Our perspective is that like any social actor, managers work under the constraints of their time and have to cope with collective contexts that no actor can create alone. Our hypothesis is that management models are co-generated under the same socio-economic changes and trends. Thus, intensity is in our view the result of historical collective processes that have changed the content of work and of management simultaneously. We will analyse later in this chapter a case study concerning bus drivers where such co-generation appears. Next, we clarify our approach to intensity.

Work intensity: some hypotheses

Our hypothesis is that intensity is the consequence of *a loss of work control or a loss of work governability* experienced at an individual, managerial or institutional level. Governability[1] is the ability to create visible objects (things, instruments, symbols, protocols . . .), that can be investigated, ruled and evaluated in order to govern. Loss of work governability means that the material, symbolic and conceptual contents of work are no easier to specify, to structure or to regulate by managers, workers or any other stakeholder. Intensity at work means that some aspects of work are invisible and, consequently, not governable. When job governability decreases, the distinction between work and ordinary life tends to vanish. Therefore, 'intensive work systems' could be a paradoxical concept, if intensity appears when work is no more distinguishable (at individual, managerial or institutional levels) in the continuous flow of someone's activities.

From the preceding proposition, the following paradox emerges: if intensity comes from vanishing boundaries of work, the researcher will face a strange un-decidable loop. He or she intends to study a phenomenon (work intensity) which is produced by the disappearing of the same phenomenon (work). How can we study something that has lost its limits, i.e. has lost the ordinary features that we used in order to analyse its content? Let us take an example: an engineer spends all his holiday trying to maintain his own technical competences. How can we know if these efforts are part of his job? Let us assume that none of his bosses asked him to work outside office hours and that no contract rule links his wages or his career to such off-work activity. Yet, managers expect engineers to personally update their expertise. The problem comes from the fact that expertise is an explicit element of the employment contract, while renewal of expertise is only an *implicit* convention of such contract. Now, if the engineer's expertise is continuously threatened by obsolescence, the quest for expertise renewal becomes unlimited and the risk of intensity increases.

Therefore, the methodological issue created is recognition of the artefactual foundations of any concept of 'work'. The medical or psychological points of view on intensity avoid this problem. The causal link between the definition of work intensity and personal distress can be left to the workers themselves and their perception of reality is then the only reality that may be claimed by a psychological approach. Our perspective is different: as intensity is linked to some lack of governability of work, revisiting the theoretical and managerial problems raised by the definition of work will guide us to a contingent view of intensity.

Work as collective action

The artefactual shaping of work

What do we call 'work'? Work has been characterized by historians 'as more essential to men than laughter' (Nougier 1965, p. 5). Such a definition of work provides no conceptual distinction between different types of activity. As humans are permanently engaged in a variety of collective activities, 'work' is the name for specific and changing activities according to a societal and historical context (Maurice *et al.* 1980). One may recognize work when there is a *salary*. But business owners and freelance artists also work. Hence, salary is obviously a too restricted sign. We may also define work by the specific knowledge it needs: when a chemist works he uses chemistry. But we can use chemistry as a hobby and a pleasant game. Obviously, any approach is built on a conventional restriction. This means that 'work' is artefactually designed, defined and distinguished and that it can be recognized and observed as such only when these design parameters and criteria are the result of a collective process.

However, such definition problems are not specific for work. We meet the same difficulties whenever we want to define any seemingly universal term concerning a form of collective action like organization, co-ordination or power. The conceptual limitations in social science theory lead us to a 'theory of collective action' (Hatchuel 1997 and 2001). Some of the basic propositions of this theory are explored below:

1   *Proposition 1.* We define a 'collective action' as an action which cannot be determined by a unique value (freedom, profit, utility) or by a unique actor's decision (the boss, the nation, the working class) (Hatchuel 1997, 2001). Hence, work is obviously a form of collective action as there is no unique value that encompasses work, and work always involves more than one actor.

2   *Proposition 2.* The preceding definition of collective action has several consequences. A crucial one is that studying collective action requires two interrelated perspectives, cognitive and relational:

  (a)   To describe a collective action, we have to describe what is known to the participants. The word 'cognitive' does not mean here pure conceptual and cerebral skills. We consider it in a broader sense: a violinist plays with all his or her senses and emotions. But this does not mean that a violinist has no reflexive learning about his/her senses and emotions.

  (b)   To describe a collective action, we have to recognize the relations that actors perceive between them. By relations, we mean any model of interaction referring to individual and collective identities or rules. Relations tell who people are by comparison with others.

Usually we separate these two perspectives. We say that there exist nations like the French or the British, but we forget to mention the cognitive procedures by which people recognize themselves or others as members of the same national group; and the problem only appears when some collective action is needed like organizing a vote about some regional independences. Conversely, we all know what mathematics is but we scarcely mention that truth in mathematics depends on the relations between mathematicians: are they all honest and independent judges of their colleagues?

This dual perspective will help to characterize forms of work and intensity at work through the cognitive and relational artefacts that contribute to its governability. Let us consider the example of a salaried doctor. Understanding the dynamics of such a job needs both analysis of which part of the medical knowledge is activated and what other people know about this knowledge. We also have to consider the meaning of being a salaried employee in such contexts. However, the core idea is that these two aspects will influence each other and their content will be transformed through their interrelation. One salaried doctor is not like another doctor, nor like another salaried worker.

Work design and confined jobs

With these premises, we can understand why a great deal of research has been devoted to what we define as *confined* jobs. These jobs are easier to analyse because they are part of a larger collective process, which rationalizes and defines them. These jobs were also highly problematic in Western countries but the fact that they were observable contributed to a strong identification of the image of work with these specific forms.

Let us take the very classic case of the assembly line. It is well known that this type of work demands extensive design work. Plant location, layout, machines, tools, tasks and procedures have to be designed and defined before the job can be described. All these artefacts still leave some room for the worker, and research has established that local autonomy is crucial for work performance. However, such jobs are 'design intensive' and assembly line workers can hardly redesign machines, products or tasks. Even participatory forms of management maintain strong limitations in the scope of intervention by the workers. We call such jobs confined jobs. The design parameters also act as work 'descriptors', which can reach high precision and pre-dictability. This is no accident: it is the goal of the intense design efforts. Even if some informal and autonomous activity remains, the large number of designed artefacts facilitates the cognitive and relational aspects of work. Thus we define confined work as work that is conceptually and practically designed to be observable and controlled by its designers or by other professionals.

Industrial history tells us that such jobs have also been an easy target for external regula-tion and critique, hence for institutional governability. The pace of the line, the monotony of rigid assignments, the de-skilling trends in such jobs have stimulated a great deal of reform policies, such as work hours limitations, health and fatigue controls, job enrichment, wage policies.

Built-in intensity regulation in confined jobs

Job confinement offers a way to discuss intensity regulation. The design effort creates the pos-sibility for both productivity and intensity observations. This means that work and intensity regulations are achieved by the same non-separable processes: stabilizing the cognitive and relational requirements.

Stabilizing the cognitive requirements

Confinement has important cognitive implications for the worker. His or her 'action world' is delineated and stabilized. Workplaces, instruments, risks, colleagues and goals can be rapidly discovered while a learning process can transform the experience into actionable knowledge. We define the operational knowledge required by these jobs as 'doing know-how' (Hatchuel and Weil 1995). This definition is valid only for the knowledge related to the tasks. One should not underestimate the tacit knowledge created by the workers, but it is hardly of the same magnitude as the knowledge required in unconfined jobs.

Stabilizing the relational requirements

Confined jobs require relational stability, clear-cut boundaries and established communication processes. Such regulations allow mobility and individual exchange, provided that training is designed. Not surprisingly, we recognize in all these features the classical bureaucracy: job confinement permits interchange of individuals and workers tend to live in a semi-closed society at work.

Confined jobs have been criticized since the 1970s for monotony and de-skilling. When work speed is too high or complexity increases, task performance demands more attention and energy – a form of intensity. However, job confinement facilitates causal analysis and direct observation of such phenomena. Public authorities can force reductions in work intensity, not only because they have the institutional power to do so, but also because these jobs are sufficiently observable and definable to offer clear objects for governability (time span, work hours, schedule, environmental rules . . .). These conditions also favour the development of work experts as legitimate prescribers of new regulations. Thus, job confinement is in itself a partial solution for intensity, a form that installs the conditions of governability.

Work intensity in unconfined jobs: a bus driver case

Confined jobs shaped the popular view of industrial work and a great deal of social policy is implicitly based on the assumption that all jobs are confined. Yet, jobs are confined only when confinement is relevant and valuable. To understand why some jobs cannot be confined and to discuss the corresponding types of work intensity, we shall examine the case of bus drivers in the Paris transport authority (Joseph *et al.* 1991; Hatchuel and Weil 1995). The case provides a distinction between prescribed and confined work that plays an important role in understanding contemporary forms of intensity.

Prescription, confinement and intensity

Bus drivers represent a large class of jobs in the service sector. Moreover, the bus driver belongs to an old lineage of trades probably beginning with the boat captain. In the ancient Mediterranean world, boat captaincy was a highly complex job encompassing both routinized actions and the highest authoritative decisions: emergency drills and jettisoning cargo. Like the bus driver today, the boat captain had to comply with a number of rules, and was at the same time given wide autonomy. In spite of obvious differences, bus drivers and ancient boat captains have common characteristics: a work which at the same time is highly prescribed and necessarily unconfined, a mix strongly favourable to intensity. Neither of these jobs can be fully prescribed, yet they are highly prescribed; both jobs are confronted with unforeseen problems to be handled with local authority. Yet, the driver has neither the heroic image, nor the legal power of the captain. Let us explore the bus driver job in more detail.

- *Highly prescribed work.* Bus drivers' work schedule is planned months in advance. They cannot decide the departure, stopping and arrival points negotiated by the unions. They are trained to drive buses in a comfortable and safe way. In some cases, drivers also sell tickets. They receive a detailed schedule of their route, which can be changed only after consent of a supervisor – if they can reach him during the drive. Modern buses have radio and information systems that allow the driver to send and receive messages to and from a regulation centre. This centre has the authority to change several prescriptions, e.g. the schedule, stopping the bus, exchange of drivers. The bus drivers' work is thus highly designed and prescribed.
- *Necessary autonomy and low confinement.* Obviously, the bus driver is not as confined as the assembly line worker is. No designer can control the traffic, the flow of passengers or their behaviour. The driver makes decisions continuously: autonomy and low

confinement are unavoidable features of the job. When speaking gently to passengers, is she working? When insulted by a passenger, is he working?

Unconfined work: enriching the definitions of work and intensity

After the assembly line worker, the bus driver example highlights a second model of intensity. Let us analyse this model with the same framework by discussing the cognitive and relational characteristics of these jobs.

- *The cognitive characteristics.* Bus drivers' know-how cannot be restricted to repetitive and stable driving techniques. They must maintain a high degree of attention to several sources of problems: the bus, the traffic, the travellers, the climate. When a problem appears, they have to understand what is happening and react efficiently and quickly. Sometimes the problem is entirely new to the driver, who cannot rely on a repertoire of programmed solutions or previous learning. He or she has to combine old or design new solutions. We have defined the forms of knowledge that are required as 'understanding know-how' and 'conceiving know-how', when one has to face a continuous flow of emerging problems and with the duty to undertake corrective action.
- *The relational characteristics.* The bus driver has to cope with a permanent flow of unstable and differentiated relations: from anonymous interactions with passengers and actors in the traffic to professional links. Smooth working is possible only if peaceful behaviour is maintained both in traffic and with customers. Otherwise, the driver is submitted to moral hazards, injuries, aggression and even violence. But each line is different, depending on the regions through which it runs, and the driver's work is also prescribed by the dynamics of the micro-society of its passengers. Bus drivers who work in difficult suburbs do not have the same perception of their job as colleagues in wealthy residential parts of the city, where people tend to complain about bus drivers.

This brief analysis of bus driving is enough to clarify the important distinction between prescription and confinement. The bus driver is highly prescribed and obviously unconfined. As this distinction is crucial for our approach of intensity, some definitions will help to clarify the point:

- *Work prescription* is defined as prescription of any formal or informal requirements bearing on the job regardless of their source. A salesperson receives prescriptions from the management but also from the clients: the relations are different in each case but the salesperson has to take account of both.
- *Work design* was defined earlier as the set of prescriptions that are formulated and implemented by the designers of the work in the company. Hence, work design is only a subset of the prescriptions required from the job.
- *Work confinement* is the ability of work designers to determine the work content and environment. This means that the designers are able to build a separate world, where their prescriptions are almost the only ones that bear on the worker. Unconfined jobs are jobs where work design defines only a sub-part of the work environment.

By distinguishing these three notions, we avoid the contradiction between prescription and autonomy. This contradiction only stands when work is confined, but it vanishes in the context of unconfined jobs where high prescription is no more the opposite of autonomy. Thus, it is possible to increase the existing prescriptions in driving or reporting to the supervisor, and simultaneously increase autonomy concerning some passenger behaviours. Confinement possibilities are clearly limited, which gives a new perspective on intensity.

New intensity: when bus driving is more than driving buses

During the last decades, bus drivers have, in many urban contexts, been subjected to new forms of intensity at work, although not from management initiatives or new work design. The first sign of a new problem was a decrease in the age of those drivers who, for medical reasons, were not allowed to drive. The bus companies have always organized medical examinations to check whether a driver is still fit for the job. Between 1980 and 1990, the mean age of unfit drivers in Paris decreased. This was an indicator that the job had changed. The reasons for the younger drivers ending their career were not confined to physical illnesses. The typical young unfit driver suffered less from vertebral–skeletal pathologies than his older colleagues, but showed more psychosomatic symptoms.

Several authors have analysed the tensions that a bus driver faces (Joseph *et al.* 1991). If we examine these observations through cognitive and relational perspectives, some intensity drifts can be roughly sketched. An increase in non-civilized behaviour and in traffic variability in the Paris region requires close understanding and design efforts from the drivers. Conversely, lack of experience and competence in these respects – typical of young drivers – could lead to provocative behaviour, creating a negative image of the bus operator and reinforcing violent or violating behaviour. Moreover, the drivers of the 1980s and 1990s were more educated and more prone to reflexivity and cognitive mobilization (Inglehart 1990). Many of them experienced a strong discrepancy between the complex yet invisible requirements of the job and its image for the average passenger as low qualified work. Trade unions reacted rapidly and organized immediate strikes whenever a bus driver was physically injured, demanding management and state policies for restoring safe work conditions.

Reconfining jobs and creating new resources: revisiting commitment

During the 1990s, the Paris bus authority launched several measures in order to reduce the number of unfit drivers and to offer new opportunities for those who had to give up driving. However, the most innovative actions were taken by a special team that organized new relations between the bus company and the most aggressive passenger populations. These actions, from organizing sport competitions to the recruitment of mediators from these populations, involved local authorities. The main goal was to prevent violence and bring people to awareness of the value of public transport as an instrument for social integration and justice. Trade unions, on the other hand, often asked for increases in bus personnel or the cancellation of lines in areas where violence was frequent.

Using our framework, all these measures can be interpreted as *reconfining strategies*. Reconfining means that something has been destroyed in the work definition and environment and a new form of confinement is needed. It sounds like more confinement again but it is the creation of a new type of governability that really matters. In this case, one important societal transformation had changed the old job environment. The ordinary civility, the normal polite behaviour of bus passengers, was suddenly recognized as an invisible resource for governability that became visible only when it began to disappear. Until then, the driver was perceived as a representative of authority, who repressed certain uncivil behaviour. Both drivers' authority and passengers' compliance formed resources that bus companies had considered as a natural gift from society.

The bus companies had two main policies: (a) let the drivers adapt to the new environment, or (b) try to reshape this environment. No doubt, the two strategies had to be simultaneously attempted. The new societal characteristics could not be completely reshaped by the bus company, but some aspects of the crisis could be prevented. On the other hand, bus drivers had also to reconstruct some aspects of the cognitive and relational content of their work. Obviously, intensity of work could be reduced, if not entirely eliminated.

In this context, revisiting the concept of commitment and its links to intensity has some theoretical value. Commitment has been a major issue in contemporary human resources management (HRM). Moreover, commitment has been linked to empowerment and autonomy. The logic was simple: autonomy and rewards create commitment and efficiency. The logic was obviously too abstract and flawed in some cases. What is commitment? Commitment comes from work psychology with roots in the notion of motivation. Strong motivation is seen as a prerequisite for high commitment. But this formulation forgets the cognitive and relational conditions implicit in this causal link. What does motivating mean for an impossible task? What type of commitment can be expected from bus drivers who are anxious about the behaviour of their passengers?

With the ambition to restore civilized relations, the Paris transport authority was fighting a new form of intensity. Yet, commitment and empowerment of drivers were not considered an acceptable managerial strategy in reaction to a new environment. The commitment of bus drivers could be restored only through an external strategy to reconfine some aspects of the environment. The bus company attempted to invent forms of relations and educational efforts towards these populations. Bus drivers received training and immediate psychological help when they had been attacked. Management also learned about the complexity of bus driving and new organizing possibilities were explored. Hence, new prescriptions appeared, but they were accepted as helpful reconfining strategies and were not seen as a reduction of the drivers' autonomy.

Finally, this bus driver case shows a form of work characterized by strong prescriptions but low confinement; changing face to face relations with customers; increasing importance of understanding and conceiving know-how. In such work, intensity is a permanent threat, but it also takes extreme forms that call for reconfining strategies. The same conceptual framework will still be useful to study another class of job situations, where demands for innovation and flexibility completely endanger job boundaries.

White collar jobs: vanishing work boundaries

In the bus driver case, there was still a large part of design in the job definition. We all think that we know in some detail what a driver's job is! This is not true for white collar jobs. Yet, the same framework can be used to characterize intensity problems in the white collar world. However, we will limit our discussion to some conceptual remarks that are open for further research on this professional category highly affected by intensity problems.

High prescription, low confinement and self-management

White collar personnel are in charge of the rules and standards of the organization. They define the main products and processes, organize control and co-ordination within the enterprise and relate to external partners. Compared with blue collar workers, they can be seen as free of any prescription. This view is wrong. White collar staff are highly prescribed actors, because they are dependent on the knowledge of others.

Let us take the case of an industrial designer or a stylist: despite being paid for his or her creativity, he or she has to take into account the engineer's views, the legal and aesthetic constraints of brands and the price and positioning strategy of the marketing department. Because any decision interferes with many others, white collar staff also have to establish prescriptions for their colleagues. The larger the number of white collar workers, the more they feel prescribed by colleagues, and the higher the number of colleagues they prescribe. We have called this mechanism 'reciprocal prescription', because work is prescribing the action of others. This is also well known as a classical source of interdepartmental conflicts. However, in spite of being highly prescribed, the job of most white collar personnel is not designed or is only poorly designed.

The new distinction introduces another form of intensity problem. For sure, white collar workers have some established goals; they receive budgets and are assigned missions. They also have to report at planned dates and are submitted to evaluation procedures. All these elements organize the logic of the job, but do not design it. White collar workers have to self-organize their work, to self-define their needs, to self-maintain their information and technical skills. We can thus define the specificity of white collar work by both limited design and important areas of *self-management*. Consequently, the combination of high prescription, weak job design and self-management clearly characterizes a different logic of intensity. The central tensions of white collar jobs derive from this permanent contradiction between high prescription and self-management.

Self-management, innovation and flexibility – the road to epidemic intensity

Tensions between high prescription and self-management do not always induce problematic intensity. Comedians or musicians experience such tensions as normal features of work. But organizational and business contexts add innovation, uncertainty and flexibility. Then the classic rationality of setting goals and looking for appropriate means is often reversed. Available means usually determine new goals and changing goals often disrupt existing means. For white collar people, work also means preparing for future changes. The white collar worker is often seen as a 'strategist' acting in a very constrained and rapidly changing environment. Yet, when contexts change too quickly, important cognitive and relational consequences endanger the possibility for self-management:

- *The cognitive characteristics.* White collar jobs require various forms of knowledge. However, high instability of goals and contexts creates a permanent shortage of useful knowledge. Understanding and combining know-how are predominantly required cognitive skills.
- *The relational characteristics.* The complex and changing interdependencies bearing on white collar work create ambiguous interfaces, competing positions and fuzzy areas of accountability. Learning from colleagues becomes hampered or biased due to rivalry and vague jurisdictions.

Such cognitive and relational tensions create intensity precisely because they are important threats to self-management. This is a crucial point for understanding intensity drifts and personal dangers, as self-management is always embedded in the processes of self-governability and subjectification.

Intensity as a crisis in self-management

When self-management cannot be achieved, hampered by cognitive and relational tensions, a new form of intensity appears. The work situation disturbs the subjectification process and reinforces the fact that work is no more efficiently self-designed and self-confined. At the end of such vicious circles, work could have lost any meaning at all. It has often been observed that white collar people can struggle endlessly for their position, legitimacy or rank – more than for their 'work'.

This introduces a fundamental distinction between the bus driver and the white collar cases. When bus drivers experience intensity, it is commitment that loses any meaning to them, yet work is still defined by existing design. When the white collar worker cannot reach self-management, work is no more distinguishable from any 'struggle for life'. If work is socially defined by a process of self-management, the only sign of intensity, which is not a medical or psychiatric syndrome, is the lost ability of people to define their own work and this is an observable phenomenon.

Intensity in the white collar world is the result of limited self-design, high prescription and self-confinement: it appears through permanent knowledge shortage, short-term solutions and relational instability. Work boundaries tend to vanish or become too abstract. Success and rewards are probably the easiest remedy, making up for slackness, discrepancies and dissension. However, this does not stop the epidemic process of intensity as disturbed self-management and reduced work governability spread in organizational contexts where interdependencies are strong.

Conclusion: some policies towards sustainability

In this chapter we have tried to understand the concept of intensity at work from a specific perspective. The main results are twofold: (a) a conceptual framework that revisits the usual descriptions of work by insisting on its artefactual design, and (b) a typology of work situations giving birth to different forms of intensity: highly confined, weakly confined and self-managed work.

1   *A framework for redescribing work.* Considering the artefactual processes that shape a work system, we have distinguished the following interdependent concepts:
    (a)   *Prescriptions* are the requirements (rules, constraints, knowledge) that bear on a work position from all possible stakeholders.
    (b)   *Design* is the part of these prescriptions that is established by the organization as a formal system in order to stabilize the cognitive and relational boundaries of a job.
    (c)   *Confinement* is the ability of the designers of a work system to (almost) completely define its material, conceptual and social contents.

2   *Types of confinement and intensity.* This framework allows the identification of types of intensity linked to the artefactual shaping of the job. Let us briefly summarize our propositions in each example of work that we have discussed: assembly line work, bus driver and white collar work. Table 4.1 offers a simplified synthesis of how each situation corresponds to the concepts presented.
    (a)   The assembly line work was the first type of work we analysed. In this case, prescriptions, design and confinement are almost the same thing. Intensity in the assembly line can be directly linked to some design parameters. Thus, regulatory policies are not different from ordinary redesign methods.

Table 4.1 Summary of the concepts and situations analysed

Work shaping ⇨ Work type ⇩	Prescription	Design	Confinement	Form of intensity	Policy
Assembly line	+++	+++	+++	Definable Observable	Job redesign
Bus driving	+++	++	++	Vanishing work boundaries	Reconfining strategies
White collar	+++	+	+	Self-management crisis	Reconfining and support strategies

Note
The + signs are only indicative of the relative scale of each work aspect.

(b)   The case of the bus driver is different. Prescriptions, design and confinement appear as different facets. New passenger behaviour and complexity of traffic tend to reduce the confinement. But these deconfining events also dissolve job boundaries. The company cannot 'redesign' the passengers and the driver will not accept violence as a part of 'work'. Therefore, any expected commitment depends on the management reaction to what threatens work definition. Management has to extend its area of intervention and rebuild acceptable work boundaries. Civilian attitudes were an implicit resource for bus work system designers. When these were endangered, the company endeavoured to create job sustainability by educational policies to stimulate new sources of civility in problematic suburbs.

(c)   The white collar worker is the most challenging problem. Intensity seems normal because work definition is difficult: prescriptions are high, while design and confinement are low. Job definition is grounded on the idea of self-management. Thus, work and self are closely interrelated. Autonomous definition of work is a sign of self-management. Yet, self-management requires some 'governability' and a positive 'subjectification process'. Intensity begins when both processes are endangered. But how can we know that they are in trouble? By asking the psychologist? Another research path is to deconstruct the cognitive and relational operations that simultaneously define self-management and work. Whatever the result, any intensity reduction policy will have to redefine work.

The issue of the white collar worker is certainly the more general problem we face when we try to define intensity at work. The white collar model tends to expand in our economies and concerns more and more workers. In a highly innovative and educated world, prescriptions tend to increase in quantity and instability; confinement tends to decrease. Hence all jobs tend to mimic the white collar work type.

So what are the available policies that could limit intensity? In this chapter we showed that reducing intensity is necessarily a reconfining strategy: a reflexive effort on the artefacts that define work and the resources that it needs. We have proposed an approach to intensity that focuses on the definition of work. Our artefactual definition of work and our collective action perspective can easily be connected to other perspectives like organizational design or resource-based theory. Yet, the main advantage is in the identification of cognitive and relational interdependencies. This offers a conceptual platform for a well-structured contingency approach to intensity and sustainability. Moreover, the concepts used avoid the equivocality of usual notions like technology, organization or structure, which are not clear predictors of work intensity. The concepts of prescription, design, and confinement fit closely the collective action process and the governability problems that shape what we call work.

Note

1 Foucault introduced the French neologism *gouvernementalité*, usually translated as 'governmentality'. With this concept Foucault tried to capture the fact that 'government' has no universal meaning and is understandable only through some class of objects installing a specific form of governmentality. In this chapter, we prefer 'governability' which is easier to understand in spite of being also an English neologism.

References

Aubert, N. and De Gaulejac, V. (1991) *Le Coût de l'excellence* (The Price of Excellence), Paris: Seuil.

Deetz, S. (1998) 'Discursive formations, strategized subordination, and self-surveillance', in A. McKinlay and K. Starkey (eds) *Foucault, Management and Organization Theory*, London: Sage.

Dejours, C. (1999) *Souffrance en France* (The Pains of France), Paris: Seuil.

Foucault, M. (1984) *Le Souci de soi* (Worries of the Self), Paris: Gallimard.

Hatchuel, A. (1997) 'Coordination and control', in A. Sorge and M. Warner (eds) *The Handbook of Organizational Behaviour. International Encyclopaedia of Business and Management*, New York: Thomson Business Press.

Hatchuel, A. (2001) 'The new horizons of management science: towards a theory of collective action', in A. David, A. Hatchuel and R. Laufer (eds) *The New Foundations of Management Science*, Paris: Vuibert (English translation forthcoming).

Hatchuel, A. and Weil, B. (1995) *Experts in Organisations*, Berlin: Walter de Gruyter.

Inglehart, R. (1990) *Culture Shift in Advanced Industrial Society*, Princeton, NJ: Princeton University Press.

Joseph, I., Laé, J.F., Bonniel, D. and Bucas-Français, Y. (1991) *Généalogie et itinéraires de l'inaptitude* (Origins and Travels of Inaptitude), Paris: RATP/Ministry of Research. Research report.

Karasek, R. and Theorell, T. (1990) *Healthy Work. Stress, Productivity, and the Reconstruction of Working Life*, New York: Basic Books.

McKinlay, A. and Starkey, K. (eds) (1998) *Foucault, Management and Organization Theory*, London: Sage.

McKinlay, A. and Taylor, P. (1998) 'Through the looking glass. Foucault and the politics of production', in A. McKinlay and K. Starkey (eds) *Foucault, Management and Organization Theory*, London: Sage, pp. 173–90.

Maurice, M., Sorge, A. and Warner, M. (1980) 'Societal differences in organizing manufacturing units', *Organization Studies*, 1, 59–86.

Nougier, L.R. (1965) *Histoire générale du travail* (General History of Work), Paris: Nouvelle librairie de France.

Smith, C. (1998) 'Labour process', in A. Sorge and M. Warner (eds) *The Handbook of Organizational Behaviour. International Encyclopaedia of Business and Management*, New York: Thomson Business Press.

Sorge, A. and Warner, M. (eds) (1998) *The Handbook of Organizational Behaviour. International Encyclopaedia of Business and Management*, New York: Thomson Business Press.

Weick, E.K. (1979) *The Social Psychology of Organizing*, New York: McGraw-Hill.

5 A resource-centred perspective

Manfred F. Moldaschl

Introduction

Taylorism and Fordism are the paradigmatic opposite poles to work-related social sciences. The post-Fordist modernization strategies seemed to guarantee simultaneously both 'good work' and 'efficiency' under new conditions. The context changed, but the promise remained the same: work design can solve the conflicts among workers, firms and societal interests. In reality a new scientific management has emerged that is human-centred, a new paradigm of post-Fordism. Organizations still report unsatisfactory and unacceptable results for their employees when implementing the 'new organization'. These may take the form of job dissatisfaction, health problems and/or increased workload. This paradigm offers such explanations as: (a) managers do not really want to share power; or they are not able to perceive the discrepancy between their ideal support of empowerment, and their actual behaviour; (b) workers are socialized under restrictive conditions and consequently refuse more responsibility. These explanations, which are substantiated in many empirical studies, tell however only half the truth.

Four theses can be formulated in this context. First, there are other fundamental reasons that are not perceived or given sufficient weight. Approaches like socio-technical systems design (STS) (e.g. Trist and Murray 1993[1]) or the organizational development movement (Burke 1993) offer categories and design perspectives adequate for the criticism of Taylorism/Fordism, but do not address the new horizons and problems of present organizational modernization. Second, the solutions for 'good work' recommended by organizational development experts have become a clear cause of intensity, as their goal of 'high involvement' of employees (e.g. Lawler 1992) has been co-opted and reinterpreted by management. Third, resources must be seen as a key category for understanding these problems – they are the missing link in the explanation of failures in the realization of 'good work'. And fourth, the measure for sustainable work systems (SWS) is a positive balance of the utilized human, social and cultural resources. The following sections will discuss these theses more deeply.

Autonomy and intensity: relational definitions

Both historical and contemporary approaches emphasize autonomy as an important dimension of good and effective work, and thus use it as a general indicator for the quality of work. Autonomy is conceptualized here as degree of functional variety and job decision latitude, a variation of Gulowsen's (1971) criteria of autonomy. One general and more or less explicit thesis in this paradigm is that qualification and workload are positively affected by autonomy and with 'high performance' as the consequence. According to this reasoning it is expected that a reduction in the horizontal and vertical division of labour increases the quality of work (Benders *et al.* 1999).

Autonomy

If new empirical results of research are taken into account, we must conclude that this thesis is no longer adequate. We must reject the idea that autonomy could be defined as a resource itself. Otherwise we could not explain, for instance, the increase of workload which often accompanies making work more autonomous. Rather, autonomy should be defined by the relation between job requirements, rules and resources (Figure 5.1).

This is the basic tenet in my theory of workload (Moldaschl 1991), which is based on the psychological action regulation theory (Volpert 1989) and Giddens' theory of structuration (1984).[2] In this theory, a work system that offers a high degree of autonomy in the conventional sense of 'degrees of freedom', 'multifunctionality' or 'variety' (*formal autonomy* in my terms) can be the opposite. If the resources provided by the work system are not sufficient to cope with these requirements, practical or *substantial autonomy* will be low. As a consequence in this case, workers tend to use their personal and social resources excessively (e.g. ignoring proper breaks and working unordered overtime), and it is likely that existing personal and social resources (e.g. health, readiness for social support) are being more exhausted than reproduced.

Intensity

Does a writer experience 'intensity' or 'stress' when he or she is very committed to his/her work and has a lot to do? There are some definitions of stress that allow this assumption (Maslach and Leiter 1997). In my view, it makes no sense to define intensity only or mainly in terms of quantity, as in the prevailing positivist mindset. What does it mean to say a job has 'too much' or 'too little' stress, a task is 'too complex' or 'too simple' (Chapter 3)? What is the 'right' or, in the terms of this book, the 'sustainable' amount of intensity, stress, complexity?

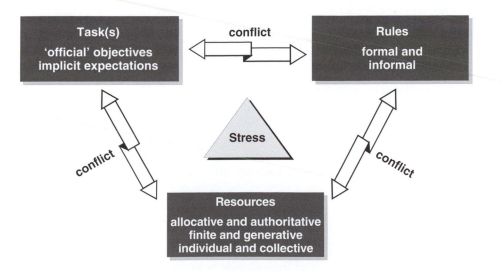

Figure 5.1 Resource-centred definition of stress: contradictory job requirements.

Can this optimum be normed, or is it individual? Work and organization sciences seem to oscillate between the normative and the relativistic poles, since they have failed to prove their norms, and simply recommend matching person and situation.

What I propose is a concept for the dialectical integration of these poles. The basic idea is to define psychological workload as a problematic relation in the context: as contradictory job requirements (CJR). A person must do something to cope with the task, which is 'actually' undoable, because resources (time, tools, information, qualifications, etc.) are lacking, or because existing rules impede action. Rules or tasks themselves can also be contradictory, as when formal and informal objectives are incompatible (e.g. in a chemical plant: 'safety first' conflicts with 'maximize plant production'). If the relation between tasks, rules and resources is contradictory, the typical result is stress and overwork, often exacerbated by social conflict. A typical stress situation in our studies was that work groups had to neglect quality control because staff were scarce. This forced them to risk failure and incur penalties. That workers have to balance conflicting goals is normal. The task only becomes contradictory if they are not allowed to regulate the balance, e.g. by changing the priorities in the given situation.[3]

This is significantly different from positivistic stressor concepts, which understand any characteristic of the real world as a potential stressor, e.g. responsibility, job complexity or quantity. It is only a statistical question here whether, or to what degree, stress or 'intensity' is 'caused' by these 'stressors'. If, for instance, a positive correlation between complexity and stress is found, the conclusion could be to go back to Tayloristic simplification in order to 'improve' work. As a relational stress theory the popular cognitive stress concept (Lazarus and Folkman 1984) can be cited. These authors also assume that resources play an important role in the genesis of stress; but they conceptualize resources only as *internal* ones, mainly competences. Thus, whether the internal resources will be sufficient to cope with the requirements of a situation is solely dependent on the individual's personal appraisal. If they do not, the employees will experience 'stress'. Stress or intensive work is here basically defined as a misfit between situational and personal characteristics, as a merely individual phenomenon. Consequently, it is possible neither to give a theoretical definition of situational stress factors, nor to give systematic recommendations as to how working conditions should be designed. As in the first approach mentioned above, everything can be a stressor, and a sufficient solution is to find a person who can tolerate the given conditions. There are parallels to Antonovsky's concept of salutogenesis (1979), which addresses resources only in the process of coping with stress, not as a constitutive element in the genesis of stress.

Another relational approach seems much nearer to the CJR model: the *demand control model* (Karasek and Theorell 1990). This was in fact my starting point. In this model, control is defined as a combination of task variety and autonomy (decision latitude). Psychological strain (not stress) is high if demands are high and decision latitude is low, and vice versa: strain is minimal if demands are low and control is high (pp. 31ff.). Thus, in terms of strain, the optimal job would be a boring one (or 'relaxed', as the authors call it, p. 70). Of course, their model is more complex, and I will only address the core difference from my model: autonomy is understood in the conventional way, and their model only includes one resource dimension as a moderating variable, namely social support. An example will show why this is unsatisfactory (see below).

In the delimitation of such concepts, the resource-centred workload theory, CJR, is basically an attempt to integrate requirements and resources, object and context in one relational definition. It is distinct from the relativistic or individualistic approach, as well as against the deterministic idea of deriving workload from a single or aggregated organizational context variable (as the degree of centralization or formalization), as is common in most stress concepts. Uncertainty, which is often modelled there as a 'stressor', has the contrary status in the CJR model. According to micropolitical approaches (as the transformation theory in labour process theory, or Giddens' structuration theory), I understand uncertainty as a central *source of power* for the workforce, because it is the realm controlled by the workers/employees, not by management.

Example: a resource-centred view on group phenomena

Considering group work, the resource-centred perspective in the CJR model treats group cohesion and social support as indicators of good work, or at least as stress moderating variables. The recommended solutions for good work of the socio-technical school (Moldaschl 2001) showed that *group cohesion*

1   is one of the major sources of resistance against management strategies, after the group members had formed an effective mode of co-operation and division of labour; and
2   is an important factor in the emergence of self-coercion within the group, a blend of group pressure and self-commitment to the redefined task, which had to be honoured under restrictive resource conditions.

Social support, on the other hand,

3   lost many of its positive connotations and its function as a resource for the workers, in as much as social support was instrumentalized by the management strategy of numerical flexibility (minimizing staff) and its emphasis on management's and workers' joint responsibility for performance. Social support lost its character as a workers' resource in the process; and
4   workers' responsibility for performance has heightened interpersonal monitoring of individual performance within work groups, often to the detriment of social support.

How do workers react to management strategies, or to their negative effects, from their own perspective? Examples of negative reactions are that they withdraw to instrumental motivation, refuse to be flexible, i.e. to rotate jobs or to take broader responsibilities. They participate less in continuous improvement processes and other development activities, restrict their willingness to co-operate and to give social support, and they decline opportunities for learning and personal development. These all contribute to often observed stagnation and frustration in processes of organizational modernization. These results cannot simply be explained by tiredness or lack of interest. They also reflect active ways of meeting the new management strategies of control by autonomy. They react sometimes with autonomy by resistance and, more often, with autonomy by feigning limited competence. This could be analysed as the efficiency of workers' control. This also shows that workers' resistance against 'good', 'rational' and 'scientific' 'best practice' models of empowerment cannot be interpreted as 'irrational' if their resource interests are taken into account.

However, looking at workers' reactions, current modernization often does not seem very effective and sustainable at all, either for employees or the company. Does this justify my earlier criticism of the idea that group work automatically leads to 'good work' and efficiency? Are the conclusions obvious: for example, allot sufficient resources, avoid overload and the exploitation of social support? No, not in general. Heuristic guidelines and recipes like these are as paradoxical as the claim: be spontaneous (at once)! Resources are contested terrains. A precarious balance must be maintained by the different actors. Management wants to exploit the rationalization potential of group work, and must react prudently to the willingness of the workers to be flexible and co-operative. Workers want to extend their freedom, but they must deal with the risk of being allotted new tasks and responsibilities when they successfully manage the former ones. They are prepared to perform at a higher level, but in flat hierarchies they must be clear of their responsibilities for personal development, promotion and financial and other rewards.

Further studies on conditions of 'good work' and 'best practice' of reorganization will not help if they stick to the rationalistic one-purpose-no-contradiction paradigm. We need another, political and micropolitical, view, asking about the divergent interests and perspectives of the involved individual and collective actors. The resource perspective is one theoretical option from which to look at the contextual embeddedness of work units like teams. Consequently, we may not ask, for instance: how much does social support reduce psychological stress, or how much does group cohesion affect performance? We must ask: how do the workers or employees regulate their efforts and resources in relation to the given context? What is the relation between internal and external resources? These questions lead to the next point.

Resources and capital: enabling conditions over time

To exploit resources does normally mean that they diminish and disappear through this process. In contrast, it seems to be clear what a sustainable use of resources should be. But it is not that trivial, because resources are different and have distinct 'logics' of reproduction. In order to assess which ways of utilization could be sustainable, we should before have a closer look at the specific resources in our field. Perhaps we can presuppose only one attribute or meaning which is common to the different types and definitions of resources and capital: they are enabling conditions for action in the present or the future.[4]

Finite, regenerative and generative resources

The basic idea of the resource-centred perspective on SWS is to analyse the production and reproduction or, better, the consumption and creation of resources in the processes of work and (re)organization. In order to meet the diversity of resources, we first have to conceptualize different qualities of resources. In an ecological analogy, it is obvious that one must differentiate between finite and regenerative resources. The latter are means for action, which get consumed in use, but can be regenerated by work or, in general, by human effort. This is the case for most material resources like tools, machines, buildings. Finite resources are generally limited, as petrol is in the material world for instance, but these limitations might not hold in the social world. Perhaps the health and sanity of people could be seen as such a finite resource. For health in general this should not be true, because physical and mental health can be re-created by human effort within certain limits.

Crucial is the assumption that there is another type of resource with a fundamentally different 'logic of reproduction' (i.e. economy): generative resources. They are means for action, which are created and amplified in their use. This is true for the most subject-bound, individual and collective competences. One consequence of this distinction is obvious: while strategies of sustainability would tend to replace or minimize the use of resources in the first two cases, this is not necessary for the third – if one respects their own cyclical rhythms and temporality. The misunderstanding of how creative human resources, like knowledge and ideas, are often being exploited with the efficiency principles applied to mineral resources, has been studied, e.g. in the case of the continuous improvement process (CIP). Results indicate that some managements drop CIP as soon as the flow of financially profitable ideas decreases (Moldaschl 1998).

These distinctions can be related to Giddens' theory of structuration (1984). Giddens defines 'structure' in categories of rules and resources in order to analyse how 'structure' is produced and reproduced by action. He sees resources as means for action, which, thus, constitute power. Control means that actors have control over resources, and this control is unequal. Furthermore, Giddens distinguishes between allocative and authoritative resources, even if he is not very clear about the purpose of the distinction. *Allocative* resources include objective or material ones (e.g. personnel capacity, tools, capacities for vocational training, knowledge). *Authoritative* resources are defined as control over means of space and time and the co-ordination of people (e.g. work organization). For our purpose, this distinction makes sense if we apply it to the material and the living or generative resources. Table 5.1 summarizes the given definitions and offers some examples.

Table 5.1 Categories and criteria for a resource-centred perspective on sustainable work systems

	Finite resources	Regenerative resources	Generative resources
Resource type	natural, biological	man made, material, objectified work	human capacities
			social relations
		cultural objectivations	cultural practices
Resource economy	exhaustive or restrictive	sparing, but expansive	lavish, but appropriate
Evaluation criteria	resource protection, resource substitution	resource productivity (efficiency of use)	resource creativity (effectiveness of creation)
Examples	physical health	physical and mental health	skills, creativity relieving routines
		explicit knowledge, knowing what	implicit knowledge, knowing how, intuition
		org. intelligence patterns of mobility and seniority	collective expertise, trust
		common language	morale; pro-social values, cultures of discourse

Temporality

Panta rhei: all things are in flux. Resources too, whether they get used or not. Even if one might find some objections to Albert Schweitzer's comment, love is the only thing that does not diminish, when we use it excessively: he accentuates these creative, anti-entropic and autopoietic forces of life which are represented and expressed in human abilities. Muscle power, for instance, gets exhausted in the present cycle of use, but it gets stronger in the next – if alternating periods of rest and maximum stress are correctly considered, along with changes in the lifecycle. The same can be assumed, for example, for experience, knowledge, motivational and moral dispositions. Knowledge, for instance, has very different ways and cycles of regeneration and generation: implicit knowledge or experience, for instance, has a different time structure and logic of reproduction from explicit knowledge.

Internal and external, social and human resources

The common understanding of human resources (e.g. in human resource management, HRM) is rooted in an individualistic understanding of human capital. Not all, but many models of HRM follow the technocratic idea to select or adapt people according to identified or presumed needs of the organization. The selection principle reads: 'the right person at the right time to the right place'. There is no difference from material resource planning, and the principle implies that one should look for the specific person who can support specific stressful conditions. This purpose fits perfectly with person-based stress concepts (see above). As an expression of methodological individualism, this understanding is undersocialized, because, for instance, professional qualifications are socially constructed and shaped, as the cultural–historical paradigm enlightens. Expertise, for instance, 'does not reside under the expert's skin' (Engeström 1992). Non-individualistic approaches alert us to the fact that, particularly in modern interactive work systems, interpersonal resources are the crucial ones: trust, common knowledge and language, cultures of interaction, professional standards. Because the resource 'knowledge' is so overemphasized and de-contextualized in present debates, another distinction has to be emphasized: between internal resources that are external to the actors and their relations, i.e. 'objective' or, better, objectified conditions. Social resources, which reside in relations between individuals, social groups and institutional actors, are, e.g.:

- network relations, e.g. trust relations that allow co-operation and reduce control effort;
- pro-social values (as a 'rational' basis for trust and co-operation);
- collective expertise (e.g. residing in 'communities of practice');
- cultures of interaction and dialogue, that foster creativity;
- relieving routines in the division of labour.

The above mentioned co-operative or pro-social values for instance have the status neither of independent nor dependent variables. They can be understood as historically generated resources, conditional results of ongoing interaction. Trust, for instance, as an effective alternative to costly control, grows with the acts of use – if it does not get disappointed. For sanctions as an instrument of control the opposite is true. Their function gets used up by use. As a means of control, sanctions can only be maintained as effective if their application can be avoided or restricted to rare exceptions. Generally, each act of utilization changes the quality of the resource, confirms or questions, consumes or reproduces, destroys or creates.

Individual human resources in the more specific sense, which are relevant for the regeneration of organizational and social entities, can be defined here as the individual 'bank' of useful skills, personal health and stability, personal relations. The person bases their performance in the task (job control) and their power in bargaining processes (workers' control) on them, and individual actors and groups can use social resources for common and peculiar, collective and individual, purposes.

Resources: a relational definition

When we identify resources in the material conditions of work and co-operation as well as in personal skills, interpersonal relationships and institutional contexts, we have to answer two questions: can everything be a resource in the observed practices? And if so, what is the benefit of a category that makes no difference? The answer to both questions can be given in one sentence: yes, and it depends. Any aspect of the real world can become a resource for action. It depends on the context. For instance, a 'useless' Brazilian frog or a Cambodian fern can become a resource in medicine if someone discovers that they produce 'useful' substances for a particular human purpose. An employee's blindness, normally seen as a handicap for the employing organization, may turn into a resource if this organization starts to offer products or services for blind customers. Thus, and instead of producing endless lists of resources, we should conceptualize the category as a relational or contextual one.

Values

My definition of resources is operational, not normative. Since there is no use of resources without purpose, values must be added. And this means it must be decided which purposes are legitimate and which values are guiding. It is, for instance, not suitable to legitimate a pure utilitarianism of the kind that every thing or relation in the world can be neglected if it is not a resource, i.e. not useful for a specific human purpose. In order to avoid such a misunderstanding in the context of a sustainability discourse, values have to be added implicitly or explicitly, e.g. transformed in heuristic codes of conduct. For example: treat any living being and any social relation as if it could imply a resource; be attentive to the diversity of resources; protect socio-diversity.

Sustainability of work systems: a model

On the basis of these distinctions, the idea of sustainability can be defined in relation to organizational solutions and strategies: they are sustainable in a social sense if they maintain and reproduce the given social and human resources or even extend them. The amount of this contribution is measured as *resource productivity*. The risk of strategies lies in the unintended (or approved) destruction of genuine bases for action. In our research network we relate this idea to the category of work systems. By a work system we understand a regulated collaborative activity on different levels: a group, a department, or a higher organizational unit. It includes, e.g., wage systems, technical infrastructure or training systems. Nevertheless, it makes no sense to cover everything with the concept of work systems. Industrial relations, for instance, should be analysed as a separate dimension. Finally, we define a contrasting pattern to sustainable work systems (as an ideal type in Max Weber's sense) and we call it *intensive work systems*. They develop by consuming (exploiting) resources that are generated and provided in the social environment of the work system or the organization. The negative balance of this exchange can be identified in the exhaustion of work motivation, low trust, long-term sick leaves, etc.; and the work situation is characterized by serious mismatches between job requirements and available resources (i.e. contradictory job requirements, see above).

Levels of sustainability: the future as contested terrain

It would be amazing but starry-eyed to think that a sustainable work system implies sustainability for each worker and all external effects. It is much more likely that we have to face severe contradictions among different levels of sustainability, and the overall sustainability represents something like a sound compromise. We have to bear in mind that the enterprise does not exist in a vacuum. An organization – whether profit-oriented or not – is embedded in a broader social and cultural context. This context enables and restricts organizational practices. The context itself gets reproduced and changed by these practices. Thus, the sustainability of work systems should be conceptualized and evaluated at least on the following levels:

- From a *worker's perspective*, a work system is sustainable when it maintains or develops (or allows one to develop) marketable qualifications and skills, social relations and personal health. This requires a match between job demands and resources, or institutionalized procedures which help to identify and change current mismatches.
- A work system or a reorganization strategy is sustainable on the *organizational level* (single enterprise perspective) when it maintains or extends the human, social and institutional resources (e.g. flexibility) of the organization.
- From a *societal perspective*, organizational strategies can only be held as sustainable if they do not stress the socially produced resources and the social system as a whole, but contribute to the generation and regeneration of resources, e.g. by qualifying their workforce, or contributing to their old age pension.

The worker's perspective does not necessarily mean the individual level (see Chapter 4), since we may not identify subject, individual and workforce. The subject as a specific person may, for instance, continuously accept conditions that are unhealthy from a medical or psychological (scientific, 'objective') point of view, if that seems bearable compared to the advantages of the job and the given alternatives (as we well know, e.g. from female assembly workers). If we talk about individuals we can do this in an abstract way, defining their interests from a scientific point of view. This is important for intervention into a specific practice, because we must take into account systematic differences between our (scientific) relevance and the subject's relevance (see Chapter 15). Furthermore, the worker's perspective may also be collective. A good example for an area exhibiting differences between individual and collective 'sustainability interests' is working time. Even if individuals are mostly interested in a maximum scope to time their working hours (including overtime), workers as a collective cannot be interested in giving away any standards and the chance of their regulation. Shop stewards face the same conflicts as scientists if they want to regulate working conditions in a way that they understand as sustainable. We can use analytical concepts like the demand control model or the CJR model as tools to study the resource situation from the worker's perspective, but they have to be combined with tools that analyse other resource balances too (e.g. the reproduction of marketable skills).

Organizational practices are obviously sustainable if the organization persists (something we can only assess for the present or the near future). This tautology reminds us that we are talking about a specific aspect – the sustainability of work. Thus, we have to show how the use of the workforce goes together with other criteria of organizational survival and success (e.g. profit, independence, image; see Chapter 14). Since there is a vast amount of literature arguing that the new work organization is able to reconcile diverging criteria, we will just look at some possible contradictions of sustainability within and between the organizational and the other levels; the following case exemplifies a clash of criteria within a company.

A West German corporation established a chemical plant in the former East Germany after unification. Its staff were highly qualified, trained to work in groups, and participated in various decision processes. The plant was planned for highly automated production, but following market changes, the efficiency of the plant fell below expectations. The corporate headquarters was dissatisfied with the plant and reduced its resources (investment, staff, autonomy) in order to increase the investment–profit ratio. In this situation, the motivated staff failed to increase the plant's productivity because they had neither the financial resources to adapt the plant's technical layout, nor the right to decide on the type and sequence of orders produced there. These matters were managed by headquarters, which optimized the conditions for more profitable plants. Consequently, qualifications were poorly utilized, and although the workers tried very hard – in sometimes conspiratorial coalition with the local management – the economic improvements were limited, for the plant and for themselves. One reason was that the local management faced the same situation: financial resources (e.g. to reward the extra-ordinary efforts of the staff) were as limited as their influence on the structure of wages or time. Consequently, the social and human resources available at the outset in terms of motivation, trust, the commitment to the existing organizational solutions and the will-ingness to try out new ones, decreased continuously. The group work process, for instance, was initiated twice and failed twice (Figure 5.2).

On a societal level we continue to ask how organizational survival and success are achieved. In addition, what do organizational practices contribute to the reproduction and welfare of its institutional environment (including ecological aspects, which we do not address here). We are aware of inter-level conflicts of interest. An enterprise may, for example, pursue a strategy of non-sustainable exploitation of specific human resources to promote its own sustainability if the costs can be externalized to society (e.g. by not contributing to skill formation and simply substituting workers if new skills are needed. The costs of unhealthy working conditions may also be externalized to the national health system). Conversely, and according to an environ-mental perspective, we can evaluate the extent to which enterprises increase, for instance, social capital and are apt to (re-)internalize their external social costs, e.g. by educating more people than they employ afterwards. The issues under which the sustainability of firm prac-tices can be evaluated are as manifold as our relational understanding of resources suggests. Industrial relations, training systems and employability, regulatory regimes and cultures in a regional, national or supranational scale are but a few examples. Under the headline of

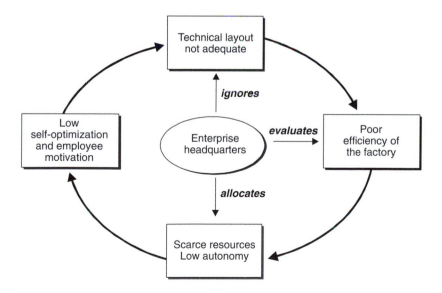

Figure 5.2 A vicious circle of resource dependence.

globalization the debate on relevant rules and resources for the competitiveness of nations increased drastically, and shows the same opposition as in organizational debates: between economics, mainly emphasizing wages and labour regulations, and broader socio-cultural explanations.

Each emphasis on one of the levels has costs and benefits. To think and act in terms of sustainability only makes sense if each level of aggregation has its own legitimacy and if one is aware that there is always an embedding context to be taken into account. It is just this view that enables us to discuss contradictions between levels of socio-economic reproduction and cultural development, and therefore opens a space for different blueprints of how the reproduction cycles on the different levels could be interlocked in overall sustainable ways. Talking about sustainable work systems in this way, therefore, gives us means to address 'side effects' systematically. The future is a contested terrain, and we should request a theoretical approach that is capable of holding this contest, instead of only 'externalizing' it into the contest of different theories.

Conclusions

What is the benefit of a resource-centred theoretical approach as presented here? At any rate, the intention is not to deliver a neo-STS approach. The idea is not a new normative 'model' for the perfect workplace in the high performance company, which is, at the same time, a positive example of sustainability. I am very sceptical that a set of rules or design principles or guidelines can be found which, if applied, could guarantee at least one of these goals. The reality is contradictory, as emphasized above. The methodological consequences of this view are discussed later (see Chapter 15). The theoretical and pragmatic intentions of the resource-centred perspective can be summarized in the following three points.

First, I propose to understand the vision of SWS in general as an *analytical* perspective on entrepreneurial practices and on how they deal with the mentioned contradictions. The resource perspective offers one framework for the production and (re)interpretation of empirical research findings on modern, autonomous, qualified work and reorganization.

Second, in practical contexts of rationalization, e.g. work design and organization development, the approach aims to draw the attention of practitioners (and consultants, action researchers) to the great variety of and the fundamental differences between the used and reproduced resources. Thus, it could perhaps generate more awareness about the specificity of handling living resources in longer time horizons, and draw more attention to the unintended effects of strategic action. And it could or should foster interest in evaluating discrepancies between planning and reality.

The distinction between intensive and sustainable work systems has, thirdly, a paradigmatic function. It lies at a right angle to the common clichés of and distinctions between Tayloristic and post-Tayloristic, hierarchical and participative, 'bad' Japanese and 'good' European models. It makes clear that both patterns of organizational modernization or rationalization can always imply a problematic creation of insecurity and intensification of work. This has been proved in the majority of recent empirical studies in various sectors of the economy, and it means that the consequences for the human capital and the social environment of the company may probably be non-sustainable if the reproduction of resources is not taken adequately into account. Thus, it is not enough to criticize Tayloristic or neo-Tayloristic strategies, in order to recommend the traditional humanistic recipes such as job enrichment, group work, participation, because these 'solutions' are or can be part of the problem. On the other hand, the SWS resource approach gives us a vision of how we could emphasize the enormous diversity of human and social capital in order to create zones of protected autonomy.

The discourse on human and social capital, which we want to influence with our SWS perspective, can be connected with a debate of which Karl Polanyi (1944) was an exponent. This debate is centred around the question about which capital and which capitalism we are talking. And when we are talking about problematic, destructive tendencies in the presently dominating neo-liberal capitalism, we can remind ourselves with Bourdieu (1977): social and cultural capital are not always and forever 'good' *per se*. It depends on the way in which and the purpose for which they are used.

Notes

1 For reasons of brevity I will only give one reference for each research approach mentioned.
2 The figure shows only the general tenet, and focuses here only on stress that results if two or more components are conflicting (symbolized by the broken arrows). The theory shares Giddens' elementary conception of *power*, which is seen as the ability to act differently, to have alternatives in coping with external requirements and conditions. Power as a meta-conception here expresses the degree to which actors in the organization can utilize rules and resources in order to maintain their autonomy. This allows a distinction between workers' autonomy on two levels: *job control* means autonomy within the job, and *worker control* means collective control over the conditions of jobs and employment, i.e. the general conditions of reproduction, as addressed in research on industrial relations. The contradictory job requirements (CJR) theory was applied in a variety of qualitative and quantitative studies (in the cited ones, and e.g. by Büssing and Glaser (1996)).
3 The theory conceptualizes four categories of negative consequence: the coercion to take risks and threat as the virtual ones; and additional effort and overload as the manifest ones.
4 Dictionaries define resources as means, or as sources of income; from the Latin: *resurgere*: to arise (again). The category of capital is often used as a general denominator for resources.

References

Antonovsky, A. (1979) *Health, Stress, and Coping*, San Francisco: Jossey-Bass.

Benders, J., Huijgen, F., Pekruhl, U. and O'Kelly, K.P. (1999) *Useful but Unused. Group Work in Europe*, Dublin: European Foundation.

Bourdieu, P. (1977) *Outline of a Theory of Practice*, Cambridge: Cambridge University Press.

Burke, W.W. (1993) *Organizational Development*, 2nd edn, Reading, MA: Addison-Wesley.

Büssing, T. and Glaser, F. (1996) 'Widersprüchliche Arbeitsanforderungen in der Arbeitstätigkeit', *ZAO*, 40, 2, 87–91.

Engeström, Y. (1992) 'Interactive expertise', *Research Bulletin* 83, University of Helsinki.

Giddens, A. (1984) *The Constitution of Society*, Cambridge: Polity Press.

Gulowsen, J. (1971) *Selvstyrte arbeidsgrupper, på vej mot industrielt demokrati* (Autonomous Work Groups. Towards Industrial Democracy), Oslo: Tanum.

Karasek, R. and Theorell, T. (1990) *Healthy Work. Stress, Productivity, and the Reconstruction of Working Life*, New York: Basic Books.

Lawler, E.E. (1992) *The Ultimate Advantage. Creating the High Involvement Organization*, San Francisco: Jossey-Bass.

Lazarus, R.S. and Folkman, S. (1984) *Stress, Appraisal and Coping*, New York: Springer.

Leana, C.R. and Van Buren, H.J. (1999) 'Organizational social capital and employment practices', *Academy of Management Review*, 24, 538–555.

Maslach, C. and Leiter, M.P. (1997) *The Truth about Burnout. How Organizations Cause Personal Stress and What to Do about It*, San Francisco: Jossey-Bass.

Moldaschl, M. (1991) *Frauenarbeit oder Facharbeit?* Frankfurt and New York: Campus.

Moldaschl, M. (1998) 'Rationality, culture and politics of production', in E. Scherer (ed.) *Shop Floor Scheduling and Control. A Systems Perspective*, London: Springer, pp. 67–90.

Moldaschl, M. (2001) 'From team ideology to sustainable work systems', *Concept and Transformation*, 6, 2 (in press).

Mudrack, E. (1989) 'Group cohesiveness and productivity. A closer look', *Human Relations*, 42, 9, 771–85.

Penrose, E.T. (1968) *The Theory of Growth of the Firm*, Oxford: Blackwell (1st edn 1959).

Polanyi, K. (1975) *The Great Transformation*, New York: Octagon Books (1st edn 1944).

Pralahad, C.K. and Hamel, G. (1990) 'The core competence of the corporation', *Harvard Business Review*, 3, 79–91.

Trist, E. and Murray, H. (eds) (1993) *The Social Engagement of Social Science. A Tavistock Anthology* (Vol. II), Philadelphia: University of Pennsylvania Press.

Volpert, W. (1989) 'Work and development from the viewpoint of the action regulation theory', in H. Leymann and H. Kornbluh (eds) *Socialization and Learning at Work*, Aldershot: Avebury, pp. 215–32.

6 A complexity perspective

*Tomas Backström, Frans M. van Eijnatten
and Mari Kira*

Introduction

A sustainable work system can be described as a system that consciously strives towards simultaneous development at different levels – individual, group/company and region/society. For example, at the lowest level, an individual wants to stay healthy and enjoy continuous learning; at group/company level, economic growth may be considered important to maintain or raise market shares; and, at societal level, the maintenance of inclusive employment opportunities may be crucial. All these different aspects interact, and materialise concurrently. In this chapter, we will use theories of complex systems as a *metaphor*. A fundamental presumption of this approach is that rather chaotic processes at the level of the parts/agents/holons lead to apprehensible patterns in the system as a whole.

We state at the outset that only a system that is continuously in a state of 'becoming' can be called 'sustainable'. Sustainability cannot be regarded as a static characteristic of a structure or a process because everything in the system is constantly 'on the move'. A definition of sustainability must take account of time as a key factor, and should focus on dynamic qualities of the system. In short, we understand sustainable work systems as complex systems. We will demonstrate how the metaphor of complexity can be used to define and understand sustainable work systems.

Some elements in the complexity metaphor

In this chapter, we suggest that a complexity metaphor can create a theoretical basis for holistic organizational change processes that may lead to sustainable work systems in practice. According to Lissack and Roos (1999, p. 10), complexity refers to:

> The collection of scientific disciplines all of which are concerned with finding patterns among collections of behaviours or phenomena. The field looks at patterns across a multitude of scales in an effort to detect their 'laws' of pattern generation or 'rules' that explain the patterns observed.

The complexity metaphor sees the organization as a whole entity composed of several wholes/parts or 'holons' (Koestler 1967; Mathews 1995; Wilber 1996). A holon is both an individual 'whole' and a part of a much larger whole, at one and the same time. The deeper meaning of sustainability can only be grasped in the multiple contexts of the employee's work group, company, family and neighbourhood.

Employing this holistic way of looking at reality, the object of study is not further divided into parts – as is often the case in analysis – but is left completely intact. The functioning of the whole in its environment is an explicit object of inquiry (Gharajedaghi 1999). A whole entity (e.g. an organization) is studied in its entirety.

The complexity metaphor points to *emergent properties*. An emergent property is a new quality that presents itself 'out of the blue' when different components intensively interact in a complex system. An emergent property is absent in the parts, but present in the whole. It is explained by the expression 'the whole is more than the sum of its parts'. Emergence as a phenomenon is an example of self-organization. It is connected with the ability to 'make sense' (which is also a main issue in Bjerlöv's account of dialogue and learning, see Chapter 16).

Looking at emergence in the field of organizations, it should be emphasized that renewal is not something managers produce just by designing a process for it. Renewal emerges from interaction between a multiplicity of stakeholders. It is not possible to point to a limited number of actors or activities responsible for a specific improvement.

According to the complexity metaphor, a complex and dynamic system may be in different states: equilibrium (E), near to equilibrium (NTE), far from equilibrium (FFE) and fatal chaos (FC). Systems go through phases of relative stability and instability. Growth is typically discontinuous, and can be characterized as involving a jump to the next level of complexity and coherence. See Figure 6.1.

The behaviour of a system on the edge of chaos can be explained in terms of the concept of 'strange attractor' (Nicolis and Prigogine 1989). A strange attractor is a complex behaviour pattern to which the system is attracted. Accordingly, the behaviour repeats itself, but each time in a slightly different manner (Marion 1999). The organization is said to be 'imprisoned' in a strange attractor when it is robust and hard to develop, no matter how much leaders or consultants try to change it. But a complex system is also able to change discontinuously by suddenly following another strange attractor. Such metamorphosis actually takes place when the system jumps out of the old, passes a ridge, and falls into a new attractor basin. The organization changes suddenly, and starts to follow a completely new pattern of behaviour.

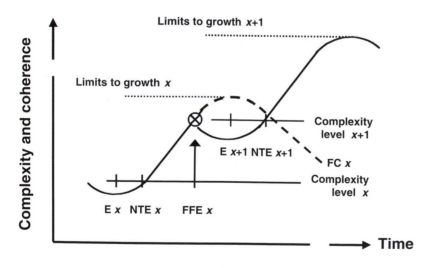

Figure 6.1 The growth curve of discontinuous growth.

Key: E = equilibrium; NTE = near to equilibrium; FFE = far from equilibrium; FC = fatal chaos; x = present level of complexity/coherence; $x +1$ = next level of complexity/coherence; ⊗ = bifurcation point.

The term 'chaord' is a name for a system that is both chaotic and orderly at the same time (The Chaordic Alliance 1999). Mind, e.g. intentions and culture, is more important in such a system than matter, e.g. technology, organization and space. The system emerges through interactions between its members and between members and the surroundings, towards ascending levels of coherence and complexity. A high degree of connectivity makes the system an unbroken unity in which nothing can exist or occur independently of the whole. A chaordic system is so dynamically complex and highly sensitive to initial conditions that any link between cause and effect is necessarily obscured, rendering its future indeterminate. Its structure is continuously cycling through a process of 'falling apart' and 'coming together again' in a novel new form ungoverned by the past (Fitzgerald 1996).

The complexity metaphor has developed in different disciplines. Encoding and decoding between model and reality differ between distinct disciplines. We especially distinguish between physical and artificial systems on the one hand, and living – autopoietic – or social systems on the other.

Key features of sustainable work systems using a complexity metaphor

There are three central features characteristic of sustainable work systems when using the complexity metaphor: (a) spontaneous and mutual alignment of individuals; (b) successful thriving in rapidly changing environments; and (c) fitness development for competitiveness. These features are briefly presented here, and will be elaborated upon in the paragraphs that follow.

1   A first key feature of sustainable work is the tendency of employees – for spontaneous and mutual alignment – to pull in the same direction. A sustainable work system is, according to the complexity metaphor, most efficiently grounded in individuals' acting and interacting without top-down or external control. Managers create and nurture conditions and affordances that allow alignment to emerge, but any such alignment must originate in the individual. Alignment is a matter of internal interaction and dialogue, promoting collective learning and self-organization, which creates a common culture, a flow of information, a frame for interpretation and a common vision. This situation makes it possible for an individual to create and reconstruct meaning and understanding, and thereby to manage the worry (psychological wear and tear) that continuous change might cause, and also to foster personal and professional development.

2   A second key feature of a sustainable work system lies in its ability to thrive in a continuously changing environment. In line with Stacey *et al.* (2000) and Stacey (2001), sustainable work can be seen in terms of the complex responsive processes involved in relating to the surrounding world through networks and adapting to external changes. There are numerous examples of companies ending up in 'fatal chaos', e.g. suffering a bankruptcy, because of a failure to adapt to change in time.

3   A third key feature of a sustainable work system is fitness development for competitiveness. The complexity perspective has been successfully used in the study of biological evolution – which focuses precisely on fitness development for competitiveness. Most organizations now face strong competition in a global market. There is a continuous striving towards increased development in complex systems (both legitimate and shadow systems) in order to be able to survive in a rapidly changing environment.

Spontaneous and mutual alignment of individuals

Individuals have a substantial role to play in a complex system. Through interaction and collective learning, they are able to create a social holon that prospers in a complex system. Further, an individual's interaction with work and other people in the system may lead to personal development that facilitates life in the complex system.

Towards common understanding through interaction and dialogue

One of Holland's (1995) seven basic characteristics of complex systems is 'tagging'. Tagging is 'a mechanism that consistently facilitates the formation of aggregates' (p. 12). One example employed by Holland is that of a banner used to rally members of an army.

What processes lie behind the aggregation of members of an enterprise? The concept of collective learning refers to the development of common understanding. A group of people working together may – through interaction – develop common understanding and 'sense-making' in relation to work and its context. Such common understanding makes it possible for individual members of the group to act in a similar way. An important form of interaction between people is 'dialogue' (Bohm 1987; see also Wilhelmson 1998, Bjerlöv 1999, and Chapter 16 on dialogue and learning). According to Ellinor and Gerard (1998, p. 21), dialogue is: 'A way of conversation in which shared meaning is created among many. Learning is accomplished through inquiry into assumptions. Dialogue stresses the whole among the parts and focuses on the connections between them.'

Opinions are expressed by talking – as too are views, conceptions and taken-for-granted assumptions concerning the task, work and organization. In dialogue, people have the opportunity to mirror their individual understanding and perceptions against those of others. Both parties speak at the same time as they think, and both hear immediately what is said. In this way, people obtain continuous, co-ordinated, mutual access to two subjectivities ('mine' and 'yours'), resulting in inter-subjective proximity. This may develop into a mechanism for the aggregation of organizational members, resulting in the development of an organizational mind, and acting as a meta-agent. Then, there is an organization capable of action in a unified way, using its holonic potential (Fitzgerald and van Eijnatten 1998).

An organization with a high degree of collective learning has advantages over organizations where competition rules. The so-called 'learning organization' will have the ability to generate collective frames of interpretation, and will thereby be adaptive to changes in the environment. Its members will act in a unified manner, and operate in synchronicity with each other. This can be illustrated using the 'shoal of fish' metaphor. When threatened, small fishes adopt a large, whale-like formation that moves very quickly, which confuses the predator.

Personal and professional development

Work in a complex system is a major challenge. How is it possible for an employee to deal with work in a complex and dynamic context? Since sustainable work systems pose such a challenge to their employees, they should also simultaneously support employees' opportunities to cope with the challenge. Accordingly, from the perspective of an individual, a work system is sustainable only when it supports employees' abilities to cope with the challenges of both work and the world in general. In a sustainable work system, an employee should be able to grow and develop – not only in a professional sense, but also as a whole person capable of navigating, functioning and prospering in a complex world.

We have already discussed learning as a key part of individual growth at work. But, since a person is not only interacting with work at a cognitive level, cognitive development in itself is not enough. Emotional and subconscious elements are also involved. A sustainable work system is sensitive to these more profound levels of interaction, and aims at the holistic development of any psychological potential that might enable employees to deal with working life. The way a person sees the world influences the way she/he perceives existing stressors and also the way she/he reacts to them (see e.g. Stellman 1997). As Csikszentmihalyi puts it: 'Subjective experience is not just one of the dimensions of life, it is the life itself' (1990, p. 192).

An example of world-image related coping can be found in Antonovsky's (1987) concept of 'sense of coherence' (see Chapter 3). Antonovsky has shown that a person's high sense of coherence – in other words, his/her ability to perceive the world as comprehensible, manageable and meaningful – enables him/her better to deal with life's stressors. In a complex organization, sense of coherence is an important psychological potential – worthy of organizational support. The work experiences of today should enable the individual to perceive the challenges of tomorrow as more comprehensible, manageable and meaningful. Semmer (1997) states that it is imperative to design work conditions in such a way that they support individuals' resourcefulness. But how can an individual's resourcefulness – internal potential – be supported? We believe that dialogue within the work system is a powerful enabler. Through dialogue, individuals can create and obtain material, cultural and social resources that support their work, and also have work experiences that are comprehensible, manageable and meaningful. The availability of such resources and 'coherent' work experiences contributes positively to an individual's ability to cope with work at both cognitive and emotional levels. Accordingly, dialogue – as described above – also has an important function from an individual's coping and developmental perspectives.

Thriving in continuously changing environments

Networking for sustainability

One way of making the surrounding world more stable and less unpredictable is to interact with it through a network. The organization also gets a chance to exert influence over markets and resources through the network. Further, networks provide a means for spreading risk:

> Their [IT companies'] leaders know there are lots of potential ways the landscape could evolve, so they form alliances with various agents that have different skills: If markets move in any particular direction, at least their companies will have presence there.
>
> (Fulmer 2000, p. 190)

The emergence of networking in social systems involves autocatalytic interaction (Marion 1999). Autocatalytic interaction is a basic feature of the complexity metaphor. It is one of the processes behind self-organization, and it also provides the basis for the natural growth of networks. Autocatalytic interaction is a concept employed by Kauffman (1995) to describe how systems – for example, organizations and networks – emerge and develop. A catalyst is something that speeds up a process. The process will take place even without the catalyst, but will run much more slowly. In an autocatalytic interaction, certain actions in the process serve as catalysts for other actions, which in turn are catalysts for further actions. In this way, any one action is reinforced by virtue of being involved in a process involving certain other actions, which are also strengthened in the same manner. Accordingly, a new order arises out of chaos locally and naturally – without control or external co-ordination, and without the consumption of energy, and in such a manner that a certain action is reinforced by other actions.

In the well-known simulation derived from game theory called 'Prisoner's Dilemma', two types of player are created – 'pure co-operators' and 'pure defectors' (Nowak *et al.* 1995). It was found that neighbour defectors exploit lone co-operators, but that four or more co-operators can hold their own in many situations. Lone defectors fare pretty well, but if a number of defectors clump together, they work to their mutual detriment. Co-operation or collaboration may also be good for companies and increase their sustainability. For example, small subcontractors with one big client may face severe pressure to fulfil the client's – sometimes almost conflicting – wishes concerning price, time to deliver, quality, and so on. There are ongoing efforts in Sweden to start up networks of small subcontractors – designed to turn them into virtual major subcontractors with an ability to develop products together with their client. They can then develop and deliver not only parts, but also whole subsystems. If this succeeds, the power balance between client and virtual subcontractor will be more even, and the subcontractors' situation more sustainable. In some of the cases, the interaction in the network is carried through at the level of the operators. This may provide an opportunity to achieve self-organization and genuine sustainability.

Adapting to external changes

Unexpected changes may come from political deregulation, technology development or uncertainty with regard to sources of future competition. Further, trade barriers have come down, and commercial organizations are expanding globally, becoming interconnected and forming alliances. Companies are also becoming much more linked to their customers and suppliers. Inter-couplings make it more likely that small changes will propagate and develop into significant and unpredictable changes, as generated by the butterfly effect (Holland 1995). And even if individual components are changing as sluggishly as ever, more things are changing at once. The future cannot be predicted.

> There are at least three major problems with the way most predictions are made: They are based on historical data, they fail to count for unique events, and they ignore co-evolution. In addition, there are some psychological challenges implicit in predictions.
>
> (Fulmer 2000, p. 68)

Another way of planning is to shape an energetic and flexible team that is capable of responding to the unanticipated, as well as to any ordinary event. This involves utilizing the ability that all complex adaptive systems have in common – to build models or 'maps' to anticipate their world.

In order to cope with changing external conditions, an organization must be able to recognize them. Organizations may have a capacity to draw a map of their surroundings, making use of the information they obtain in interaction (Marion 1999). Interaction with the environment has an impact on the organization in the sense that the organization's members engaged in that interaction will remember the relations and patterns of action that have been exchanged. Through collective learning, this part of the environment becomes a part of the actual world of organization members and, thereby, of the organization itself.

Several conditions have to be met to enable such impressions to form a 'map'. The organization has to be stable enough to build up a memory, while, at the same time, being sufficiently dynamic to create a changeable map from constantly arising individual experiences. In other words, the organization must be 'on the edge of chaos'. Few shared meaning structures and too little interaction within the organization cause rigidity, and also an inability to update a common map. On the other hand, over-extensive interaction and too great a sensitivity to impulses from the outside rapidly prompt major changes in the mapped image in various parts of the organization, so that no one knows which map will serve as the one to be shared. Fulmer states:

> There are at least five general characteristics of an adaptive organization's structure: It tends to be relatively decentralised, has high spans of control, makes extensive use of temporary structures, has a powerful information system, and constantly evolves the structure.
> (Fulmer (2000, p. 179)

To map an unstable environment is too complex to be managed within a simple organization structure. Rather, the organization must be divided into small, manageable tasks assigned to different individuals or groups; to function as a unit the departments or teams must be integrated and co-ordinated by feedback, or include slack or be built of interdependent parts (Marion 1999). A sustainable way of reducing the impact of an unstable environment is to introduce organizational slack (stock piles of resources) to deal with unanticipated problems or demands. Systems divided into specialities, where tasks are performed sequentially, may experience problems of failure due to brittleness. If a system component – at either individual or organizational level – has slack reserves, it can feed on these when any one section fails. Organizational slack offers opportunities for reflection and learning, and also for dialogue. Further, change and development demand slack, including the presence of fitness scouts who explore alternative solutions to organizational problems.

Fitness development for competitiveness

The enterprises of today are not as stable as they once were. Every day we hear of mergers, outsourcing and other commercial rearrangements. This does not necessarily mean that work systems are unsustainable (see also Chapter 9). As stated above, sustainable work systems are always on the move – in a state of 'becoming'. We go on to explain what 'sustainable becoming' might mean.

Development in complex systems

Although a sustainable work system is always one in the process of further development, its types of development may be twofold:

1 *Continuous development.* Although exterior aspects of a holon may be constantly changing, the interior of the holon, i.e. its dominant intentions and culture, is maintained (Wilber 1996). The holon continues to behave as a whole. It remains to be recognized by its environment. Members of the holon derive personal meaning and identity from their membership.

2 *Discontinuous development.* A holon has the capacity to change its form and function, and adopt a new identity – whenever necessary, and when the holon is sufficiently mature. This is a transformation process or metamorphosis – like becoming a butterfly from a caterpillar. Members may form a new holon when the identity of the old is lost. A new holon normally emerges spontaneously.

These two forms of development can be clarified by employing the strange attractor concept (Nicolis and Prigogine 1989), see above, p. 66. The specific strange attractor an organization follows is reproduced by the dominant frame for interpretation or the 'legitimate system' (Berger and Luckmann 1966). Further, the concept of a 'shadow system' (Stacey 1996a) indicates an underlying process, making it possible for an organization to undergo metamorphosis and start to follow a new strange attractor.

Over time, it is supposed that an organization develops a system to perform its primary tasks to ensure survival. This is the purpose of an organization's legitimate system, with its dominant schema. Legitimization imposes order in an organization by ascribing meaningfulness to its actions. And it justifies the institutional order by giving normative rank to its practical imperatives. However, it is important to understand that legitimization has both cognitive and normative elements. Legitimization does not just attribute value, it also involves knowledge. Incipient legitimization is present as soon as a system of linguistic objectification of human experience is conveyed. 'That's the way it's done' is the first answer to the child's question 'Why?' It is the self-evident foundation of knowledge that all subsequent theories must rest upon, and – looking at matters the other way around – that they have to achieve if they are to become part of tradition. Theories can legitimize parts of the organization's actions in terms of a distinct body of knowledge. The legitimate system may develop continuously, but a strongly changing environment may impose demands for discontinuous adaptation and improvement. How is this possible?

Reality is socially defined. But definitions are always embodied; that is, concrete individuals or groups of individuals serve as definers of reality. It is important not just to pose the abstract question 'What?' about reality, but also the sociologically concrete question 'Says who?' Most organizations are pluralistic. This means that in parallel with the legitimate system, shadow alternatives develop – driven by recessive symbol systems. The legitimate system strives towards the status quo, the shadow system towards change. Different social groups have divergent sympathies with regard to various theories, and will consequently become the carriers of one rather than another. A theory demonstrates its superiority not only through its intrinsic qualities but also through its usability in terms of the carrier group's social interests. Dialogue and talk become transformational when they rise to another level of awareness – creating a shift in an individual's structure of thinking, and his/her ways of acting in connection with the work task, of relating to others' knowledge, and of trying to understand something in a new way. If the legitimate system has defects in fitness, there is an opportunity for the shadow system to grow in strength. And, when time passes, the shadow system can suddenly take over, outperform the legitimate system, and itself become the new legitimate system (Stacey 1996a). This takes place when a large number of independent initiatives for change reinforce one another and merge into a significant movement. Emergence is achieved via political interaction and collective learning (Stacey 1996b). Political interaction means that people identify an issue and promote opinion in favour of it; they build coalitions, convince others and negotiate with still others for support.

Development of inner holonic capacities, those possessed by shadow systems, is a key to the adaptive ability of an organization. External pressure for fitness imposes demands on internal dynamics. Thus, it is a disadvantage for the organization if all members are proximally or strictly tied to the core of the legitimate system. It is an advantage if there is room for experimentation, and for fitness 'scouts' to roam well beyond the boundaries of conventional thought (Marion 1999). And there is also a need for effective internal interaction, which can generate the collective learning that builds up the shadow system and makes possible the political struggle between different theories.

Organizational requirements for the emergence of sustainability

The lesson so far is that interaction in an organization may lead to common understanding, creation of resources and the ability to 'manage' or thrive in the surrounding world – in short, an ability to evolve towards sustainability.

The organization has to combine stability and instability, i.e. to be close to the edge of chaos – to be able to reach sustainability. The complexity metaphor tells us that diversity among agents is vital if the aggregate is to be able to undertake complex behaviour. Internal conditions and an environment that allows the organization to operate at the edge of chaos have to be created and nurtured. Fulmer describes this as a three to five year process, grounded in shared individual learning: 'To make large scale shared learning a reality, organizations must encourage and reward at least four core values: external focus, diversity, responsible risk taking, and openness' (Fulmer 2000, p. 159).

Organizational activities important for shared learning are the dissemination of experiences and information within the organization, opportunities for dialogue and common reflection, and the shaping of strategies for collective acting on the part of the organization (Dixon 1994). All these elements are key building blocks in collective learning in organizations, and they underline the importance of communication between members of the organization at all levels.

Integration and added value

The complexity metaphor, as we have presented it in this chapter, combines several levels (individual, organization, society), several stakeholders (managers, workers, customers, suppliers) and several processes (cognitive, social). Simultaneous interaction is its central feature. We have focused on the holon 'organization', which consists of several other holons: 'the individuals.'

What is the added value of the complexity metaphor for sustainable work systems? On the basis of Fitzgerald's (1996) five statements about chaordic properties, complexity science can be regarded as capable of combating the following shortcomings of current approaches:

1   Except when a psychodynamic approach is adopted, the study of work often seems to be reduced to exterior aspects only (i.e. what can be accessed by our five senses or their extensions) – leaving out more subtle, non-observable interior aspects (the thoughts and introspections of individuals and collectives).

2   With the exception of some culture and group process studies, the world of work is treated as the sum of a multiplicity of distinct, independent, separate parts – leaving out the emergent properties of wholes and their environments.

3   The future of work can hardly be predicted (by considering significant unilateral cause–effect relationships). We seem to neglect the fact that – in our complex world – causes and effects interchange continuously, in dynamic, non-linear feedback networks. This means that we can only know the present; the future may be unknowable, even in principle (Stacey 1996a, 1996b).

4   We constantly intervene in our work systems, in order to prevent decay. We are changing work structures and procedures. By doing so, we may prevent the work system from developing autonomously at the same time.

5   Progress and growth in the work organization are unlikely as long as a steady state of equilibrium and stability is maintained by the use of control mechanisms. We cannot let

go of control and by the act of controlling we may prevent the system from travelling by itself from equilibrium to the far from equilibrium conditions where creativity reigns (Fitzgerald and van Eijnatten 1998).

Research into work and work organization would profit from incorporating the complexity of the whole situation. Such an approach would necessarily be both integral (or holistic) and longitudinal – simultaneously taking into account the history of the system. Applied to sustainable work systems, what specific behaviour patterns in work situations can be labelled as involving 'intensive work'? We are accustomed to looking for analytical critical incidents – such as an increase in short-term sick leave among professionals, or the stress that results from an inability to cope with contradictory demands by managers and project supervisors. But what is really needed is to find the broader picture – the strange attractor that operates in these situations. Can we define 'the strange attractors of intensive work' – where all aspects remain integrated, rather than analysed – in a way where there is enough room for context, and in which attention is paid to the time factor? What work systems are causing these patterns, and what patterns are producing these work systems?

Can we identify behaviour patterns and work systems that are particularly harmful to health? And can we design work systems that are producing 'sustainable' attractors for both the humans involved and the organization? Sustainable work systems can be 'imprisoned' by different strange attractors. One of them can be described as competitiveness that is accompanied by individual growth, and also by a culture that equally respects all members of the organization. A sustainable work system that is typically under the control of this sustainability attractor produces outcomes of benefit to all stakeholders, rather than serving the interests of one single elite group at the expense of those of others. A sustainable work system governed by such a sustainability attractor offers opportunities for interaction that contribute to the development of individuals, groups and organizations, and also to that of the region or society as a whole.

Defining sustainability as a 'strange attractor' has many advantages. It stresses the dynamics of the process, it points to the wholeness and the complexity of the system, and it draws attention to the discontinuous development of the system in terms of jumping into other attractor basins.

In short, a sustainable work system is not a state; it is a dynamic process. It concerns changeable values – mutual growth and discontinuous development, simultaneous consideration of all stakeholders – rather than a set of rules and structures. This is a *how* question, not a *what* question. We do not ask what resources we have, but show how resources may emerge when we need them. Each organization itself has to define its own unique dynamic solutions, but the concept of a sustainable work system may help it to see how sustainability might be achieved.

References

Antonovsky, A. (1987) 'Health promoting factors at work. The sense of coherence', in R. Kalimo, M.A. El-Batawi and C.L. Cooper (eds), *Psychosocial Factors at Work and their Relation to Health*, Geneva: World Health Organization.

Berger, P.L. and Luckmann, T. (1966) *The Social Construction of Reality. A Treatise in the Sociology of Knowledge*, New York: Doubleday.

Bjerlöv, M. (19991) 'Lärande I verksamhetsanknutna samtal. En studie om prat och lärande i möten på en arbetsplats' (Learning in work-based discourse. A study of talk and learning in meetings at a workplace), Stockholm University, Department of Education/Solna: National Institute for Working Life, doctoral thesis no. 89.

Bohm, D. (1987) *Unfolding Meaning. A Weekend of Dialogue with David Bohm*, London: Ark Paperbacks.

Chaordic Alliance, The (1999) Online. Available: http://www.chaordic.com.

Csikszentmihalyi, M. (1990) *Flow. The Psychology of Optimal Experience*, New York: Harper Perennial.

Dixon, N. (1994) *The Organizational Learning Cycle*, London: McGraw-Hill.

Ellinor, L. and Gerard, G. (1998) *Dialogue. Rediscover the Transforming Power of Conversation*, New York: Wiley.

Fitzgerald, L.A. (1996) *Organizations and Other Things Fractal. A Primer of Chaos for Agents of Change*, Denver: The Consultancy.

Fitzgerald, L.A. and Eijnatten, F.M. van (1998) 'Letting go for control. The art of managing in the chaordic enterprise', *International Journal of Business Transformation*, 1, 4, 261–70.

Fulmer, W.E. (2000) *Shaping the Adaptive Organization. Landscapes, Learning, and Leadership in Volatile Times*, New York: AMACOM American Management Association.

Gharajedaghi, J. (1999) *Systems Thinking. Managing Chaos and Complexity. A Platform for Designing Business Architecture*, Boston: Butterworth-Heinemann.

Holland, J.H. (1995) *Hidden Order. How Adaptation Builds Complexity*, Reading, MA: Perseus Books.

Kauffman, S.A. (1995) *At Home in the Universe. The Search for Laws of Self-organization and Complexity*, New York: Oxford University Press.

Koestler, A. (1967) *The Ghost in the Machine*, London: Hutchinson.

Lissack, M. and Roos, J. (1999) *The Next Common Sense. Mastering Corporate Complexity through Coherence*, London: Nicholas Brealey.

Marion, R. (1999) *The Edge of Organization. Chaos and Complexity Theories of Formal Social Systems*, Thousand Oaks, CA: Sage.

Mathews, J. (1995) 'Holonic organizational architectures', *Human Systems Management*, 15.

Nicolis, G. and Prigogine I. (1989) *Exploring Complexity. An Introduction*, New York: Freeman.

Nowak, M.A., May, R.M. and Sigmund, K. (1995) 'The arithmetics of mutual help', *Scientific American*, June, 76–81.

Semmer, N. (1997) 'Individual differences, work stress, and health', in M.J. Scharbracq, J.A. Winnubst and C.L. Cooper (eds) *Handbook of Work and Health Psychology*, Chichester: Wiley.

Stacey, R. D. (1996a) *Complexity and Creativity in Organizations*, San Francisco: Berrett-Koehler.

Stacey, R. D. (1996b) *Strategic Management and Organizational Dynamics*, 2nd edn, London: Pitman.

Stacey, R.D. (2001) *Complex Responsive Processes in Organizations. Learning and Knowledge Creation*, London: Routledge.

Stacey, R.D., Griffin, R. and Shaw, P. (2000) *Complexity and Management. Fad or Radical Challenge to Systems Thinking?* London: Routledge.

Stellman, J.M. (ed.) (1997) *Encyclopaedia of Occupational Health and Safety*, 4th edn, Geneva: International Labour Organization.

Wilber, K. (1996) *A Short History of Everything*, Dublin: Newleaf.

Wilhelmson, L. (1998) 'Lärande dialog. Samtalsmönster, perspektivförändringar och lärande i grupp-samtal' (Learning dialogue. Discourse patterns, perspective change and learning in small group conversation), Stockholm University, Department of Education/Solna: National Institute for Working Life, doctoral thesis no. 88.

7 Institutional contexts

Bob Hancké[1]

Introduction

This chapter discusses the influence of institutional frameworks on work intensity and sustainability. It tries to make sense of the general observation among students of work that, despite decades of internationalization and the transfer of 'best practices' in organization, different countries keep on exhibiting marked variation in work organization and job contents; in order to do so, the chapter combines neo-institutionalist (Powell and DiMaggio 1991; Hall and Soskice 2001) and neo-contingent (Sorge 1991) insights to produce a political economy of work organization. The main argument of this chapter is that a comparative institutional perspective on both intensive work systems (IWS) and sustainable work systems (SWS) helps understand different trajectories of IWS and different possibilities of SWS in different countries.

A few conceptual clarifications on the analysis are introduced here. For the purposes of this chapter, institutions are defined as both legal and quasi-legal frameworks and of the constraints imposed by the presence of actors (such as labour unions, works councils and employers' associations) endowed with rights and resources resulting from these frameworks. Also, for the sake of the argument here, I will concentrate on workload issues (in line with the resource perspective on IWS–SWS), but I believe that the broad analytical framework proposed here is helpful for other perspectives on IWS–SWS as well.

The next section will rapidly review the main positions on comparative studies of work, in order to introduce the analytical framework presented in the following section. I will then build on that framework to discuss differences in work intensity, and conclude by raising the question what this implies for SWS.

Understanding varieties of work

Not more than a decade ago, there was a tendency in the comparative sociology and political economy literature to link positive economic and social outcomes with the 'correct' mix of such institutions. Neo-corporatism (i.e. strong labour unions, wage equality, etc.) predicted lower inflation and unemployment in OECD countries (Schmitter 1981; Cameron 1984; Soskice 1990). High value added product market strategies, as pursued by German and Swedish export firms, relied on a mixture of high skills, high wages and co-determination institutions (Piore and Sabel 1984; Streeck 1992). Conversely, countries with the 'wrong' institutional set-up – such as the USA, France or the UK – had an economic performance record (in terms of inflation and unemployment) which was dismal, while social problems (exemplified by wage inequality and crime) abounded.

These arguments about the role of institutional frameworks have increasingly come under fire from different angles. One broad counter-argument is that work everywhere is being redesigned – on a neo-craft basis in one version of the argument; on a neo-Taylorist basis, according to the other (Appelbaum and Batt 1994; Herrigel 1996; Sabel and Zeitlin 1997; Katz and Darbishire 1999). It has, however, become increasingly clear that both these mutually exclusive positions appear to cover large sections of modern working life simultaneously: some work settings are changing to reintegrate conception and execution, while others push the separation of conception and execution (and the exploitation that came with it) to extremes.

The second broad counter-argument (see Womack, Roos and Jones 1991 for its best-known version) states that a convergence towards a single best model is taking place, which combines the most beneficial features of the Japanese and American systems. However, even in the highly mature car industry, the sector that the argument is based on, work remains differently organized in different countries (Dore 1990; Jürgens *et al.* 1993; Streeck 1996). This is more than an irritating finding: it suggests that more is going on than just the market weeding out the inefficient systems, especially regarding the northern European versions of work systems.

The final broad position in the debate on the future of work is associated with the position adopted in this book: existing work systems increasingly come under pressure, precisely because their survival depends upon their capacity to extract resources from their workers; what is needed is a different model of work systems (and their design). However, while decades of experimentation with work design have taught us that such attempts often fail because of institutional and other constraints, they have given us little in the way of substantive knowledge about these constraints.

This chapter attempts to specify these constraints by proposing a comparative institutional framework to understand the different experiences in different capitalist countries. For convenience's sake, the framework presented here relies on a rough distinction between two models of work/production – mass production and knowledge work – and two models of institutional frameworks – deregulated market economies, as found in the USA and the UK, and co-ordinated market economies, as found in most of the northern European countries, particularly in Sweden and Germany.[2]

The core argument presented here is that work intensity in the different work and production settings follows different patterns in liberal market economies and co-ordinated market economies as a result of the different institutions governing internal labour markets and workers' participation. Understanding those differences offers insights both into how intensive work systems developed and into the degrees of freedom for designing SWS.

Institutions, sectors and product market strategies

How do institutional frameworks influence product market strategies? In order to answer this question, I will review two broad models of work systems around which many of the contributions in this book are organized: mass production and knowledge work. Mass production is understood here as the production of standardized goods (and services) using low and semi-skilled labour, or slightly more extended to include frontline management tasks, but without changing the basic notion that the conception of goods, services and processes is separated from their execution. The prototype for this mass production work is the car worker. Knowledge work can follow a mass production model (for example when established design routines are applied to a multitude of different specific cases), but it generally refers to a work system in which broad principles are used to solve highly unique, specific and idiosyncratic problems. The prototype of this work situation is found in the medical profession, but it now also includes software design, consulting, engineering, and other design-oriented work situations.

Varieties of capitalism

These different modes of work organization are, however, embedded in different institutional frameworks, the immediate result of which is that work is organized differently in different countries (for full details on the analytical framework, see Soskice 1999; Hall and Soskice 2001). Detailed comparative studies of work organization demonstrate without exception that the organization of work is as much a result of the struggles between workers and management over skills, job contents and the division of labour more generally, as it is driven by the search for more efficient production techniques (see e.g. Sabel 1982; Maurice *et al.* 1986; Lane 1989; Jürgens *et al.* 1993). Institutional frameworks, endowing the different parties with power resources, powerfully shape both form and contents of these struggles, and therefore influence their outcomes (Berger 1981; Kern and Schumann 1984; Piore and Sabel 1984; Soskice 1999; Hall and Soskice 2001).

For the sake of this chapter, I will simplify these institutional arrangements and concentrate solely on the institutional frameworks that govern training systems, internal labour markets, forms of workers' participation and labour relations.[3] Two broad ideal-typical patterns can thus be discerned.

The first consists of systems where workers' training is organized across firms, which provides workers with deep-industry skills that are portable across companies. These skills arrangements, in turn, are policed by strong industry-level labour unions as well as firm-level co-determination arrangements, such as works councils or institutionalized company or plant-level labour union sections (engineers' associations play a similar role for knowledge workers – Lütz 1993). The outcome of this first system is that workers and companies are mutually dependent upon one another: the workers' skills, which are accumulated over time, are central to the company's well-being, while the worker is enticed to make a career in the company through long-term career planning. These settings are found in most northern European countries, which we will call the co-ordinated market economies.

The second is commonly associated with the Anglo-American model. Here, training follows a pattern whereby workers obtain a general education and training is then 'topped up' in the company. Industry-level arrangements for training play little or no role in providing workers with skills. The role of labour unions is restricted to negotiating wages for particular job categories, and protecting the interests of their members during conflicts. As a result of these strategic choices, companies have an incentive to treat their workers as variable capital: careers are usually short term, or, when they are long term, governed by seniority agreements, which keeps older workers on the basis of years worked, without necessarily finding a basis in skill levels. The economies where these arrangements are found – typically the Anglo-Saxon economies – will be called the deregulated market economies.

Sectoral models of work and varieties of capitalism

Both in mass production and knowledge intensive sectors, these institutional frameworks have very different effects on how work is organized. Mass production in deregulated market economies typically follows a pattern of low skilled work, low labour productivity (related to low investment in capital, which itself follows from the low wage option, since it does not impose permanent rationalization as a production strategy) and the goods produced are low value added. Organizational change typically is conflictual and aimed at increasing external flexibility. In the co-ordinated market economies, in contrast, work in mass production is a negotiated affair, for two fundamental reasons. Semi-skilled work in this system still relies on a host of 'social' or 'organizational' skills in these economies: working in teams, discussing production processes with engineers, early involvement in product and process engineering, highly effective but idiosyncratic systems of quality control, etc. In short, the workers have a series of both technical and non-technical skills, which make them indispensable to management. Furthermore, labour relations institutions, which often have semi- or quasi-constitutional rights in the company, assure that management sticks to its end of the bargain.

Similar distinctions can be drawn for customized and batch production systems. In these sectors, typified by the chemical or the machine tool sector, the organization of work as well as decision-making are typically much more decentralized, and the workers are more highly skilled. In the co-ordinated market economies, this implies that management faces a permanent problem of how to make sure that its skilled workers and technicians are putting in the appropriate effort (the monitoring problem, as it is called in the management literature – Milgrom and Roberts 1992). This is ensured through two mechanisms: peer monitoring and long-term career planning (including regular subsidized retraining and promotion programmes). In the deregulated market economies, this particular set-up has led to a situation whereby the skilled workers control access to the job. Since technical training does not take place before the worker enters a company, the skilled workers are responsible for training the next generation. This, combined with their strategic position in the company, gives them the possibility of tightly controlling entry into the labour market. Labour unions are, in this setting, primarily the official agents protecting the crafts.

These broad institutional distinctions are relevant even for new sectors, located on the boundary between classical production and service work, as typified in the software and biotech industries. Broadly speaking, two very different segments make up these new sectors. The first are the Silicon Valley/Route 128 groupings of extremely innovative small firms, who heavily rely on the skills of their workers (Saxenian 1996). However, since the risk of failure is large in these sectors, firms have to use large monetary incentives to obtain workers, and workers have to be certain that their skills are not obsolete after failure, which reduces their willingness to invest in company-specific skills. Thus the types of innovation in these segments tend to rely on general transferable skills, and knowledge production is organized in such a way that it is relatively easily codifiable (and can therefore be appropriated by the company) (Soskice 1997; Casper *et al.* 1999). The second segment is situated in the more stable segments of business software and platform biotechnology. These rely on long-term careers, and innovation is based upon accumulated, often industry- or company-specific knowledge and organizational skills which are of a considerably more tacit nature (Casper *et al.* 1999).

Interestingly, the deregulated market economies tend to specialize in the first, so-called radical innovation segments, where careers are governed by short-term considerations; in contrast, knowledge work in co-ordinated market economies is concentrated in the more stable segments, where long-term mutual dependence between companies and employees is the rule (Hall and Soskice 2001).

This short review has offered a framework for understanding how and why we encounter wide variety in work organization in different sectors and countries. The institutions governing training systems, work organization and labour relations systematically interact to produce outcomes whereby companies adopt different strategic equilibria, congruent with these institutional frameworks. How does this conceptualization shed light on questions of work intensity in different sectors and countries?

Varieties of work intensity

If work systems vary along such broad institutional lines, work intensity is bound to follow different paths in different settings as well. That is the central point in this section: different institutional frameworks produce different forms of IWS. This is so because institutions produce constraints on management and provide workers with different resources for negotiating work system reorganization.

Mass production

Work reorganization in mass production sectors has been the topic of a large literature, generally confirming the basic idea that different product market strategies lead to different outcomes in work organization, and that these outcomes are systematically related to differences in the institutional frameworks (Turner 1991). However, the neat distinctions initially proposed by these authors are increasingly being called into question. Since the early 1990s, the reorganization of companies in the German car industry, long considered as one of the test cases for this argument (see Streeck 1996), has followed not one (institutionally determined) path, but at least two (Schumann 1998 and Chapter 11 below). The first is the trajectory conventionally associated with the German (and more broadly northern European) high skill, high participation model; the second is called 'structurally conservative' and follows a model which instrumentalizes (but thereby also weakens the emancipatory qualities of) workers' participation.

Understanding what is going on here requires careful comparisons between work settings in different systems. The generalization of ISO 9000 in the mass production sectors of coordinated market economies provides such a comparison. ISO 9000 is a quality management system which prescribes a series of procedures for companies to follow in order to make their quality control system more transparent – both internally and to outsiders. The relevance of ISO 9000 for the IWS–SWS debate lies in the fact that they impose hard rules for documentation of and a systematic reflection on work practices. Put simply, they force every worker to permanently monitor his or her work and search for mechanisms to improve it.

Because of its origins in the American defence sector, with its general Tayloristic orientation, we could expect the ISO 9000 system to push companies to adopt singular best way models of work organization under conditions of high international competition (where direct production costs provide important competitive advantages). This is not the case. In Germany, the structure around the works councils and local unions has provided workers with the possibility of steering the process of implementation of ISO 9000 to safeguard the autonomy and qualifications of the skilled workers in the car industry. In France, in contrast, where local labour union sections are notoriously weak, and works councils have very few hard rights in negotiating new forms of work organization, the generalized adoption of ISO 9000 standards led to an integration of previously fragmented quality control functions, but within a broad neo-Taylorist work organization (Casper and Hancké 1999). A similar argument applies to the introduction of ISO 9000 in industry in the Anglo-American economies (Tuckman 1994).

What this suggests is that the institutional frameworks profoundly influenced how ISO 9000 was introduced in different countries. The German setting produced a negotiated introduction of ISO 9000, safeguarding many of the elements of autonomy and skills associated with the northern European model. Workers were able to mobilize institutions of work organization as a power basis from where to influence processes of work reorganization (see also Turner 1991 on the introduction of teamwork). The result was a negotiated form of work intensity, which was policed by the existing institutions of labour relations.

Conversely, in the deregulated market economies, ISO 9000 is much closer to the Taylorist ideal-type. Roughly speaking, the hierarchies associated with the Anglo-American models of work organization also became the mould for the introduction and implementation of ISO 9000. As in Germany, they certainly contributed to a change in work practices – often including a rise in skill levels and decentralization of decision-making – but these ended up being guided by conceptions of work that were close to the previously existing systems. Since workers in these economies have very few institutions that can support them in negotiating work reorganizations, ISO 9000 reproduced the old order.

Moreover, and perhaps more to the point, both the US and UK are largely abandoning mass production industry altogether. Since the mid-1980s, these countries have de-industrialized at a faster pace than the northern European countries under the threat of south-east Asian competition. This raises the question of whether work intensity in the Anglo-American economies is increasingly related to the fear of job loss (Katz and Darbishire 1999).

In the mass production sector, institutions therefore provide different matrices for work intensity, because they provide workers (and their representatives) with different institutional resources to negotiate work reorganization.

Mass production industries have frequently offered paradigmatic examples in the past: the mechanisms found there provided a heuristic for understanding developments in other industries as well. How does this general argument on the role of institutions in guiding work intensity help us understand the evolution of work in other types of industry?

Knowledge work

Knowledge work is, generally speaking, characterized by high work intensity. Often it is project- rather than time-based, and individual careers are closely linked to the success of a project. However, there are some indications that knowledge work contains different risks in different countries, which can be meaningfully linked to the broad institutional patterns of labour market organization.

In deregulated market economies, the dominant pattern could be called institutionalized self-exploitation: growth in human capital is a direct result of individual achievement. In general, there are very few institutions to promote and protect labour standards. The outcome is, on the part of both workers and companies, a short-term orientation, which is compensated by a high-powered incentive structure to reward and retain valuable employees.

While this has been a relatively stable pattern for the last decade, the extremely low unemployment in the Anglo-American economies today, with aggregate rates of around 4 per cent and chronic labour shortages in the knowledge intensive sectors, may be putting a lot of pressure on this system. In order to retain their workforce, many companies in the US are resorting to human resources policies which bear a striking resemblance to what is standard fare on many continental European labour markets: increased workers' participation and training programmes, child care and part-time work provisions (*Economist* 25 March 2000). This (admittedly sketchy) evidence suggests that the labour market power of knowledge professionals – itself the result of the highly open labour markets within which they operate in deregulated market economies – may compel companies to take into consideration the quality of work, including intensity, in order to retain their qualified workforce.

to highlight institutionally 'incompatible' and therefore ultimately frustrating SWS strategies (e.g. those based on high skill and works councils in countries with highly open labour markets and competitive product market regimes)?

A related question can be raised regarding co-determination schemes. If indeed they influence the shape of work intensity, do they also provide different spaces for designing SWS? Without falling prey to a naïve form of institutional determinism, it seems rather unlikely that SWS which rely on high workers' involvement will be very successful in liberal market economies, which are organized around entirely different principles.

The basic message of this chapter is therefore relatively simple. Good work is not created in a vacuum, but is in part a product of and contributes to the institutional frameworks within which it exists. Awareness of these broader institutional constraints and opportunities – even if they are often more flexible in practice than we can predict – will ascertain that SWS design and implementation principles are compatible with the institutional framework that the work systems are embedded in, and contribute to the viability of the corporate strategies they give rise to. Thus they will not simply be ignored or, worse, rejected as if they constituted an alien body, but stand a better chance of finding their way into new work practices.

Notes

1   My thanks go to my colleagues in the SALTA–SWS workgroup, and to David Soskice, Steven Casper and Donatella Gatti for useful discussions related to the topic of this chapter.
2   A few caveats are in order here. First, this 2×2 distinction is heavily informed by research in production sectors, especially in the traded goods sectors (such as cars, chemicals and machine tools). While it may be possible to extend the perspective to services in general, and even public services in particular, it is not at the heart of this chapter. Second, the distinction between deregulated and co-ordinated market economies is equally broad. Some countries do not readily fall into these categories (e.g. France, Italy) and it does not take into account very well the possibilities of firms to 'escape' their institutional frameworks. Some of these more dynamic aspects will become more central in the treatment of different forms of IWS.
3   These institutional frameworks are not just stand-alone arrangements but are linked to and rely upon other institutional frameworks, such as the ones covering financial systems, inter-firm relationships and competition regimes (see Hall and Soskice 2001).
4   Informal conversations with IG Metall representatives suggest that, with the downturn in the sector since late 2000, grievances among workers have built up and the number of works councils and union representatives in the software sector is rising.

References

Appelbaum, E. and Batt, R. (1994) *The New American Workplace*, Ithaca, NY: Cornell University Press.
Berger, S. (1981) 'Introduction', in S. Berger (ed.) *Organizing Interests in Western Europe*, Cambridge: Cambridge University Press, pp. 1–23.
Cameron, D.R. (1984) 'Social democracy, corporatism, labour quiescence, and the representation of economic interest in advanced capitalist society', in J.H. Goldthorpe (ed.) *Order and Conflict in Contemporary Capitalism. Studies in the Political Economy of Western European Nations*, New York: Oxford University Press, pp. 143–78.
Casper, S. and Hancké, B. (1999) 'Global quality norms within national production regimes: ISO 9000 norm implementation in the French and German car industries', *Organization Studies*, 20, 6, 961–85.
Casper, S., Lehrer, M. and Soskice, D. (1999) 'Can high-technology industries prosper in Germany? Institutional frameworks and the evolution of the German software and biotechnology industries', *Industry and Innovation*, 6, 1, 5–24.
Dore, R. (1990) *British Factory–Japanese Factory* (first published 1973), Berkeley: University of California Press.

Hall, P.A. and Soskice, D. (2001) 'Varieties of capitalism. The institutional foundations of comparative advantage', in P.A. Hall and D. Soskice (eds) *Varieties of Capitalism. The Institutional Foundations of Competitiveness*, Oxford: Oxford University Press, pp. 1–68.

Herrigel, G. (1996) *Industrial Constructions. The Sources of German Industrial Power*, Cambridge/New York: Cambridge University Press.

Jürgens, U., Malsch, T. and Dohse, K. (1993) *Breaking from Taylorism: Changing Forms of Work in the Automobile Industry*, Cambridge: Cambridge University Press.

Katz, H.C. and Darbishire, O. (1999) *Converging Differences. Worldwide Changes in Employment Systems*, Ithaca, NY: Cornell University Press.

Kern, H. and Schumann, M. (1984) *Das Ende der Arbeitsteilung?* (The End of the Division of Labour?), Munich: Beck.

Lane, C. (1989) *Labour and Management in Europe. The Industrial Enterprise in Germany, Britain and France*, Aldershot: Edward Elgar.

Lütz, S. (1993) *Die Steureung industrieller Forschungskooperation* (The Steering of Industrial Research Co-operation), Frankfurt am Main: Campus.

Maurice, M., Sellier, F. and Silvestre, J.-J. (1986) *The Social Foundations of Industrial Power*, Cambridge, MA: MIT Press.

Milgrom, P. and Roberts, J. (1992) *Economics, Organization and Management*, Englewood Cliffs, NJ: Prentice-Hall.

Piore, M.J. and Sabel, C.F. (1984) *The Second Industrial Divide. Possibilities for Prosperity*, New York: Basic Books.

Powell, W.W. and DiMaggio, P.J. (eds) (1991) *The New Institutionalism in Organizational Analysis*, Chicago: University of Chicago Press.

Sabel, C.F. (1982) *Work and Politics*, Cambridge: Cambridge University Press.

Sabel, C.F. and Zeitlin, J. (1997) 'Stories, strategies, structures. Rethinking historical alternatives to mass production', in C.F. Sabel and J. Zeitlin (eds) *Worlds of Possibility. Flexibility and Mass Production in Western Industrialization*, pp. 1–33.

Saxenian, A. (1996) *Regional Advantage. Culture and Competition in Silicon Valley and Route 128*, Cambridge, MA: Harvard University Press.

Schmitter, P. (1981) 'Interest intermediation and regime governability in contemporary Western Europe and North America', in S. Berger (ed.) *Organizing Interests in Western Europe*, Cambridge: Cambridge University Press, pp. 285–327.

Schumann, M. (1998) 'New concepts of production and productivity', *Economic and Industrial Democracy*, 19, 1, 17–32.

Sorge, A. (1991) 'Strategic fit and the societal effect. Interpreting cross-national comparisons of technology, organization and human resources', *Organization Studies*, 12, 2, 161–90.

Soskice, D. (1990) 'Reinterpreting corporatism and explaining unemployment. Coordinated and non-coordinated market economies', in R. Brunetta and C. Dell'Aringa (eds) *Labour Relations and Economic Performance*, London: Macmillan, pp. 170–211.

Soskice, D. (1997) 'German technology policy, innovation and national institutional frameworks', *Industry and Innovation*, 4, 1, 75–96.

Soskice, D. (1999) 'Divergent production regimes. Coordinated and uncoordinated market economies in the 1980s and 1990s', in H. Kitschelt, P. Lange, G. Marks and J.D. Stephens (eds) *Continuity and Change in Contemporary Capitalism*, Cambridge: Cambridge University Press, pp. 101–34.

Streeck, W. (1992) *Social Institutions and Economic Performance*, London: Sage.

Streeck, W. (1996) 'Lean production in the German automobile industry? A test case for convergence theory', in S. Berger and R. Dore (eds) *National Diversity and Global Capitalism*, Ithaca, NY: Cornell University Press, pp. 138–70.

Tuckman, A. (1994) 'The Yellow Brick Road. Total quality management and the restructuring of organizational culture', *Organization Studies*, 15, 5, 727–51.

Turner, L. (1991) *Democracy at Work. Changing World Markets and the Future of Labor Unions*, Ithaca, NY: Cornell University Press.

Womack, J., Roos, D. and Jones, D. (1991) *The Machine that Changed the World*, New York: Harper & Row.

Part 3

Illustrations

Realizing aspects of sustainability

Part 2 presented a range of paradigms, concepts, conceptual frameworks, ideas and 'lenses' that can help us examine the emerging practice of sustainable work systems. Sustainability is a complex phenomenon that is emerging as a response to human and societal need. Yet, realizing sustainability in the context of work organization presents major challenges.

This section of the book – *Illustrations* – is intended to provide a few examples of work systems in different contexts, nationally and industrially, which realize facets of sustainability. The illustrations are not success stories but examples for learning that can provide important lessons for our understanding of sustainability and its realization. The individual examples address one or more facets or features of sustainability for those employed in the organization and for the organization itself, i.e. social and economic sustainability. The examples are practices that emerged in the interplay between intensity and sustainable work and are examined to varied degrees from different theoretical frameworks. We look at intensive and sustainable work systems through different lenses to see as much as possible, very much like natural scientists describing our physical world look at cells through microscopes and stars through telescopes. The observation lenses are chosen to respond to and respect the characteristics of each system or analysis level in question. However, what unites our lenses is their focus towards work, towards individuals and organizations at work. Sustainability and competitiveness have often been recognized as essential goals of our society, but the discussion has stopped at societal level, ignoring the organizational and individual levels.

Chapter 8, 'Integrating product and personal development', provides an illustration of how the work intensity of a new product development (NPD) environment in the software industry was transformed to a sustainable work system by the deployment of a platform-based work design mechanism. The chapter advances a framework that explores the interplay between platform-based NPD work and sustainability. The framework is utilized to examine the complex dynamics in a software development firm and addresses three central issues of sustainable work, namely the key design requirements, potential cause-and-effect relationships between NPD features and sustainability and the role the platform-based architecture can play in enhancing sustainability at the team and organizational levels.

Chapter 9, 'Sustainability in a rapidly changing environment', explores sustainable change in the telecom environment. The business area studied is new product development. The studied unit went through a thorough renewal as new managers were appointed and its field of activity and its ways of organizing work were changed. Sustainability is related to processes concerning four different aspects of the ongoing business: in products, in organization structure, in principles related to how work is organized, and for individuals. In a rapidly changing environment sustainability can be understood as the ability to interpret and deal with the complexity, alterations and dynamics – through time and over the levels – of non-synchronized processes.

Chapter 10, 'Values and stakeholder relations', focuses on the financial services sector which is possibly an extreme example of the impacts of the new economy, encompassing deregulation, downsizing, outsourcing and restructuring (mergers and acquisitions). The sector is faced with the delicate balance between transaction economies (rationalizing trans-actions) and relational orientation (maintaining trustful relations with customers). The chapter describes the bank's individual and corporate sustainability over the last twenty-five years by a sensitive balance of different stakeholder needs and aspirations. It analyses a bank's uti-lization of values, culture and personnel policies to reinforce the employees' security, professional identity and redirected competences, orientated to maintaining strong relations with customers. High investments in personnel in a branch context are matched by its com-mercial success: a win–win for social and commercial sustainability.

Chapter 11, 'Group work and democracy', demonstrates that the new forms of work organization require a reassessment of some basic assumptions of socio-technical thinking in manufacturing. By comparing cases with very different impacts on the workers, some aspects of sustainability in group work settings in the car industry are highlighted (resource perspec-tive, dialogue, negotiated workloads) and a framework for analysing group work from the perspective of sustainability is proposed.

Chapter 12, 'Institutional support for developing SMEs', brings in an illustration of sus-tainable practices in a network-based enterprise. Over the past decades, better fulfilment of goals for the organization and better jobs for its employees have been at the centre of much discussion regarding enterprise development and, in a large number of cases, specific projects have been carried through with a win–win ideal. In this way, many elements of SWS have been tested in a market-controlled context. This chapter describes examples where attempts to create wide employee support for an SWS process through a bottom-up approach have been successful in enterprise networks.

The last chapter in this part, 'An innovative coalition succumbs to bureaucracy', illustrates the co-operation between management and unions, major corporations and small companies, companies and public authorities in creating a coalition. The coalition was extremely active in maintaining individual sustainability through employability, ensuring re-skilling and out-placement of potentially redundant workers. Company sustainability was facilitated by maintaining the competence quality of the workers. Regional sustainability was achieved through ensuring the supply of qualified human resources in the manufacturing industry. The example also illustrates the sensitivity of such coalitions to their institutional context and how single changes in relationships can reverse developments.

8 Integrating product and personal development

A.B. (Rami) Shani and James B. Sena

Introduction

For many businesses, new product development is the single most important factor driving success or failure. For these businesses their strategic focus is directed at those imperatives that will increase the likelihood of the success of their new product development (NPD) process (Schilling and Hill 1998). One of the emerging challenges in NPD is the increased intensity of work and its consequences (Delbecq and Weiss 2000). Finding alternative ways to ensure success requires addressing the firm's capability to continuously improve the sustainability of the NPD processes.

Work intensity is viewed as a socially constructed phenomenon that is embedded in the increasing rate of change in the nature of NPD work (Olin and Shani 2001). In the context of NPD, changes in the software development industry seem to occur at many levels: the rate of technological hardware development is increasing and new software products are being introduced into the marketplace; individuals are required to put continuous effort into acquiring new knowledge and skills; expectations and pressure to reduce NPD cycle times are increasing; individuals are under pressure to integrate a variety of knowledge bases into the process; and last, organizational members are pressured to integrate customers (and at times suppliers) into the process. Two major causes of work intensity are scope creep (unplanned changes to the scope of work as the product development progresses) and the actual delivery of the finished product to the customer (time to market). Another negative consequence of the increasing work intensity seems to centre on the difficulty in retaining talented software development engineers and management information system specialists. As turnover increases, it is accompanied by a loss of knowledge and understanding of core processes. As information technology becomes a critical success factor, especially within firms whose product is the actual development of a software product, loss of key personnel has a major impact.

The main thesis of this chapter is that one way to address some of the increasing work intensity issues in the NPD work environment within the software development industry is the deployment of a platform-based work design. Here, a firm would adopt a modular approach to new product development, and realign its structure, processes and product architecture. We term this work design 'platform architecture'. At the most basic level, platforms provide a basic core that is altered and enhanced to produce product variants with different features (Muffato 1999; Zhang and Doll 2001). A product platform may be defined as the set of parts, subsystems, interfaces, manufacturing and operational processes that are shared among a set of products and that facilitate the development of derivative products with cost and time savings (Ebrahimpur and Jacob 2001; Krishnan and Gupta 2001). Sharing common software architecture across a product line brings a core set of knowledge and assets to the development process. Complexity, development and maintenance costs are reduced and the production of documentation, training materials and product literature is streamlined. This approach means that the firm would need to undertake certain knowledge-based activities including identification of core competences and might even consider such alternatives as outsourcing of some of its tasks.

The objective of this chapter is to propose a platform-based architecture framework as an alternative work design configuration for managing and sustaining a complex new product development project with special emphasis on individual and business sustainability. We address these relationships with a specific focus on the team interfaces through an illustrative case of product development in a software firm wherein new products both enable and result from component and object reusability. The chapter is organized in four parts. Following this introduction, we introduce an alternative framework that is based on a synthesis between socio-technical systems and strategic thinking. Next we briefly describe our methodology, and this is followed by an overview of the SDF company and its product development process. The analysis of the company, its NPD process and sustainability provides the basis for the discussion and conclusion.

Towards an alternative framework

Given the complex nature of new technology, standard approaches may not suffice to explain or appreciate the potential of new work forms, such as the platform architecture. In this chapter we recognize and integrate the strategic and socio-technical character of a software product development process and apply the principles of socio-technical system and strategic analyses to decisions that must be made as the product passes through the various stages of development.

The socio-technical systems (STS) perspective was developed in the 'old' economy as an alternative organization design theory (van Eijnatten 1994). Yet, Pasmore (2001) and Shani and Lau (2000) convincingly argue that socio-technical system thinking is of high relevance to companies in the 'new' economy. Many streams of STS evolved over the last fifty years of research and practice in different parts of the world. Yet, at the most basic level, the socio-technical system perspective considers every organization to be composed of a social subsystem (the people) using the tools, techniques and knowledge (the technical subsystem) to produce a product or a service valued by the environmental context (Trist 1982; Taylor and Felten 1993; Pasmore 1994; Shani and Sena 1994). While every organization is perceived as a socio-technical system, not every organization is designed according to socio-technical system design principles, methods, processes and philosophies (Kolodny and Dresner 1986; Hanna 1988; Adler and Docherty 1998). The economic performance of firms based on socio-technical system design principles has been significantly better than comparable organizations using conventional designs (Hanna 1988; Pasmore 1993; van Eijnatten 1994). The degree to which the design of the technical subsystem, social subsystem, and the environmental context are integrated determines the success and competitiveness of the organization (Pava 1986; Shani, Grant and Krishnan 1992).

This chapter provides an opportunity to examine the relevance of socio-technical systems to the 'new' economy and sustainability. In order to link new product development and socio-technical systems with sustainability we propose a new comprehensive framework that identifies six factors that affect performance and sustainability. We believe that our framework would be useful in attempting to understand why new product development efforts result in specific outcomes and to anticipate those changes that may lead to improved results. Figure 8.1 portrays system performance and sustainability as an outcome that is influenced by the causal relationships among the five other factors.

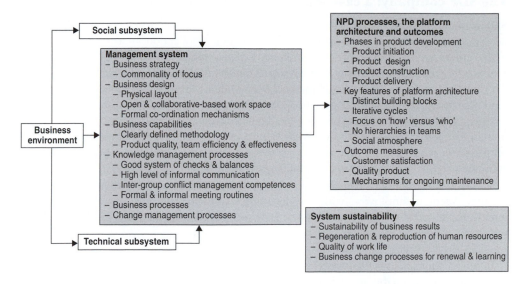

Figure 8.1 Towards a comprehensive framework of new product development and sustainability.

The *business environment* is comprised of elements and forces in the marketplace in which the firm competes. The *social subsystem* refers to the people who work in the organization. Individual attitudes and beliefs, competences and skills, relationships between group members, relationships between supervisors and subordinates, relationships between groups, cultures, traditions, past experiences, assumptions, values, rites, rituals, work habits and practices, and emergent role systems are all integral parts of the social cluster. The *technological subsystem* refers to the tools, techniques, devices, artefacts, methods, configurations, procedures and knowledge used by the organizational members to acquire inputs, transform inputs into outputs and provide outputs or services to clients or customers. *Management system* refers to the systems that attempt to link the environmental, technical and social subsystems. Business strategy, business design, business capabilities, business processes and change management processes provide the key elements. Of special interest are the knowledge management processes because they directly relate NPD to the platform architecture. The overall management system provides the context within which new product development efforts are designed and developed.

Methodology

The research reported in this chapter sought to address the dynamics of a fast growing software development firm. This research relates to a five year period in the evolution of the company. The ongoing changing firm demographics coupled with the fast company growth set the stage for the examination of work intensity and sustainability.

The data collection involved ethnographic observations of activities and decisions in the firm, the keeping of a diary, the periodic sharing of data and ongoing semi-structured interviews with staff regarding their views of the firm, their working experiences and the firm's success. One of the authors served as a special consultant and a participant-observer in the development of software agents for the product described in the case.

The SDF company: a case study

SDF is in the business of building, implementing and supporting agent-based 'co-operative decision-making' tools for distributed problem solving. Application areas include: facilities management, transportation planning, military logistics and control and engineering design. SDF has its origins in a university-based research facility. SDF's differentiating factor has been the development of an agent-based methodology to deal with spatial problems for organizing engineering design with respect to space management, space constraints and storage priorities from an architectural perspective. Their approach used a series of agents to assist human decision-making. Issues such as division of responsibility, shared direction, control of part-time workers and full-time employees from both the university and SDF working on common projects and sharing responsibilities and facilities are addressed.

The firm made significant use of agent technologies, an extension of the platform architecture. Agent technologies, with respect to the software industry, are self-contained, intelligent, adaptive software capsules that are used as building blocks to construct complex software products. Through the use of collaborating expert agents product development provides the flexibility and range needed for product design sustainability. Heterogeneous, semi-autonomous, knowledge-based software components are integrated into co-ordinated applications. Through the use of interoperability standards and methods information can flow seamlessly through an application across heterogeneous machines, computing platforms, programming languages and data and process representations (Lander 1997).

The organization of SDF

On the surface, the organization of SDF does not appear to be untypical for a software development firm. However, the various departmental units function with a minimum of supervision, behaving in a manner that resembles an internal form of outsourcing. Frequent meetings, a good infrastructure of networks and electronic communications, and a well thought through layout of workspace facilitate the firm's operation. Figure 8.2 presents the firm's organizational structure. Much of the product work is conducted by co-operative supporting groups existing within the department structure. Also depicted in the organization chart is the organization of the product teams. The leadership of the product team is divided between a product manager and a technical leader.

Software development is by its nature an intensive work situation because of cyclical development, pressure to reduce development time, self-absorption in the task and challenges at hand, a highly competitive global market, keeping abreast of ongoing technological innovations, and increasing personnel turnover rates. At the micro level there are pressures to get the product to market even when it may not be complete or meet all of the specifications. The dual leadership is intended to address these problems by assigning external and internal direction and as a check-and-balance control mechanism.

Within the product structure responsibility and direction of the support groups are divided and/or shared between these two leaders and the various departments (e.g. testing, customer support and training). Disputes or differences have to be resolved through discussion or are brought to senior management for resolution. This has not been a significant problem because the work content and work constituency are relatively homogeneous. New products evolve from existing products and involve technology transfer and adherence to grounded technologies that utilize SDF's spatial agent approach.

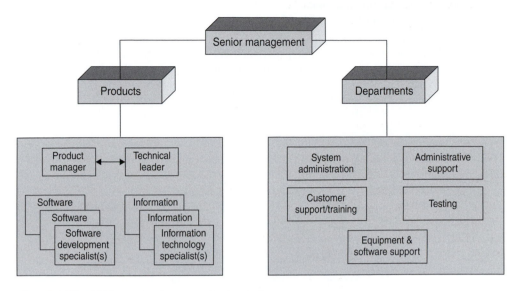

Figure 8.2 The SDF organization: organizational chart.

The product development process

SDF has a well-defined process for product development that typifies the platform-based architecture (Figure 8.3). As in many firms there are several points where iterative cycles are depicted. In these cycles work intensifies and converges – a spiralling, repetitive, centring process. Preceding the product development process is the product initiation phase where the RFPs (requests for proposals) are prepared. This involves customer liaison and knowledge acquisition. As in most organizations of this nature the goal of such an iterative process is the awarding of a contract.

Responsibility for specific product development elements is divided among the product manager, the technical leader and various support groups. In Figure 8.3 we show this division by grouping the various tasks on panels contained on the platform. The product leaders are shown in parallel panels. The support groups are depicted as blocks that overlap the product team's responsibility areas/panels. The design and development phase depicts the system requirement activities as being jointly shared by the presentation and design activities – these are mainly the responsibility of the technical leader. However, the technical leader must draw from the programming team, requiring him or her to deal with a programmer pool consisting primarily of part-time workers and a small cadre of experienced programmers. The estimating and scheduling activity is also jointly shared.

The choice to have a dual set of product leaders – the product manager and the technical leader – is a clear example of the rationale for stocks of knowledge. The technical leader ensures that the product evolves by developing co-ordination mechanisms to support software version control, libraries of shared and reusable code and the application of agent-based technologies. We could think of these as storage banks (sources of knowledge) on the platform. The technical leader oversees the production of the software team; makes assignments and reviews the work of the software developers; and co-ordinates and schedules testing and quality control. The product manager interfaces with the technical leader but is not involved in the actual software development. Instead the product manager handles the external interfaces with the customer and management. Knowledge about customer needs and expectations can be tempered and translated to agent technologies using a standardized framework for work definition.

The hardware, services and supplies, management and customer liaison, training and documentation are the responsibility of the product manager in co-ordination with the service groups. When the product work is completed the product is delivered to the customer by both the product manager and the technical leader. Since SDF deals primarily in a military

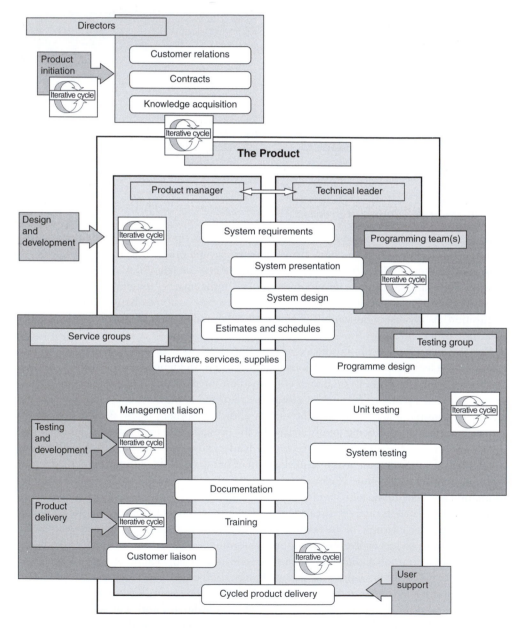

Figure 8.3 The product development process at SDF.

environment most of their contracts are modular and spread over a series of years or periods. There is not always a clear, precise product delivered. Instead products evolve by adding features and capabilities. SDF markets a core product that consists of a basic set of agents. The typical system can be retrofitted to a particular customer – the system is then tailored to the configurations and special needs of the customer. Each product takes on a particular flavour by adding agents, most of which have been previously developed and are then modified to meet special customer needs, or new agents that are specifically developed to meet unique needs for the customer. This agent-based technology is one reason that accounts for SDF's success and explains its ability to sustain product development and viability.

The firm's structure revolves around the product teams. The departments exist to support the product teams much like support units in a production environment. The teams are an amalgamation of various specialities, some of which are solely housed within the product, while other areas, such as testing, quality control, service, customer liaison and training, are independent of the product. These units, especially testing and quality control, from a delivery perspective, are integral parts of product development. Enabling the structure is an intricate set of networks that support and enhance the communication.

The organization design is characterized by three key elements: differentiation, co-ordination and integration. In the illustration of a typical product development that follows we track a product through its development cycle. Since knowledge compared to other assets is characterized by intangibility, tacitness and action relatedness, it is more difficult to manage in comparison to other organizational assets. The choices made to facilitate co-ordination influence the organization's ability to accomplish goals. The designer's choice about how to bind together the tasks and activities influences the extent to which the different stocks of knowledge held by individuals will be shared and acted upon.

An illustration of product development

The purpose of the product that we are focusing on – the collaborative infrastructure assessment tool (CIAT) – is to provide operational support for the berthing of ships, the management and maintenance of piers and the surveillance of waterfront operations. For this product an agent-based system is partnered with human decision-makers to reach a consensus solution to a complex problem.

Product initiation

The directors of the firm operate as the initial and primary contacts with the client. Once a need is identified, dialogue is initiated with the client. As the work scope materializes product managers and technical leaders are introduced into the dialogue. In some cases area experts or consultants are brought in to assist and augment the knowledge acquisition required. This is a key aspect of the platform architecture – a more stable, specific product goal.

Product design

The design of the CIAT product consisted of identifying system requirements, deciding on a format for system presentation and specifying the system design. The spatial agent technology employed relied on the acquisition of data by artificial intelligence techniques in the form of data definition and rule specification. The initial customer contact was the product manager. Here the data collection and rule acquisition process were defined. Area specialists, consisting of system analysts from the programming teams, collected the requisite data. The database schema and rule base were initially defined – this process was one of refinement, an iterative cycle leading to greater and greater detail. The platform approach encompassed an instrument that was clear, concise and consistent.

A set of reusable software and hardware formulations is used to construct a product. Work on the system presentation is a joint effort with the product manager and the technical leader and his/her staff. The customer was initially shown and approved a front-end without unfolding the to-be-completed functionality. In the platform architecture approach the interface can be conveniently tailored to user specifications.

All of the agents are defined jointly or selected for use from an existing agent repertoire by the technical leader and the product manager along with area experts during the product design phase. The product manager and the technical leader together compile the estimates and schedules for the product construction. Arrangements need to be made with programming teams, testing groups and service groups, as well as preparing for documentation and training. The groups are independent of the product itself. They transcend the product, existing as entities beyond the product work. *This is a key element for sustainability.* Since they have major ongoing products with the military that are now in the maintenance mode these business areas must exist to support those products but on the other hand they can ramp up to provide the needed services for new product developments.

Product construction

The product construction consists of parallel operations. The technical leader and the product manager work somewhat independently. The computer programs are written by the programming team. Reusable modules are deployed – taking advantage of existing technology/expertise and work already tried and tested. *This is another ingredient in sustainability, since they do not have to create a new product from scratch.* The programming team members may be involved in multiple developments at the same time. The product definition and design are such that coders and programmers are somewhat interchangeable.

As modules are developed they are turned over to the testing group. Each module goes through a variety of tests – unit testing of each module and system testing of the modules together. The testing group is accustomed to working with agent technologies and is familiar with their presentation system. Before any product is presented to the customer it is tested for internal reliability and adherence to specifications. As the testing and programming proceed documentation is initiated. An independent group produces professional quality manuals, online and web-based materials. They liaise with the technical leader, the programming team and the testing group. When the production of the software reaches a stage where the user needs to be involved (and since the documentation is to be presented to the customer) the documentation staff accompany the product manager and area expert to the customer site. While the programs are being developed, tested and documented the service group arranges for the purchase and configuration of the network and workstations.

Product delivery

After the equipment becomes operational the new software is installed by the technical leader and area specialists. Here the user testing and development is supported by the service group and the technical leader. Training is conducted simultaneously and documentation needs are noted. Over a five year basis the CIAT product evolved jointly as the customer and SDF set priorities and defined scopes of work for each iteration of the product – agents and functionality were added and changes in technology were taken into account and accommodated. The system architects took care during each of these iterations to ensure that each new/evolved product form consisted of a set of components that could be included on a modular basis, thus making a configurable, sustainable product set.

The CIAT product development and sustainability

There are several factors that make the firm unique with respect to supporting and enhancing business sustainability. There is a clear and understood path for product development. The team was supported by permanent support staff throughout the development. In the software development industry, the typical project lifecycle ends upon delivery of the product. At SDF the design choice is to keep a small nucleus for the actual development and beyond. There is not the project 'ramp up – team assembly' that often occurs in software development. In the ramp-up product environment team members are assembled and scheduled much like contractors and move in and out of the development based on the use of their skill-set. As a result, there is no individual allegiance or identification with the product. At SDF the responsibility for identification with the products resides with the project manager. The teams and the team clusters (e.g. programming, testing and service) provide the identification, sustainability of stability and the long-term balance. The responsibility for the various tasks (e.g. quality control) resides within the teams at all times.

The intelligent agent and modular software components form a software warehouse that allows SDF to roll out alternative product versions based on the new users. Once an agent is developed it stands as a sub-product or feature that can be interfaced or included in the system. In this way business results can be sustained and maintained efficiently. The firm has a nurturing and supportive culture and an open space-based work configuration that allows for both formal and informal work environments. The emphasis seems to be the successful development of the new product or version in terms of delivery time and product quality. The focus is on 'how' best to design the agents not 'who' is doing the design or how creative one specific person is with respect to others.

In the product development there are several points where iterative cycles occur. These cycles constitute passages of refinement and product clarification. Before a contract is negotiated and formalized time is set aside in order to develop shared understanding of the purpose and scope. The customer knows what the final product is. Constraints and deliverables are clearly specified. *This is an important aspect in sustainability – developing a moving target can be counter-productive.*

As the design and development proceed there are iterative cycles on both the product manager and technical leader sides. Information sharing and decision-making mechanisms are facilitated through both informal and formal deliberation arenas. In the software groups we observed that face to face dialogue and mediated help sessions seem to be an important aspect – almost as much as using formal help desks and online retrieval from technical libraries. Even though the scope and purpose have been initially defined, clarification and refinement of details are viewed as an ongoing process. The driving force for the ongoing deliberation is the shared fundamental norm that says 'it is better to develop the product correctly the first time rather than having to do expensive remakes'. We observed that there was very little redo in any of the SDF products. In the product construction phase the iterative cycles play several roles. Obviously the software coding and testing is a repetitive cycle. As errors or problems are noted corrections and solutions are made and the cycle repeats. The intermediate product is run past the customer as it passes through stages of development. Equipment and the network infrastructure installation, training and documentation all are iterative processes as well, that must interface with the software product as it reaches completion.

The SDF culture emphasizes the need for individuals to maintain and develop their technological expertise. The firm invests continuously in its human capital using a variety of mechanisms. All employees are expected to spend at least 10 per cent of their work time in continuing education by taking outside training, in-house training, attending workshops and conferences, and through self-study. Formal seminars and forums are held weekly to share expertise and to provide the big picture – the firm's plans, current and proposed projects, and technological developments. During the growth of the firm, care has been taken to ensure that new employees are fully integrated. There is an overall caring and personal development-oriented culture that is projected, encouraged and modelled by senior management. Specific efforts have been made to develop and retain permanent staff. In contrast to other firms in the software industry SDF has a very low turnover rate.

Discussion

Many relevant issues can be discussed in the case. However, due to space limitations we will identify only a few questions for further research. The areas that we advance in this section include: What are some of the key design requirements that can facilitate sustainability? What are some of the key cause-and-effect relationships between NPD features and sustainability? What is the relationship between NPD, sustainability and learning mechanisms? How can the platform architecture facilitate and enhance sustainability?

The study of new product development in the case provides an initial support to the argument that sustainability can be designed and managed in the NPD environment in various ways. These 'various ways' can be described as a set of dimensions which fit neatly into the platform architecture schema, each of which fulfils a necessary requirement for achieving sustainability. The set of necessary but not sufficient requirements for achieving sustainability can be referred to as design requirements. Looking at the case the following are a few of the design requirements that seem to have been utilized: legitimate formal and informal arenas for exchange of ideas were created; the continuity of support and improvement efforts for the products was maintained over a long period of time; the composition of the team reflected the totality of the business functional areas of expertise; goals, scope and purpose for the teams were defined and refined on an ongoing basis; and there were effective processes for implementing continuous improvements during the NPD process. The deployment of modular-based components at various phases of the product development cycle mirrors the platform architecture.

The design dimensions represent different possible ways to respond to the design requirements. Design dimensions can be conceived on a continuum. The following are a few examples: the team members may be on a continuum from one to several functional areas; the team members may be on a continuum from same to different levels in the firm; and goal setting may be on a continuum from team level to organization level. Along each design dimension there would be a range of choices that the organization designer needs to make. This is especially true in the configuration of the specific platform for product launching. The potential cause-and-effect relationships among the design requirements, design dimensions, platform architecture and sustainability are an area that requires significant research efforts in the future.

Platform-based work design provided the foundation for sustainability at both the team and organizational levels. The modular-based design allowed for simultaneous autonomy and scope boundary for work at different levels and phases. The iterative cycles enhanced ongoing knowledge acquisition, the flow of information and continuous improvement of the NPD process. Scope creep was reduced by adhering to the modules and boundaries defined in the platform architecture. The time to market for the product was ensured through the use of the agent structure.

One of the key findings from the case is that SDF established some type of legitimate forum for the exchange of ideas and actions. From an organization design perspective, the forum is seen as a mechanism with a structural configuration and processes that are devoted to improvements and learning (Purser, Pasmore and Tenkasi 1992; Stebbins and Shani 1995). The iterative cycles approach coupled with the deliberation mechanisms for information sharing and view typified by the product architecture provides an ongoing opportunity to improve and sustain business results and a way to foster learning at all levels and across all levels of the firm. Our case suggests that not only is a learning mechanism (such as mentoring and face to face dialogues) an integral part of sustainability but that the type of learning mechanism is a clear managerial choice that has a significant influence on the organization's ability to develop and nurture sustainability. The very way that the firm chooses to lay out the work environment and the support patterns facilitates and establishes the ongoing learning environment.

Conclusion

Work intensity and sustainability in the new product development environment in the software industry emerged as major challenges in the 'new' economy. As was argued in Chapter 3 in this book, work intensity leads to the consumption of human resources, while sustainable work systems are characterized by the opportunities for individuals to continuously regenerate resources, skills and knowledge. It was further proposed that a work system is sustainable when it maintains or extends the human, social and institutional resources of the organization. This chapter has advanced and utilized an integrative framework, based on socio-technical and business strategy thinking, to explore the interplay between platform-based NPD work and sustainability.

The study of new product development in the SDF company illustrates that the proposed integrative framework can be a useful analytical tool to examine the dynamics of work intensity and sustainability in the 'new' economy. Furthermore, it provides an initial support to the argument that sustainability can be designed and managed in the NPD environment in various ways. Design is viewed as a formulation of choices between a clear set of alternatives. It was further argued that the 'various ways' could be described as a set of dimensions, which fit neatly into the platform architecture schema, each of which fulfils a necessary requirement for achieving sustainability.

Learning mechanisms seem to have played a critical part in sustainability at SDF. This finding supports similar arguments and findings reported in Chapters 15, 16 and 17. As we have seen, the establishment of mechanisms for information sharing and deliberations at SDF provided an ongoing opportunity to improve and sustain business results and a way to foster learning at all levels and across all levels of the firm. Managers at SDF made choices about the design and deployment of specific learning mechanisms. The platform-based architecture for NPD work seems to provide a context that has the potential of fostering a work environment that can increase the organization's ability to develop and nurture sustainability. Yet, as we have seen at SDF, the complexity and nature of NPD work in the software industry illustrates the need for further research in order to understand the full impact of platforms on sustainability in an increasingly competitive and uncertain environmental context.

References

Adler, N. and Docherty, P. (1998) 'Bringing business into sociotechnical theory and practice', *Human Relations*, 51, 3, 319–45.

Delbecq, A.L. and Weiss, J. (2000) 'The business culture of Silicon Valley. A turn-of-the-century reflection', *Journal of Management Inquiry*, 9, 1, 37–44.

Ebrahimpur, G. and Jacob, M. (2001) 'Restructuring for agility at Volvo Car Technical Services (VCTS)', *European Journal of Innovation Management*, 4, 2, 64–72.

Eijnatten, F.M. van (1994) *The Paradigm that Changed the Work Place*, Assen/Stockholm: Van Gorcum/Arbetslivscentrum.

Hanna, D.P. (1988) *Designing Organizations for High Performance*, Reading, MA: Addison-Wesley.

Kolodny, H.F. and Dresner, B. (1986) 'Linking arrangements and new work designs', *Organization Dynamics*, 14, 3, 33–51.

Krishnan, V. and Gupta, S. (2001) 'Appropriateness and impact of platform-based product development', *Management Science*, 47, 1, 52–68.

Lander, S. (1997) 'Issues in multiagent design systems', *IEEE Expert*, March/April.

Muffato, M. (1999) 'Introducing a platform strategy in product development', *International Journal of Production Economics*, 60–1, 145–163.

Olin, T. and Shani, A.B. (Rami) (2001) 'New product development and sustainability. Learning from Ericsson'. Paper presented at the 8th International Product Development Conference, EIASM, Enschede, The Netherlands, June.

Pasmore, W.A. (1993) 'Designing work systems for knowledge workers', *Journal for Quality and Participation*, July–August, 83–91.

Pasmore, W.A. (1994) *Creating Strategic Change*, New York: Wiley.

Pasmore, W.A. (2001) 'Action research in the workplace. The sociotechnical perspective', in P. Reason and H. Bradbury (eds) *Handbook of Action Research. Participative Inquiry and Practice*, London: Sage, pp. 38–47.

Pava, C. (1986) 'Redesigning sociotechnical systems design. Concepts and methods for the 1990s', *Journal of Applied Behavioral Science*, 22, 3, 201–22.

Purser, R.E., Pasmore, W.A. and Tenkasi, R.V. (1992) 'The influence of deliberations on learning in new product development teams', *Journal of Engineering and Technology Management*, 9, 1–28.

Schilling, M.A. and Hill, C.W.L. (1998) 'Managing the new product development process', *The Academy of Management Executive*, 12, 3, 67–81.

Scott, G.M. (1998) 'The new age of new product development. Are we there yet?' *R&D Management*, 28, 4, 225–36.

Shani, A.B., Grant, R. and Krishnan, R. (1992) 'Advanced manufacturing systems and organizational choice. A sociotechnical system approach', *California Management Review*, 34, 4, 91–111.

Shani, A.B. (Rami) and Lau, J. (2000) *Behavior in Organizations*, Boston: Irwin-McGraw-Hill.

Shani, A.B. (Rami) and Sena, J.A. (1994) 'Information technology and the integration of change. Sociotechnical system approach', *Journal of Applied Behavioral Science*, 30, 247–70.

Stebbins, M. and Shani, A.B. (Rami) (1995) 'Organizational design and the knowledge worker', *Leadership and Organizational Development Journal*, 16, 1, 23–30.

Taylor, J.C. and Felten, D.F. (1993) *Performance By Design. Sociotechnical Systems in North America*, Englewood Cliffs, NJ: Prentice-Hall.

Trist, E.L. (1982) 'The evolution of sociotechnical systems', in A.H. Van de Ven and W.F. Joyce (eds) *Perspectives on Organization Design and Behavior*, New York: Wiley, pp. 19–75.

Zhang, Q. and Doll, W. (2001) 'The fuzzy front end and success of new product development. A causal model', *European Journal of Innovation Management*, 4, 2, 95–112.

9 Sustainability in a rapidly changing environment

Lena Wilhelmson and Marianne Döös

Introduction

Learning, development and sustainability all have positive connotations. The *processes* they denote are easily thought of as being as harmonious and unproblematic as the outcome. Such processes, however, require change and new thinking that expands earlier understanding, leaving old paradigms and entering new ones. This is painful and laborious for individuals as well as organizations. This duality is an assumption behind this chapter where light is shed on the complexity of sustainability. As in several chapters in this volume sustainability is looked upon in a dynamic way:

> only a system that is continuously in a state of 'becoming' can be called 'sustainable'. Sustainability cannot be regarded as a static characteristic of a structure or a process because everything in the system is constantly 'on the move'. A definition of sustainability must take account of time as a key factor, and should focus on dynamic qualities of the system.
>
> (Chapter 6)

An understanding of sustainability benefits from being thought of as a process. Here we discuss sustainability as including periods of comfort, growth and equilibrium, as well as phases of pain, fractures and labour. The aim is to use a case study for critical reflection and thus elaborate the sustainability concept by highlighting its complexity.

A sustainable work system is seen as a system where management and employees consciously strive for the personal growth of employees as a means for development of competitiveness. Moreover, we agree with the idea of the resource-centred perspective where sustainability is defined in relation to organizational solutions and strategies which are seen as 'sustainable in a social sense if they maintain and reproduce the given social and human recourses or even extend them' (Chapter 5).

A unit within Ericsson Telecom AB[1] provides the empirical background. This unit underwent a thorough renewal during 1995–9. New leadership took form; it changed its field of activity and its ways of organizing work (Wilhelmson and Döös 2000). The original research focused on production and activity issues, such as possibilities to organize for the enhancement of learning and competence development.

A secondary analysis[2] offers an opportunity to reflect upon the issue of sustainability over time, in a rapidly changing environment. As a result, sustainability is placed in relation to phases of development over time in four different aspects of the ongoing business: in products, in organization structure, in principles for how to organize work, and for individuals. Within those aspects phases of ups and downs were traced and related to the issue of sustainability.

A brief case presentation is followed by a description of fluctuations in the aspects mentioned above, intertwined with more analytical reasoning and observations. Finally we discuss the issue of sustainability over time in this changing environment.

The case

The unit strived for autonomy[3] within the larger whole of the mother company and its tradition of hierarchy and strict rules, which had resulted in bureaucratic stiffness, according to managers in the unit. Keeping up with a continuously changing world had created a need for flexibility and learning. An important part of the renewal work concerned achieving a situation where employees act as knowledgeable individuals making decisions based on their own interpretations of the current realities. There was a need for individuals to be responsible and able to handle change. Organizational structures and ways of working that were coherent with and lead to such understanding and acting among the organizational members were thus required.

Visions and ideas

Visions and ideas were the basis for the renewal. The visions of the managers, as well as other dedicated and driving persons, were explicit and important as guiding stars for co-ordinating all the changes. The visions were clearly in line with sustainability on several levels: the nation, the company, the unit and the individual. An important and unusual part of the vision was that 'added value for the individual' was regarded as of *equal* importance as 'profitability for the company' (Company pamphlet 1997) in the striving for a non-hierarchical organization. Reciprocity in responsibility for fulfilling shared assignments, keeping promises of delivery dates and quality meant a qualitatively new and wider involvement in the complete product development process for almost everyone. Organizing work in teams and small 'virtual companies' were important means to reach these goals.

When the managers tried to organize work according to those ideas, it can be seen as putting the sustainability concept into operation. The changes can be characterized as empowering,[4] which might be problematic for the individual engineer, imposing high intensity caused by market requirements. This issue was, however, not raised in the study.

Important events

The change process is largely viewed through the visions and reality descriptions of managers and key actors,[5] i.e. from a managerial perspective. A rough overview of important events in the unit during the years 1995 to 1999 is presented below:

- 1995: the first merger and dual leadership;
- 1996: teamwork and improvements;
- 1997: renewal work: changes in products, technology, organization and competence;
- 1998: the second merger and a cultural clash;
- 1999: the unit is split and organizational principles are abandoned.

The first merger

The unit was formed in 1995, when two newly appointed managers (a male and a female) agreed to merge their units and to lead the new unit together, and a co-leadership took form.

At this time the unit ranked as number 19 out of 23 local design centres (LDCs).[6] It was:

> one of the most expensive LDCs, never delivering on time, never within budget, with a varying quality in its products and with a large employee turnover . . . there was a thick layer of problems on top of everything that was good.
>
> (Manager)

A way to deal with this was to emphasize the importance of 'keeping promises and delivering on time with quality'. This was the first vision, clearly articulated and quite down to earth.

Improvement work

Some 400 improvement activities were carried out in order to reduce the gap between current reality and the vision. Large meetings were held with all personnel, external speakers were invited and workshops arranged. All this aimed at making everyone conscious of the vision and its implications. The unit also moved into a new open-space building – a decision that was forced on the employees by the two managers – making communication easier. Teamwork was implemented, initially against the will of several managers and other employees.

After a year the improvement activities were paying off; now the unit was ranked as number 3 out of 34 LDCs. Did this give rise to complacency? No, the two managers raised new issues: 'Where is the market heading? Now when we do things right, are we doing the right things?'

Renewal work

In 1997 the answer to the second question was – No! Leaders on different levels of the unit had identified the need for change:

> We started to look around. What is happening within telecom, within datacom, what is happening in the world? Telecom is declining, becoming a commodity, while datacom, infocom and multimedia are growing. And here we are, working on our signals. No one will pay our costs for products that can be taken from the shelf.
>
> (Manager)

The unit management decided to leave telecom, eliminate cash cow products and move into the Internet telephony business. Together with many of the personnel they undertook a thorough restructuring of the unit to make this change of products and technology possible. 'To embrace the whole chain', i.e. emphasizing the importance for engineers to take responsibility for a wider task and to be acquainted with all the steps in a product development project, was now formulated as a second vision. A new organizational infrastructure was built on the basic principles behind the vision to support creativity and learning, to make new product development possible and to create the right and competitive competence quickly. The amount of changes caused worry and insecurity at all levels of the unit. Employees had to alter old habits and their ways of thinking and acting in work. All this was considered necessary due to the competitive pressure from the outer world. At the same time the renewal work had created a strong feeling of uniqueness and pride among many organizational members, not least among the key actors.

The critical second merger

Early in 1998 the unit was merged with another Ericsson unit.[7] The aim was to strengthen skills and competences needed for the new types of products. Data-part engineers were experts on software for Internet telephony applications, possessing necessary datacom knowledge. Tele-part's skills concerned the performance issues reached through the improvement and renewal work. Out of the merger evolved the third vision: 'to make Ericsson the leading supplier of IP [Internet–protocol] telephony services'.

However, the merger soon resulted in a severe cultural clash that never was resolved. Tele-part management did not realize the full importance of really getting the new organizational members 'onboard the team train'. Data-part was supposed to bring in new competence, but it turned out that this competence was heavily loaded with a culture of 'gurus, cowboys and experts'. According to managers and key actors in Tele-part, the culture was both rather elitist and hierarchical and still 'without sufficient order', e.g. concerning delivery time and the documentation of the software development process. The two fundamental principles for managing work – to work in teams and to have autonomous product companies – became conflicting at this time. Since the two parts did not share work tasks, the ideas and the culture of teamwork and shared responsibilities were never really transacted. Keeping the level 'telecom quality' in the project process that was achieved back in 1996 turned out to be problematic and this period was hard on several individuals – both at designer and management levels.

The split

At the beginning of the summer of 1999 the unit was again divided into its two original parts. This decision was taken on the level above the unit and was essentially based on the idea to organize around similar products that belong together. In Tele-part the spirit was still there, still relying on the renewal principles and on coming products, but after the split organizational principles were put on ice for the time being. In Data-part the product developed and was reaching the market, which created new demands. Further improvement work was discussed, teamwork was now wanted also here, as a way to handle problems with quality, economic control and delivery on time.

In 2000 and up till now, one can see how visions and organizing principles are coming about again in different ways in several organizations within and outside Ericsson, carried by managers and members with experience from this journey through change.

Fluctuations over time

The amount of change inside and outside the unit certainly does not mean linear development over time. Here follows an account of fluctuations in the four respects mentioned earlier, with phases of positive development and strength as well as of struggle and weakness.

Fluctuations in products

The products are the solid ground for the unit's existence. The history shows definite ups and downs in this respect. In the beginning the unit was poor on production as the ranking showed. But the potential for better performance was good and after a year of improvement activities the unit was already at its peak, delivering upgraded software for the AXE telephony system. From this strong position management decided to change the field of activity from mature cash cow products in traditional telecom technology to an entirely new area of Internet telephony, with emphasis on datacom technology. In moving from the well-established ground, production once again became shaky. It takes time before new products are conceived, developed and sold. Learning the logic of datacom is time consuming and work tasks therefore take more time. But the decision to shift products has still shown to be positive in the long run. When the unit was split, new products were about to be launched.

Several new products gained high market share and still do well. Approximately 160 ideas were generated and evaluated, of which the most promising ones were developed in product companies. In retrospect, these products often continued to live on together with the managers, project leaders and engineers who initially developed them. A living product creates a sustaining environment for its developers, as it goes into more industrialized phases from being an invention. Within the shelter of a successful product, project leaders and engineers can make use of developed competences and skill; they can rely on important experiences. Even if the product over time belongs to various units in the enterprise, a core group of people seems to follow the product on its way to maturity.

Fluctuations in organization structure

Being part of a large company, dealing with fast moving product development, also means to be acting in an environment that is rapidly moving and changing its structure. The general principle for organizing is that every product should belong to the correct product area and business unit, which implies recurring merging and splitting adjustments and restructuring activities all over the global company as new products are moving along.

The organization structure thus fluctuates a great deal over time. The two merger decisions were made on the initiative of the unit itself, but the decision to split was made on a higher level in the enterprise. The unit was initially unstable after the first merger, but it soon regained stability as the two managers took firm hold of the development. The unit stood strong when looking for a partner to strengthen competence and credibility as they entered a new technology area. The second merger proved not to be a very healthy one. The invited datacom unit had a strong identity of its own. It was not possible to integrate speedily or easily. Data-part retained its strong identity, guarding its boundaries as a company within the company, working with its own product, which was very close to market launch. Tele-part was at the same time weakened by the transferring strategy[8] and its new products were still immature. At the time of the split Data-part was less robust. It had difficulties entering a more industrialized phase, difficulties in delivering on time with quality, and it was about to start new improvement work.

Fluctuations in organizational principles

On the overall level, ideas and principles guiding development seem to grow continually stronger in the minds of managers and key actors. In practice, however, those principles were meeting resistance, especially in the merger between Tele-part and Data-part. They found themselves in a cultural clash concerning organizational principles. Tele-part had strong guiding visions realized in practice. Data-part had a way of doing things that in many ways was contradictory to the visions. This clash was never handled openly. The organizational principles from Tele-part lived on until the split, when they finally collapsed.

The infrastructural means to realize the visions were mainly teamwork and small virtual product companies. Responsibility for products and competence was divided. Competence coaches were appointed to benefit the individual engineer, and with the task of staffing projects and product companies. Teamwork, development of organizational competence and learning in the work tasks were seen as the main road to new knowledge.

According to the managers and other key actors, teamwork was considered fundamental for bringing the guiding ideas and visions into operation. In the following section teamwork as an organizational principle is analysed in more detail and we switch to an interpreting and analytical mode, for a better understanding of one of the working ingredients with consequences for sustainability issues.

A project leader with former experiences both as competence coach and as product manager gives the following definition of 'team':

> It is a group that isn't too big, maximum eight people, probably less, that have a common goal, that they strive towards during work hours, and that it's their main task to reach this goal together, which often, in our setting, means designing something for a certain point of time and quality . . . and that must be the most important for each and everyone . . . and also that you gain from the exchange so that you help each other when problems are around.
>
> (Project leader)

Teams were created and trained on all levels in the unit: co-leadership, competence coaches as a team of their own, engineers working in project teams of three to four individuals and seen as self-responsible and self-managing. Also, cross-functional teams were created for special tasks in the projects.

The teamwork principle stood strong during the first years. But employees come and go and new teams were established without getting team training. In Data-part teamwork was looked upon with suspicion. This part was carrier of a totally different set of organizing principles, even if those principles were informal and never explicitly formulated. So, depending on various circumstances, the teamwork principle lost ground as time went by.

After the split Data-part changed attitude. After some time it discovered the need for a structured project process and teamwork. The quality department now carries on with establishing genuine teamwork and characterizes this as the 'heart of our challenge'.

How teamwork makes a difference

An example will illustrate how teamwork makes a difference in software development work. Inspired by the holon concept of chaos theory (Fitzgerald and van Eijnatten 1998) we highlight the differences between working with new product development as an individual and as a team member. A definition of the holon concept as presented in Chapter 6 is: 'A holon is both an individual "whole" and a part of a much larger whole, at one and the same time.'

The planning process in individually distributed work tasks ('Individual model' in Figure 9.1) is compared with the same type of process when work tasks are shared in a team ('Team model' in the figure). The comparison aims at showing working ingredients or mechanisms that make a difference for individuals, in situations of time pressure and deadlines, and when ups and downs occur in, e.g., products or customer interest.

In a planning process, when work tasks are individually distributed, the project planning meeting has a co-ordinating character.[9] Individuals act as holons on their own before, during and after the meeting where they get information from the project leader and from other

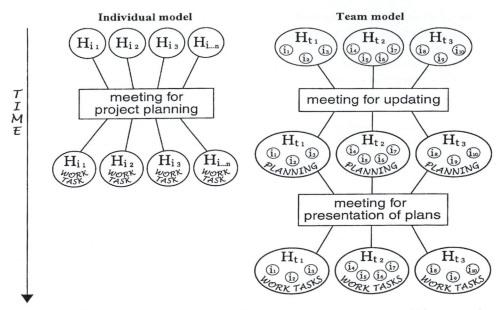

Figure 9.1 Working in small work teams implies differences in the planning process within new product development projects.

Key: H = holon; i = individual; t = team.

individual holons working within the same project. The information concerns the state of work tasks, mainly in terms of whether they are on time or not. Each individual holon has his or her defined responsibilities and pre-planned work tasks to cope with, tasks that no one else is much interested in.

A different planning situation and process is when designers are organized in teams.[10] Each team is responsible for a specific part of the product. Instead of individual holons we have a team holon, where individuals belong and share work tasks. When it is time for planning for the next period, there is an updating meeting within the whole project. Then the team holons enter a process of communication, for their own planning, jointly identifying and interpreting the team's tasks. Thereafter a new meeting on project level follows, where each team briefly presents its plans (tasks and time consumption). Finally they go back to work, with other updated team members around to discuss problems and share tasks with, although each individual holon has his/her responsibilities.

The specific team holons are not supposed to last over time in this case. They are temporary constructions related to a certain work task period within a specific new product development project. Yet teams are considered important in the construction of what can be regarded as sustainability both on the organizational and the individual level. The organization enjoys sustainability since decisions are better understood and owned by the task executors who actually develop or test the products. When it comes to the individual engineers and their experience of working in teams, they say it gives them the possibility to learn from work tasks in a more efficient way. Participation in planning processes and co-responsibility in work tasks means shared creation of meaning. Close co-operation and mutual responsibility give opportunities for collective learning (see Chapter 16). Working together in genuine teams makes dialogue an important working ingredient, when the task is to develop new products, since this task is dependent on continuous learning.

The team model for project planning supports working in iterations and making decisions en route, depending on earlier experiences, encountered difficulties and possibilities, as well as changes in demands and goals. It seems more suitable to handle the recurrent uncertainties involved in the new product development type of work. To work in integrated/genuine teams is, according to project leaders and competence coaches, a way of sharing knowledge. At the same time it diminishes the need for management. A group can take on a larger task. The risk of misunderstandings is reduced when people need to talk to each other and work out a way of communicating that makes it possible to carry out a joint task. However, the unit management also prefers the team organization because it is difficult for employees to resist peer pressure. There is a risk that peer pressure in teams also increases intensity for individuals in their struggle to meet deadlines.

Fluctuation in individual development

On the individual level sustainability fluctuates, not only due to intensity, but also in connection to the organizational principles above as well as in connection to products and product development. How the individual can profit from experiences and go on to new tasks in a sustaining way seems to be connected to work role and work tasks. Managers and other key actors talk about their experiences in quite a different way from engineers. To lead renewal work gives managers a general perspective by learning about organizational principles and strategic matters. Concentrating on technical development in a product gives the engineer fresh factual knowledge along with competence to co-operate to reach a goal.

Managers and key actors

Managers and key actors get stronger when they create visions and transform those into organizational principles used to build organization structures. The strength comes to a large degree from being a group of devoted people, discussing these matters, learning from reinforcing new ideas. When the common frame falls apart, they go in different directions, truly disappointed, as their organization principles were not strong enough to keep the unit together. They are weakened for some time, but find new grounds where they start over again. The well-developed relations between these key actors are also sustaining over time. With values, visions and goals built out of common experiences relations live on. One year after the split one of the managers starts to gather some of the key actors in his new unit to reuse the experiences they have made together.

The managers point at several lessons learned in order to be more sustaining in renewal work. They emphasize the importance of their co-leadership; together they could create the strength needed to keep on struggling when problems appeared. To sustain in the task of leading renewal work is not easy on your own. At the same time the struggle for implementing new ideas and visions may lead to keeping to those as sacred cows. It is important to be aware of the risk of being trapped in the visions, not allowing continuous improvements when a goal is reached.

Engineers and developers

The broadening of work tasks was meant to make people act consciously and well tuned to each other and to the overall task; to get the product out on the market on time. This meant being involved in the new product development in a way where the individual engineer comes closer to the customer and the product as a whole, not only working with some detail on his/her own. For this the individual needs information and knowledge about the project as well as the customer, the competitors and the product, apart from the specific knowledge of the task of his/her own team. Knowledge of this kind is strengthening and the foundation for co-responsibility.

Working in a business where change is ever-present means that the designers become skilled at rethinking and restarting. To handle the changeable reality people seem to develop strategies with the function of finding something settled and solid, that goes beyond what is changing. To formulate personal goals, like developing one's competence, also exceeds temporary changes in work tasks and projects. Knowledge that problems are always around to be solved also contributes to the feeling of stability. It is part of the work and belongs there, as do uncertainty and vagueness to the commonplace. In one way or another each person forms his/her task and uses it as a handle to hold on to. To change tasks has become a habit; you leave the old task behind and grab the new one: 'If only you know how it is supposed to be, what it looks like. So that you get hold of the task. You get acquainted with the new, so it works out well' (Engineer).

Many engineers/developers have a strong identification with the work task,[11] as they enjoy being at the technology frontier. To acquire new knowledge is for most engineers of great sustaining importance in their career development. Competence is hard currency if one wants to be valuable on the labour market. In the follow-up inquiry the engineers mentioned new technical knowledge as the most important result of all the changes that took place in the unit. The painful technological shift, to start developing Internet telephony applications, meant high demands on learning for individuals and this strengthened their standing in the long run. Engineers and developers also mention experiences of how to work in projects and groups as important learning acquired in the unit. Through this they built new contact nets. They appreciate the competence they got from working collectively, and having learned the importance of how to develop good project processes, how to keep a project in good order. This was the start of their new working life. When the unit was divided and the organizational principles were no longer in use, the engineers stood strong with new knowledge.

Fluctuations and the concept of sustainability

This case points to the importance of time and phases for sustainability. Looking back over a period of six years, it becomes evident that the occasion chosen for looking for sustainability in an organization makes a big difference, since we are dealing with processes that are not synchronized. Over time products, organization, principles and individuals go through phases of development that are on many occasions not in tune with each other.

When the unit splits products stand strong but the small company structure falls apart. Organizational principles disappear for the time being as the key actors are spread. Individual engineers stand strong with their products – going on to new units. Managers move on to new leading positions. People find new tasks, being an experience richer. These ongoing processes can be illustrated as in Figure 9.2.

In the very beginning production was poor, organization structure was weak, managers were struggling for improvements in organizational principles, employees were used to not being responsible. The improvement and renewal work caused a lot of painful and threatening changes for both middle managers and designers/engineers. It was not possible to carry on old habits. Before the merger with the datacom unit this laborious work had paid off: production was highly rated, organizational principles were highly regarded and the unit was no

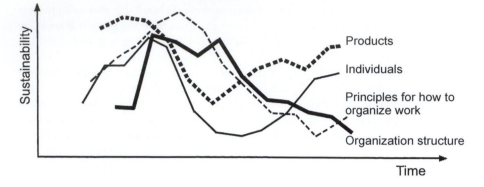

Figure 9.2 A schematic picture visualizing the ups and downs of sustainability over time and in the four different aspects of the ongoing business.

longer under threat. Teamwork along with good planning processes for projects had been established as an organizational principle. Employees were to make decisions for themselves, e.g. choosing which competence coach to belong to, which project to work in and which new skills to develop. This was sometimes hard on the individuals: 'it was like applying for a new job', one engineer said. The co-leadership was strong, especially together with other key actors. People in the unit had become proud of themselves; self-esteem was higher according to managers.

Soon after the second merger the picture becomes more blurred. New products are developing, but it takes time to reach the market. Organization structure is once again weakened. The two units remain different parts and do not integrate into one whole, which to some degree depends on differences in core values concerning organizational principles. Data-part is not interested in teamwork or detailed process planning. The principles are weakened, no longer seen as the obvious way to organize work, even if Tele-part still works in that way. Competence coaches meet difficulties staffing the product companies now when they all need more people than are available. Individual engineers are not so disturbed by all this; they are fully occupied with the interesting work tasks and learning new skills. In Data-part engineers also struggle with intensity problems, being too few and having to depend on consultants to a large degree. Being three managers does not work out well.[12]

Although the unit and the specific small company organization ceased to exist, and although the change processes caused individuals pain and suffering, reality is too complex to say that this is not an example of sustainability. Visions, ideas and ambitions live on, as do products that successfully reach their customers.

Organization principles are reinvented after some time. Individuals earned new competence, maybe with a larger capability to manage change. Contact nets and relations are built upon in new environments. In this way new resources have been generated, for the company in the creation of new competitive products and for the individuals in gaining new competences. In this way the struggle and the creation of new thoughts and experiences can be reused in new settings. Sustainability for individuals and products seems to go on within and without the unit – at least in this kind of business with the task of new product development, living under the conditions of short product lifecycles and sharp competition.

Discussion

How then can the concept of sustainability be understood and developed in the light of this case? Only to connect sustainability to the organizational level, in this case to the unit, definitely seems to be too narrow a way of looking at it. The concept of sustainability covers a complex phenomenon when seen over time and in different aspects. This case shows some of the complexity to be handled when managing non-synchronized processes. Periods of weakness and struggle were the cradle for thinking and action, leading to transformation and change that open up for continuation.

To sustain involves a capacity for change, both on an organizational and an individual level and it is not the same thing as a harmonious life. The decision to change field of activity and develop software for Internet telephony can be seen as a leap into a new 'strange attractor'[13] (see Chapter 6). To handle this kind of change invariably also includes pain; it has the character of transformative learning (Mezirow 1991). When surrounding conditions put pressure upon us to alter our cognitive structures, our ways of thinking, this has some very painful aspects to it. It can be seen as a process of accommodation (Piaget 1970) also on the level of an organization. To ask the question: 'Are we doing the right thing?' was crucial. It contributed to competitiveness in high tech development within the enterprise, new products were invented, employees developed new skills, and managers developed new organizational thinking.

In this work environment, sustainability for individuals is mainly realized by gaining good experiences and self-esteem that enhance the possibilities to go on to new tasks in new similar environments. The individual finds sustainability in his/her own development of competence, making use of changes, seeing them as opportunities to work with new products and regarding work processes as learning. The main importance then is not whether a specific project, product or unit survives. There is always a new task to define and go on with. As changes are struggled through, the individual makes experiences that are useful for future work.

Knowledge can be developed in a team that works closely together, both in doing the work task and when it comes to interpreting information. Jointly it is easier to make sense of information and develop new, transformed knowledge out of each and everyone's own experiences. Knowledge that is jointly produced has a more stable character than knowledge that is individually produced (Berger and Luckmann 1966). In this respect collectively created knowledge can be an important part of sustainability for organizations as well as for individuals, as it brings a broader line of perspectives, several persons' knowledge and experience. The knowledge thus created will in turn probably work in the direction of speed and efficiency, since employees are able to handle extended work tasks in a more qualified manner.

The vision of the empowered engineer developed by managers and key actors can be seen as an example of how prevailing emancipatory concepts concerning people and knowledge are of importance for the possibility to create work conditions that can contribute to sustainability for the individual employee.

To see individuals as holons, together building an organization, might help us see the importance of giving individuals the opportunity to grow strong. For the individual engineer to have the power to make decisions for him/herself and the team he/she belongs to, all of this was of importance to the two leaders. They were influenced by contemporary ideas[14] about teamwork and organizational development, and together with other key actors they made their own mix adapted to their present reality. They developed a skill both in creating and communicating ideas and visions. New collective meaning structures (Dixon 1994) were established; new organizational forms were created.

In conclusion, sustainability can be understood as the ability to interpret and deal with complexity, alterations and dynamics. To develop new products and adjust the organization to cope – through creating a new organization structure, developing new organizational principles and supporting competence development, all at the same time – we see as an example of a serious effort to reach sustainability. Learning is a key feature in such a developmental process.

Discussing sustainability requires both an awareness of which aspects to include and consider, and a time perspective long enough to experience the phases of ups and downs. The results of our analysis point to the importance of focusing on several units of analysis, when aiming at understanding sustainability in practice as well as a theoretical concept. This certainly poses problems for the possibilities to interpret sustainability empirically at a specific workplace at a specific time. It is also important to stress that what can be learnt from this rapidly changing environment might not be of immediate relevance for more stable and mature activities.

Notes

1 A large globalized Swedish telecom company.
2 The data cover 1995–2001, with the main data collection during spring 1999, mainly through small talks, informal observations, meeting attendance, semi-structured interviews (23) and two group reflections. We were in contact with management, project leaders and quality people as well as designers/engineers. After the main data collection there have been sporadic, recurring contacts with representatives of the unit. In autumn 2000 two managers were interviewed and a simple follow up inquiry was made with previous interviewees and other contact persons from the unit.
3 The unit was autonomous in some respects, e.g. being exempted from some rules, but clearly dependent on others, e.g. to which business unit they belong.
4 For a discussion on the 'empowerment' concept, see e.g. Appelbaum, Hébert and Leroux (1999).
5 We have chosen 'key actors' (*eldsjälar* in Swedish) as a way of naming the group of people engaged in leading the renewal work. Several leading persons within the unit acted as key actors; along with the two managers there were the human resource manager, project leaders, product managers, competence coaches and those working with quality issues. Quotations come from interviews with these key actors if not otherwise stated.
6 Index measuring software quality, delivery on time, price performance, productivity and service.
7 From here on those two parts of the unit will be labelled in the following way: Tele-part is the original unit and Data-part is the new part included through the merger. The main empirical base of the study is obtained from Tele-part.
8 The decision to give away its safe money-making products sometimes also meant transfer of staff as well as products.
9 The individual model comes from the testing of software for telenet systems in another Ericsson unit, from a study conducted during 2000 (Dixon *et al.* forthcoming).
10 This example deals with developing software for a specially designed video conference in Tele-part.
11 Something that might also easily lead to unhealthy intensity, as mentioned by, e.g., Brödner and Forslin in Chapter 2.
12 We are aware that many power games certainly must have occurred, but since this was not the focus of our study we have chosen not to look upon the renewal work from that perspective.
13 The power of habit makes us act in approximately the same way over and over again. We follow a track. But now and then we start to imagine a new way of acting and thinking, and a strange attractor is created in our mind. The more we get used to this new alternative the more likely we are to take a jump and move to this new strange attractor, and follow this new track, i.e. acting differently.
14 Such as Dixon (1994, 1997), Drucker (1994), Edvinsson and Malone (1997), Hammer (1996), Katzenbach and Smith (1993), Senge (1990) and Morgan (1998).

References

Appelbaum, S., Hébert, D. and Leroux, S. (1999) 'Empowerment. Power, culture and leadership – a strategy or fad for the millennium?' *Journal of Workplace Learning*, 11, 7, 233–54.

Berger, P. and Luckmann, T. (1966) *The Social Construction of Reality. A Treatise in the Sociology of Knowledge*, Harmondsworth: Penguin.

Dixon, N. (1994) *The Organizational Learning Cycle. How We Can Learn Collectively*, London: McGraw-Hill.

Dixon, N. (1997) 'The hallways of learning', *Organizational Dynamics*, Spring, 23–34.

Dixon, N., Döös, M., Wilhelmson, L. and Backlund, T. (forthcoming) *Functioning at the Edge of Knowledge. A Study of Learning Processes in Software Testing Teams*.

Drucker, P. (1994) *Managing in a Time of Great Change*, Oxford: Butterworth-Heinemann.

Edvinsson, L. and Malone, M.S. (1997) *Intellectual Capital. Realizing your Company's True Value by Finding its Hidden Brainpower*, New York: Harper Business.

Fitzgerald, L.A. and van Eijnatten, F.M. (1998) 'Letting go for control. The art of managing in the chaordic enterprise', *International Journal of Business Transformation*, 1, 4, 261–70.

Hammer, M. (1996) *Beyond Reengineering. How the Process-centred Organization Is Changing Our Work and Our Lives*, London: HarperCollins.

Internet Group, The (1997) Company pamphlet, Stockholm: Ericsson.

Katzenbach, J. and Smith, D. (1993) *The Wisdom of Teams*, Boston: Harvard Business School Press.

Mezirow, J. (1991) *Transformative Dimensions of Adult Learning*, San Francisco/Oxford: Jossey-Bass.

Morgan, G. (1998) 'From bureaucracies to networks. The emergence of new organizational forms', in G. Robinson Hickman (ed.) *Leading Organizations. Perspectives for a New Era*, Thousand Oaks, CA: Sage, pp. 283–6.

Piaget, J. (1970) *The Principles of Genetic Epistemology*, London: Routledge & Kegan Paul.

Senge, P. (1990) *The Fifth Discipline. The Art and Practice of the Learning Organization*, New York: Doubleday/Currency.

Wilhelmson, L. and Döös, M. (2000) *Förändringens resa. Om kompetens och organisatoriskt nyskapande på Ericssons Internet Group* (The Journey of Change), Solna: National Institute for Working Life.

10 Values and stakeholder relations

Peter Docherty[1]

Introduction

This chapter presents a number of key factors that have been influential in developing and maintaining the sustainability of a service company in relation to its personnel, customers and owners. First, the chapter presents some properties of services including the special significance of relationships to customers. The service example chosen to illustrate these is a bank. The strategic balance required to achieve sustainability in this sector is outlined.

The main factors affecting sustainability for the individual in the bank context are security and professional identity, personal development, workload, respect and fairness regarding management and rewards. From the company perspective, the sustainability factors addressed are long-term profitability, equity value and customer satisfaction. The role of the formalization of company values in mission statements and company strategies and practices as cornerstones for sustainability is described. Finally, current challenges to sustainability are outlined.

The character of services

Responsibility for stakeholders

Grönroos (1990) identifies four characteristics of a service: they are more or less intangible; they are activities or series of activities (processes) rather than things; the customer/user often participates in the process of producing the service; and services are often produced and consumed at the same time.

Services are a very heterogeneous field. This example is taken from the type of service in which the service provider takes some responsibility for the future welfare of the client. The current interaction between the service provider and the client is handled in relation to an assessment of the overall holistic perception of the client's short- and long-term needs and aspirations. The behaviour of the provider is guided or controlled partly by internalized values, norms, attitudes and mental models as well as by external organizational, professional and societal rules, regulations and laws. These elements are most apparent in such fields as human services, the traditional professions and in the public civil services. The core element in services is the centrality of direct interaction between the service provider and the client. In this relationship trust and perceived responsibility are key factors for the service provider. Key elements of the relationship, interaction, between the two are: commitment, mutual respect, mutual benefits, power dependence, shared knowledge, distinctive competence, communication skills and organizational linkages (Prim 1999).

Sustainability entails attaining and maintaining balance between different interests, goals, elements and forces in the organization's total situation. In the financial sector, the business strategy must attain balance between two key areas: transaction economics and customer–client relationships.[2] Transaction economics is often concerned with cost reduction and rationalization. This may entail the utilization of information and communication technology (ICT) applications in the extension of self-service facilities such as automatic teller machines (ATCs), smart cash cards and the Internet. It also covers resource control in the dimensioning of the branch office network and staffing levels, and organizational issues such as the distribution of authority and responsibility between levels and units.

Client relationships are of great importance in the banking sector in which so many services entail giving advice and making decisions, often under uncertainty, on matters of great significance for the client in both the short and long term. These decisions require local and holistic evaluations of the client's situation and place high demands on the bank personnel's competence regarding banking, and social and moral competence. The latter is related to the complexity of the client situations to be evaluated and the impact of advice given and decisions made on the future 'financial health' of the client. The growing share and import of these services in the business and the growing public demand that financial organizations should be held responsible for their advice and asset management, together with the financial institutions' moves to meet these demands, makes it meaningful to refer to the emerging development of professionalism.

Trust between service provider and client

The concept of 'trust' is taken to signify and represent a co-ordinating mechanism based on shared moral values and norms supporting collective co-operation and collaboration within uncertain environments. Allan Fox (1974, pp. 67–8) argued that the essential character of all trust relations is the reciprocal nature of trust. Trust tends to evoke trust, distrust to evoke distrust.

Issues of trust have become the focus of attention in organizational theory and research (Kramer and Tyler 1996; Lane and Bachmann 1998). The interest has been further stimulated by the growth of non-face to face, computer mediated forms of communication and commerce, where trust tends to become identified as a key, if problematic, issue by designers and users. In many services and other businesses the issue of trust is related to the utilization of ICT to extend self-service routines and establish virtual trading (Knights *et al.* 2001). How does technology-based self-service impact on relationships?

The financial services can be said to be in, or even to be, *the* business of trust. The creation and maintenance of trust relations is a fundamental condition of their existence. Financial services are dependent on the establishment and sustenance of a climate of public trust in financial institutions and their representatives (Dodd 1994; Morgan and Knights 1997).

Values and culture in business

A value is an enduring belief that a specific mode of conduct or end-state of existence is personally and socially preferable to alternate modes of conduct or end-states – values entail attention to both means and ends (Rokeach 1969). Values are global beliefs that underlie attitudinal processes. In particular, they serve as the basis for making choices (Connor and Becker 1994, p. 68).

Meglino *et al.* (1989, 1991) explicitly define organizational culture in terms of values and the concept of strong culture in terms of value congruence among organizational members. Value homogeneity among members allows managers to make safe assumptions about the likely behaviours of their subordinates when first order control mechanisms (such as rules) or second order mechanisms (such as direct supervision) are not present.

The integration perspective in cultural research is based on the assumption that people in a culture share a common set of values, a common set of norms that are clearly expressed and understood by the vast majority of people identifying themselves with the culture (Martin 1995). Usually a charismatic leader has generated the set of beliefs and values, and his or her role in propagating them is often cultivated through stories and myths that are well known to members of the culture.

In formulating its value base, management has the difficult task of balancing the legitimate interests of clients (sound economic services and reliable and trustworthy relations), personnel (security, identity, health, well-being and development) and the shareholders (owners) (economic viability, development and returns). Examining personnel's perspective more closely from positive experience, Pfeffer (1997, pp. 65–6) maintains that seven dimensions characterize systems producing profits through people, namely employment security, selective hiring of new personnel, decentralization of decision-making and self-managed teams as the basic principles of organizational design, comparatively high compensation contingent on organizational performance, extensive training, reduced status distinctions and barriers, and extensive sharing of financial and performance information throughout the organization.

Looking at negative experience, Maslach and Leitner (1997) relate burnout to the mismatch between the nature of the job and the nature of the person doing the job in one or more of the following areas: work overload, lack of control over one's work, too little reward for work, lack of community and positive connection with others at work (fragmenting personal relationships, undermining teamwork, working separately – not together), unfair treatment at work (regarding respect and confirmation of self-worth and conflicting values): what is really important for us? Are we doing what we say? Do we agree with the company's values?

The financial services sector

Banking is an example of a sector in which the dysfunctional impacts of the extensive and often less well-thought-out application of modern management doctrines and methods such as downsizing, outsourcing, utilizing intermediaries (contingent employees) and other rationalizations have often resulted in extremely intensive work situations. Considering client relationships, ICT has been used positively to improve client information systems and less positively in the creation of call centres. The 1980s saw some significant deregulations of banking activities in Scandinavia. In some cases, it was not a question of easing regulations, but of taking them away altogether. One example was the removal of limits on mortgaging. This led to a marked increase in the mortgaging of commercial real estate. When the real estate bubble burst in the early 1990s, many banks had to be rescued from bankruptcy by the government.

The trend to consolidation via mergers and acquisitions has been a distinct characteristic of the Nordic financial market in the 1990s and into the new decade. Several major banks have merged. At the same time deregulation has led to a blurring of the boundaries between different parts of the financial services sector, for example between insurance and banking, and between retail and investment banking. Banks have entered insurance by diversification or acquisition. Insurance companies have entered banking mainly by diversification. The development of IT has spurred the creation of niche telebanks with a few branch offices concentrated on major cities. The current trend holds for the entire Nordic scene. Successive deregulation has allowed companies outside the financial sector to establish business in the financial transaction sector. Retail chains such as J.C. Penney in the USA and ICA in Sweden are typical examples. Given the marked similarity in the strategies of key players in the sector, the acquisition and development of skills and knowledge and their organization may be expected to play a central role for a bank's success in the marketplace.

Svenska Handelsbanken

This section presents the Svenska Handelsbanken and its management's values as formulated in key policies and practices. These are related to the bank's long-term performance and to sustainability.

Svenska Handelsbanken aims to be an universal bank, i.e. a bank which offers its private and business clients the full spectrum of banking and financial services. Examples of such services are loans, real estate financing, payments, investment banking, trading, factoring, and leasing and insurance. Besides offering a broad spectrum of services the provision of a large network of branch offices is considered as being a basic component in the concept of a universal bank. In fact the extensive branch office network is seen as one of the bank's most important competitive advantages and not just an alternative channel.

Svenska Handelsbanken's basic idea is that the client should be its central focus and not its products. To achieve this, the bank has a marked decentralization of the bank's business to its branch offices. The local branch office has total responsibility for a co-ordinated and qualified service to each of its individual customers. It is individual contact persons in the local office who make all the decisions regarding their customers. This principle was introduced in the bank in the early 1970s and is regarded by management as its most important source of stimulation and personal development for personnel.

In the late 1990s asset management assumed a prominent strategic role in the bank. The 1990s saw the rapid automation of routine transactions from about 20 per cent to over 70 per cent. This has led to more and more qualified tasks being delegated to branch offices. The work at branch offices is increasingly made up of giving advice concerning investment and payments and granting credit.

Self-services via the Internet were launched in the late 1990s with the aim of reducing the volume of routine payment and deposit/withdrawal transactions in the bank office. This released personnel for the more qualified services requiring the design of specific solutions to the client's needs. These developments in business activities require significant developments both in the knowledge and skills of office personnel and in their support functions and systems.

The bank's emphasis on the client relationships is reflected by an emphasis on the branch office network. Svenska Handelsbanken has no plans to close branch offices while its major competitors, which are less focused on customer relations, closed between fifty and eighty branch offices in 2001 (Svanelid 2001).

> I don't believe in competing with technology. The only defensible competitive advantages that exist are our personnel's quality, its organization and its ways of working. Here we have our unique competitive advantage. That cannot be copied.
>
> (CEO, Svenska Handelsbanken)

The bank's formal value statement – the cornerstone of the business culture

The bank's activities are based on a fundamental view of personnel and clients based on confidence and respect. The company has a strong culture. This is an important management tool in a strongly decentralized organization (Kaufman 1960). The individual units in the decentralized organization cannot function without a clear set of common values as to how the organization is to work. However, the power of the value base depends less on its formal document than on how it guides the behaviour of the members of the organization. To ensure a certain stability and a 'red thread' in the company's activities the culture is only gradually modified to meet changes in the company and its environment. Even the culture is the subject of a continual dialogue within the bank.

Svenska Handelsbanken's culture is based on a number of clearly formulated values, maxims and principles that guide how the members of the company do business and how the company is run. This is, in itself, not an uncommon phenomenon in the business world. What is special in this instance is the extent of the diffusion of the values in the organization and the degree of acceptance of and adherence to the values by individuals in different functions, levels and geographical locations in the organization. It is to all intents and purposes 100 per cent in each case.

The values were first spelled out and interpreted in a booklet written by the CEO about twenty-five years ago. This is revised roughly every five years, though the revisions usually entail the reformulation of a single principle or the addition of a further one, plus nuancing, clarifying, updating the interpretations of the principles in the light of business and societal developments in the preceding period. The value statements basically reflect how the company regards its primary stakeholders: clients, personnel and owners (shareholders). The fundamental ideas behind these formulations are presented here.

Focus on clients

The client is the primary focus in all planning, actions and decisions in the business.

A good relationship with a client must be built on mutual understanding and respect, entailing honesty, sincerity and empathy. These may well be expressed through advising against the client's wishes, recommending alternative solutions to those they envisaged. The final decision on an issue is, however, the client's. Advice given must be what the bank regards as best for the client and must not be swayed by considerations of the bank's short-term profit. This is essential for long-term credibility. Sustainable service requires in turn that the bank's personnel are highly competent, more so than their colleagues in other banks.

Active marketing initiatives of specific services to clients must be based on a careful analysis of the clients' situation as distinct from across-the-board campaigns. Not all products are suitable for all individual clients.

The customization of services to individual clients naturally requires the delegation of full responsibility and discretion for clients to the branch office. The clients must know they are dealing with a decision-maker and not a messenger. It is the person responsible for the client who decides the conditions pertaining to the service. It is also important that the branch office is responsible for all clients within its geographical area, including major companies. This naturally entails matching the competence and experience of the branch office personnel to its clients. This requires a clear allocation of responsibility and a simple organization with a focus on flexibility and decisiveness rather than on long-term planning.

It is also essential that 'all business is local', i.e. that the district served by the branch office is not so large that the office personnel cannot be well acquainted with their clients. This value emphasizes that the bank's ties with its customers and its professional knowledge and insight are fostered by close physical proximity to its clients. A characteristic of the infrequent mis-judgements regarding bad loans has been, for example, that they were given to clients geographically (and socially) distant from the branch responsible.

Personnel should always bear in mind that it is the clients' and company's money that is being spent, so that this must be done with due moderation and consideration.

A cobbler should keep to his last. Business should focus on core skills and activities and management should be very wary and restrictive regarding diversifying into new fields of activity. Such moves may be justifiable, e.g. the decision to move into life insurance – but not insurance in general. This cautious spirit contributed to restraining the bank from making the painful mistakes many competitors made in their ventures into the real estate business in the late 1980s, early 1990s.

A major general development in the bank is the introduction of the 'personal client respon-sibility' principle. The system is not as yet fully implemented across all branch offices. It entails assigning each client a personal contact person who is responsible for the bank's service and the client's 'financial health'. This innovation demands considerable efforts in personal devel-opment for branch office staff. The use of call centres is very limited.

Focus on personnel

The bank may be regarded as exceptional in its expressed aim to offer its employees secure employment. No one, for example, has been made redundant on account of insufficient work in the last hundred years. This in its turn requires very special attention to competence and career development. Competence development is not simply a matter of formal train-ing but also learning at work through a dialogue between office personnel and managers. Organizational experiments are also conducted for learning purposes. Leaders and man-agers are, in principle, developed and selected from within the organization and are not recruited externally. Similarly, life-time employment sets demands on reward systems regarding both salaries and profit sharing.

Personnel with client responsibility are required to have a basic level of banking knowledge.

The bank employees have considerable discretion to react to the input from the client. They are encouraged to act independently to reach an agreement with their clients. Management formally acknowledges that granting such discretion will entail mistakes being made, but judges that these are well outweighed by the atmosphere, attitudes and relations created between the bank's personnel and its clients.

Providing the individual employee with responsibility, authority and competence to deal independently with a client requires the specification of moral limits if the individual is not to be exposed to the risk of self-exploitation. This requires the careful formulation of limits and goals for individuals, teams and offices and their continual follow-up and evaluation.

Focus on owners

The primary focus is profitability. Business transactions and decisions must generate profit. Economic result orientation permeates the management control system. Svenska Handelsbanken has generally been regarded as the most successful Nordic bank in the 1980s and 1990s. It is also among the best in the world regarding cost efficiency, with fewer people in its branch office network. Similarly it is careful to avoid costs that are not important for clients. As a branch office is responsible for its economic results, it has considerable degrees of freedom in the conduct of its business, including staffing levels.

Key competence development and management practices

The competence model

Having defined personnel competence as a key means of competition, management initiated a major competence development project in 1992 with the aim of reviewing the bank's current approach to competence development. The goal of the project was to produce a generally accepted description of the career and development paths in the corporation, which would be easy to understand and follow and which would stimulate personnel to further development in the whole corporation.

The focus of the project was competence from the perspective of the individual employee. The framework of the project was the corporation as a whole. The same basic model is used throughout the organization. The 'model' is divided into four levels or steps. The first corresponds to basic competence for new employees and then the levels increase progressively to the fourth which is reserved for individuals who are very competent generalists with long and broad experience.

These four levels are divided into three different areas: (a) work content, (b) authority and responsibility and (c) competence. The minimum demands for each of these areas is defined for each level. In the branch office model the area 'work content' is divided up into three sub-areas, namely payments, placements and finance. Taken together these three sub-areas cover all the work that may be involved in dealing with a client. Authority and responsibility may cover parts of or the entire business a client has with the bank.

The third area is headed 'competence', which the bank defines as covering 'experience, skills, contacts, networks, values, will/commitment, energy and capacity'. At the lower levels the demands are principally on mastery of rules and routines, technical systems and product knowledge. At higher levels the demands increase on such components as IT, sales and negotiation skills, social skills and experience. Some factors in the competence model, such as 'business acumen', 'decisiveness/power to act', 'good judgement' and 'quality', are not operationalized within the competence model but are used in personnel evaluation.

Individual planning and evaluation

The bank aims at clarity, simplicity and precision in the organization. Everyone should know what is expected of them. An important practice in this context is the personal planning and evaluation meeting between office personnel and their manager. The meetings deal with the follow-up and evaluation of last year's plan and an examination of options and ambitions to draw up new goals and plans for the coming year. The topics dealt with are the individual's competence development and assignments and goals in the branch office's business. These two issues interacting as personal development through on-the-job and action learning is a main strategy in the bank. The competence development discussion usually takes its point of departure in the competence model. Work assignments and goals take their point of departure in the branch office plans. After the meeting the individual and his or her manager should be clear about the lessons drawn from last year and the plans made for the coming year, including personal and team targets in different areas.

Moral competence – an emerging factor

Armon (1993) found in a longitudinal study that many people matured through a five stage developmental sequence in which what they valued at work became less instrumental, and more heavily directed towards the pursuit of such values as ethical conduct, assistance of other individuals and having a positive net impact on the world at large.

As mentioned earlier, there is a strong public interest in professional behaviour, which is shared by bank personnel. This ethical behaviour has been termed 'moral competence' by Brytting (2000a). This has two sides: the personal shouldering of responsibility and the competence embedded in the formal organization. The aim of moral action is *bonum commune*, the common good. The good of the individual is closely coupled to the common good. Moral competence in working life is the ability to handle morally concerned situations. Moral competence entails taking responsibility for our own and others' welfare even in a long-term perspective. Moral competence has distinct components. Value rational competence is expressed in actions which are consonant with the actor's own value system. Goal rational competence rests on reflection on external means and goals, often in the context of effectiveness, and is guided by the goals and rules in the organization. Burnout is often caused by the absence of reasonable moral commitments that give meaning to work (Martin 2000, p. xi). Emotion-based competence is guided by 'inner attention', reducing mental unease or tension.

The area of moral competence is receiving increasing attention. Taylor (1989) points out that work often includes a 'moral space', presenting individuals with situations, demands and expectations requiring action that form them as 'moral subjects'. More and more companies are endeavouring to create common values as a means for integrating, guiding and managing businesses conducted in decentralized forms (Brytting and Trollestad 2000). Moral competence includes some form of memory function that ensures continuity and learning. It may be more or less formalized. To maintain and develop moral competence requires suitable arenas: places that facilitate the exercise of communicative ability, for moral competence develops socially through dialogue.

Culture and performance

How has the company performed?

Customer performance

The bank's customer loyalty as measured by a survey in 2000 is high (Docherty 2002). Customer loyalty is strongly related to a number of indices measuring different behavioural and attitudinal aspects of the relationship between the bank's contact persons and the clients, such as the responsible behaviour of the former towards clients, their communication of critical change information to clients and their competence as perceived by clients.

Two university research institutions annually conduct customer surveys for a considerable number of subscriber client companies in Sweden. According to their 'Customer Satisfaction Index' results, Svenska Handelsbanken had more satisfied customers than the sector average during the entire 1990s. It occupied the highest place among the major universal banks for private clients and for all years but one for company clients during this period.

Personnel performance

The bank is one of the very few, if not the only, bank dedicated to offering its staff secure employment and career development. In the severe period at the beginning of the 1990s when 10,000 jobs were lost in the bank sector and some banks laid off as many as 30 per cent of their staff, Svenska Handelsbanken reduced its staff by some 382 – by not re-employing new staff when current staff retired. Recent developments in the bank mean that the work is rapidly changing character, becoming more responsible, more qualified and to some extent more intensive. The management and competence review systems result in each individual getting a personal competence development plan and specific individual and team goals, together with regular feedback during the year. The profit sharing system introduced in the mid-1970s is based on the bank's relative performance, i.e. payment is made into the fund when the result is greater than the average for Nordic bank corporations. It has been very successful so that the personnel are now major owners in the bank.

Owner performance

The bank is regarded as one of the most successful Nordic banks. Figure 10.1 shows that the bank's interest rate on its own capital after standard tax (currently 28 per cent) has been higher than the weighted average of the other banks on the stock market for the past fifteen years

Figure 10.1 Return on owners' equity after standard tax.

Note: Return on owners' equity after standard tax is calculated as the operating profit minus standard tax (currently 28 per cent) in relation to the average owners' equity. Owners' equity includes the capital share of untaxed reserves and minority share. Average owners' equity is calculated as the average of balance brought forward and the reported quarterly profits. The average owners' equity is adjusted for the dividend on reconciliation day and the new share issues paid for by the final payment day.

(Annual report, 2001). (In the period 1991–3 several of the other banks required government intervention to avoid bankruptcy.) The bank's shares are valued above the general index and are highest in the sector. The bank also had the lowest costs of any Nordic bank in this period – low costs being regarded as a prerequisite for offering clients competitive conditions.

The relationship between culture and performance

Previous research

The causal link between strong culture and corporate performance was seriously questioned at the end of the 1980s. Wilderom *et al.* (2000) analysed ten studies of this question carried out in the 1990s. Taken together these indicate the existence of a coupling between them. Denison's studies of high involvement organizations with a clear mission and widely shared organizational values being more effective seem to hold only for large firms (Denison and Mishra 1995). Wilderom interprets the work of Calori and Savin (1991) and Denison (1990) as indicating that having a strong culture is good for an organization only for a few years.

The organizational culture construct combines elements of tacit knowledge, social interconnections and specificity that make a culture-based competitive advantage unique and extremely difficult for competitors to fathom and imitate (Barney and Hesterley 1996). A culture-based advantage may thus be assumed to lead to a sustained record of superior performance. In this context the culture may function as an informal co-ordination and control system or as a reinforcement through endorsing personnel's values (Maslach and Leiter 1997).

Professionals have large areas of professional discretion concerning advising clients and influencing clients' views, e.g. investment brokers advising about investment opportunities.

Considering 'care for clients', professionals have duties to provide appropriate *care* services, as well as to *take care* to meet their responsibilities (be competent, exercise caution, avoid carelessness). *Caring about* clients implies also a significant degree of altruistic motivation, valuing their well-being and wanting to help them for their sake. It also embraces loyalty to groups of persons affected by one's work, including colleagues, communities within organizations, and the wider public.

In Svenska Handelsbanken

Considering the results presented from the bank in the previous two decades, it seems safe to say that the bank shows a positive relationship between its organizational culture and performance. The bank has succeeded in balancing its economic and client relational business goals. In addition it has succeeded in realizing personnel goals which underpin these.

Considering the previous research on this relationship, the bank is a large company (cf. Denison 1990). Its culture is continually developing in dialogue and has exhibited a positive relation for decades (cf. Calori and Savin 1991; Denison 1990). The other banks are either not able to or not interested in following this bank's experience (cf. Barney and Hesterley 1996). The observations on professional discretion are supported by client perceptions of their contact person at the bank (Bjerlöv, Docherty and Söderberg 2002).

Striving to maintain the balance of sustainability

A positive result in this case study is that management have succeeded with their value base in balancing the business idea with the bank personnel's professional identity. They have a

clear role in their special relationship with given clients to provide personal service customization based on the client's total situation in the long term. The position of 'contact
person' offers balance among various rewards from meaningful work: skill satisfaction (participating skilfully in the conduct of a profession), moral caring (in contacts with clients and
colleagues) and compensation (in terms of money, authority and recognition).

However, the bank personnel face a number of difficult balancing issues in their daily work:
balancing client aspects, such as balancing client's immediate assignment against their total situation; balancing the clients' personal interest against their total social responsibilities (e.g.
family, children); balancing disinterested advice against selling the company's products.

The managers face special sustainability issues too. The continuous improvement of performance expected by the market can lead to real problems in maintaining balance among
transaction economics, client relationships and the personnel's health and well-being. The
organizational slack in the organization is felt to be very small and the good working milieu
is perceived by some to be threatened in the near future.

Notes

1 I wish to acknowledge financial support from the Swedish Council for Work Life Research and the
Swedish Agency for Innovation Systems in conducting the bank studies cited here. I would also like
to express my thanks to colleagues with whom I have discussed this: Monica Bjerlöv, Peter Cressey,
Odd Fredriksson, Philippe Lefebvre, Ragnvald Sannes, Rami Shani, Mike Stebbins and Gösta
Steneskog.

2 Current developments in the banking sector are resulting in the office work with payment services
declining and that with advisory and problem solving services increasing. Thus I use the term
'client' in this chapter.

References

Armon, C. (1993) 'Developmental conceptions of good work. A longitudinal study', in J. Demick and
P.M. Miller (eds) *Development in the Workplace*, Hillsdale, NJ: Lawrence Erlbaum.

Arvedson, L. (1998) *Downsizing: När företag bantar* (Downsizing: When Companies Slim), Stockholm:
Trygghetsrådet.

Barney, J.B. and Hesterley, W. (1996) 'Organizational economics. Understanding the relationship
between organizations and economic analysis', in S.R. Clegg, C. Hardy and N.W. Nord (eds)
Handbook of Organisational Studies, Thousand Oaks, CA: Sage, pp. 115–47.

Bjerlöv, M., Docherty, P. and Söderberg, I. (2002) 'Management by trust'. Paper presented to the
Labour Process Conference, Strathclyde University, 2–4 April.

Brytting, T. (2000a) *Att vara som Gud. Moralisk kompetens i arbetslivet* (Being Like God. Moral Competence
in Working Life), Stockholm: Liber.

Brytting, T. (2000b) 'Mycket vill ha mer' (The haves want more), Stockholm: Svenska Dagbladet, 14
February.

Brytting, T. and Trollestad, C. (2000) 'Managerial thinking on value-based management', *International
Journal of Value-Based Management*, 13.

Calori, R. and Savin, P. (1991) 'Culture and economic performance. A French study', *Organization
Studies*, 12, 49–74.

Connor, P.E. and Becker, B.W. (1994) 'Personal values and management. What do we know and why
don't we know more?' *Journal of Management Inquiry*, 3, 67–73.

Denison, D.R. (1990) *Corporate Culture and Organisational Effectiveness*, New York: Wiley.

Denison, D.R. and Mishra, A.K. (1995) 'Toward a theory of organizational culture and effectiveness',
Organization Science, 6, 204–23.

Docherty, P. (2002) 'Organisatorisk hållbarhet: en känslig balansprocess' (Organizational sustainability:

a delicate balancing process), in I. Söderberg, J. Wallenberg and L. Wilhelmson (eds) *Svenska arbets-platser* (Swedish Workplaces), Stockholm: National Institute for Working Life (in press).

Dodd, J. (1994) *The Sociology of Money. Economic Reason and Contemporary Society*, Cambridge: Polity Press.

Fox, A. (1974) *Beyond Contract. Work, Power and Trust Relations*, London: Faber & Faber.

Grönroos, C. (1990) *Service Management and Marketing*, Lexington, MA: Lexington Books.

Kaufman, H. (1960) *The Forest Ranger. A Study in Administrative Behavior*, Baltimore, MD: Johns Hopkins University Press and Resources for the Future Inc.

Knights, D., Noble, F., Vurdubakis, T. and Wilmott, H. (2001) 'Chasing shadows. Control, virtuality and the production of trust', *Organization Studies*, 22, 2, 311–36.

Kramer, R.M. and Tyler, T.R. (1996) *Trust in Organizations. Frontiers of Theory and Research*, London: Sage.

Lane, C. and Bachmann, R. (eds) (1998) *Trust Within and Between Organizations: Conceptual and Empirical Applications*, Oxford: Oxford University Press.

Martin, J. (1995) 'Organizational culture', in N. Nicholson (ed.) *The Blackwell Encyclopedic Dictionary of Organizational Behavior*, Cambridge, MA: Blackwell.

Martin, M.W. (2000) *Meaningful Work. Rethinking Professional Ethics*, New York: Oxford University Press.

Maslach, C. and Leiter, M.P. (1997) *The Truth about Burnout. How Organizations Cause Personal Stress and What to Do About It*, San Francisco: Jossey-Bass.

Meglino, B.M., Ravlin, E.C. and Adkins, C.L. (1989) 'A work values approach to corporate culture. A field test of the value congruence process and its relationship to individual outcomes', *Journal of Applied Psychology*, 74, 424–32.

Meglino, B.M., Ravlin, E.C. and Adkins, C.L. (1991) 'Value congruence and satisfaction with a leader. An examination of the role of interaction', *Human Relations*, 44, 481–95.

Morgan, G. and Knights, D. (eds) (1997) *Regulation and Deregulation in European Financial Services*, London: Macmillan.

Pfeffer, J. (1997) *The Human Equation. Building Profits by Putting People First*, Cambridge, MA: Harvard Business School Press.

Prim, I. (1999) *Relationship Marketing of Services. An Analysis of Service Quality and Service Encounters through Relational Norms – a Dyadic Approach between Bank Account Managers and SMEs*, Gothenburg: EIASM 9th Workshop on Quality Management in Services.

Rokeach, M. (1969) *Beliefs, Attitudes and Values. A Theory of Organization and Change*, San Francisco: Jossey-Bass.

Svanelid, T. (2001) *Framtidens bank* (The Bank of the Future), Stockholm: Finanstidningen/Framtiden direkt 20010414.

Taylor, C. (1989) *Sources of the Self. The Making of Modern Identity*, Cambridge, MA: Harvard University Press.

Wilderom, C.P.M., Glunk, U. and Maslowski, R. (2000) 'Organizational culture as a predictor of organizational performance', in A.N. Askanasy, C.P.M. Wilderom and M.F. Peterson (eds) *Handbook of Organizational Culture and Climate*, Thousand Oaks, CA: Sage.

11 Group work and democracy

Martin Kuhlmann

Introduction

For more than a decade, work organization and especially teamwork have been hotly debated topics in the discussion about reorganization of production. At least in theory, most firms declare that they are moving beyond 'Taylorism' and that teamwork or group work improves the work situation especially in production. The far reaching restructuring of production work which took place during the 1990s, especially in the car industry, has meant that this industry is a relevant field for investigating problems of intensity and sustainability. Here new approaches to production work have been most ambitious. The rush towards new forms of work organization was often initiated under the label of lean production coined by the IMVP (International Motor Vehicle Project) at the Massachussetts Institute of Technology (MIT) (Womack *et al.* 1990).

This chapter does not attempt to give an overview of the ongoing debate on team or group work. Instead the results of a German group work study will be presented to get a closer view of the problem of intensity or sustainability of work systems. The main questions are: What are the characteristics of work systems that are leading to a more sustainable work situation for production workers? Is it possible to extrapolate some criteria for sustainable group work systems? It is pointed out that the concepts of resources (see Chapter 5) and dialogue (Chapter 16) are important steps forward to analyse risks and opportunities in modern working life. And what will also be seen throughout this chapter is that both dialogue and resources are referring to the level of groups of workers and not individuals. While the resource perspective outlines some material and social conditions of sustainable work systems, the guiding principle of dialogue highlights important aspects of the social processes that have to exist.

While the car industry is still the leading sector in the adoption of teamwork, attempts to remodel work along the lines of teamwork can be found in most industries in several European countries. Some firms tried seriously to overcome the often stated inefficiencies of 'Taylorism' even before lean production became the buzz word of the 1990s (Kern and Schumann 1984; Brödner 1985; Berggren 1990; Forslin 1990; Schumann *et al.* 1992; Jürgens *et al.* 1993). But the results of the work by MacDuffie and Pil (1997) and by Durand *et al.* (1999) show that work organization in cars changed profoundly in the 1990s. MacDuffie and Pil found that Europe was quickest to adopt post-Taylorist work practices like job rotation, task integration, shop floor training and especially teamwork.

How prevalent is teamwork in Europe? The EPOC Project, a survey of about 5,800 managers of workplaces (manufacturing, private and public services) in ten major European countries, found the idea of teams to be 'useful but unused' in Europe (Benders *et al.* 1999). While the European average for at least some form of delegation of decision-making rights to work groups is 36 per cent, only 4 per cent of cases include decision-making rights in several areas and affect the majority of the workforce. It is important for our discussion of group work and sustainability to realize that the term 'teamwork' is used to denote very different organizations with very different consequences for the work situation of production workers (Appelbaum and Batt 1994; Gerst *et al.* 1995; Sandberg 1995; Camuffo and Micelli 1997; Kochan *et al.* 1997; Kuhlmann and Schumann 1997; Shaiken *et al.* 1997; Benders and Van Hootegem 1999; Durand *et al.* 1999). Empirical studies of the work reality of the team concepts in North American car plants often criticize advocates of lean production-type work teams like Womack *et al.* (1990), Adler and Cole (1993) or Kenney and Florida (1993). These applications have resulted in work intensification and a much higher level of forced work discipline. This kind of teamwork often means working harder and not necessarily smarter. It has been characterized as 'management-by-stress' (Parker and Slaughter 1988). According to many empirical studies it leads to stricter work rules, a higher workload, new forms of peer pressure and serious problems with occupational health (Babson 1995; Graham 1995; Lewchuk and Robertson 1997; Landsbergis *et al.* 1999). This teamwork is an obvious example of intensive and unsustainable work systems.

In Europe, the debate is more diverse and the assessments of the workplace outcomes of new forms of work organization are more mixed. In some firms and plants there have been serious attempts to develop forms of group work which live up to the promises of socio-technical workplace reform and lead towards enriched and more co-operative work in production, better chances to cope with the workload and more influence over daily working conditions. In Germany and Scandinavia, unions have become strong supporters of anti-Taylorist workplace reform. They have often actively put pressure on management at the enterprise level to develop a work organization based on group work as a step towards a more human workplace, more healthy work and a more rewarding and productive work situation.

The empirical base for this chapter is a wide range of in-depth case studies undertaken between 1993 and 1999 mostly in the German car industry. Our research methods were: (a) workplace observations lasting for several shifts, (b) in-depth interviews with managers, workers, shop stewards (*Vertrauensleute*) and people from the works council (*Betriebsräte*) which took one to three hours, and (c) a standardized questionnaire, where we always included the entire group in each work system under observation which means ten to twenty people on each shift.[1] The fieldwork in each case took one to three weeks, and the results were discussed and validated later during workshops with managers, workers and their representatives.

Group work: levels of development – impacts on work situation

Although the group work cases of our sample had some characteristics in common, there were also important differences. The implementation of group work was the subject of negotiated agreements between management, works councils and labour unions in most of the firms studied. These agreements stated that the new work organization should not only enhance economic performance but should also improve the work situation of the employees by actively involving them in the organization of their work. The group work systems agreed on by both sides varied. In all our cases they included: (a) some form of task integration, job enrichment and job rotation; (b) more self-organization on the level of the work groups (in the sense of how to organize the work system as a whole and how to handle daily tasks); (c) some form of training (for every group member, and the newly established roles like the group spokesperson); and finally (d) completely new forms of institutionalized self-organization such as elected group spokespersons. The latter are ordinary working members of the group who also play a co-ordinating role replacing the former sub-foreman (*Vorarbeiter*). The regular group meetings to discuss how things should be done and to solve all kinds of social and operational problems are organized by the workers themselves. They have the authority to invite the foreman (*Meister*) or any other manager or expert. In some enterprises new procedures of industrial engineering were implemented where the setting of performance standards, work rates and staffing levels were no longer the sole preserve of industrial engineers but the subject of negotiation between the foreman and the group, instead.

The new work organizations gave rise to a wide spectrum of outcomes despite broad similarities in the formal agreements on which they were based. These outcomes ranged from a very positive evaluation by the workers, through predominantly ambivalent consequences for the work situation of the employees, to clearly negative results and strong criticism. One of the main conclusions of our study is that workers' perceptions of new work organization depend to a limited degree – if any – on personal characteristics like age, gender, length of service or level of education. Our analysis of the data showed that the main factor in eliciting positive or negative reactions is the type of work organization itself. Based on our workplace observations and interviews, we identified several aspects that constitute specific organizational profiles. We found very different levels of group self-organization and task integration. These are the most important aspects of the work organization profile. Finally, by comparing the projects we differentiated three levels of development of what we call self-organized, task integrated group work (Figure 11.1).

The empirical findings from our sample clearly demonstrate that the closer work organization corresponds to the ideal-type of self-organized and task integrated group work, the more positively working conditions are judged by the employees (Figure 11.2).

Regarding the workers' perceptions, our analysis is based on the survey answers from 1,017 workers whose work situations were classed as 'highly developed' (N = 538), 'reasonably developed' (N = 350) and 'less developed' (N = 112). The workers' ratings of the impact of the introduction of group work on their working conditions were classed as a deterioration, no change or an improvement. There was a clear relation between the level of development in the work situation and the percentage of workers experiencing improvements in their working conditions, skill requirements, decision discretion and interesting work.

Considering the stress and pressures of work there is a clear relation between the level of development of the work situation and the percentage of workers experiencing higher performance requirements, less difficulty in meeting such requirements, more autonomy, more possibilities to co-operate and more resilience.

A *high level of development* is characterized by a broad spectrum of tasks integrated into the groups. This renders the work of the group members more skilled and adds task variety. Group spokespersons, who continue to take part in the daily work, are elected by the members without interference from supervisors; moreover, regular group meetings allow the members to discuss problems, and develop group cohesion and collective responsibility. Along with the enrichment of work and the increased autonomy in carrying out the necessary tasks, the evaluation of the working conditions is very positive. The employees consider this type of group work as advantageous even in relation to the pressures and stress engendered by the work situation. This can be explained by the enhanced scope for self-directed regulation, the positive impact of switching between different tasks, and the improved opportunities for mutual support within the teams.

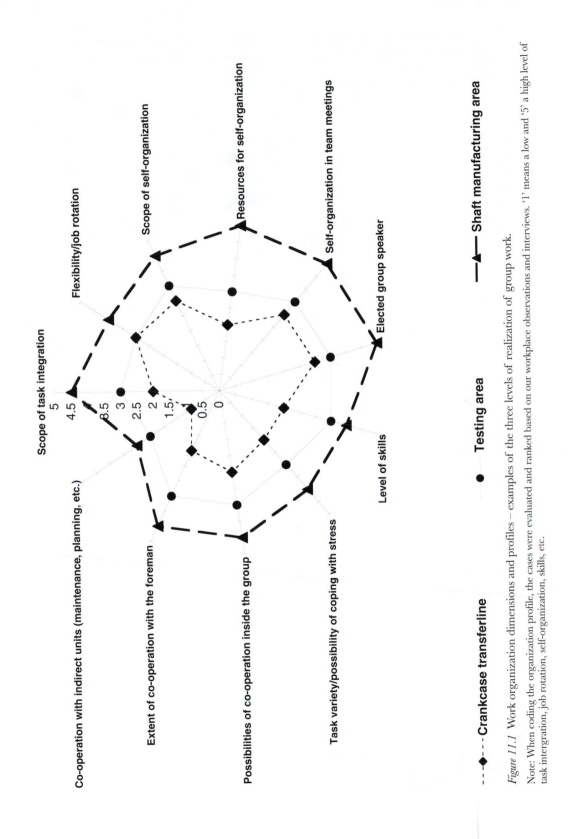

Figure 11.1 Work organization dimensions and profiles – examples of the three levels of realization of group work.

Note: When coding the organization profile, the cases were evaluated and ranked based on our workplace observations and interviews. '1' means a low and '5' a high level of task intergration, job rotation, self-organization, skills, etc.

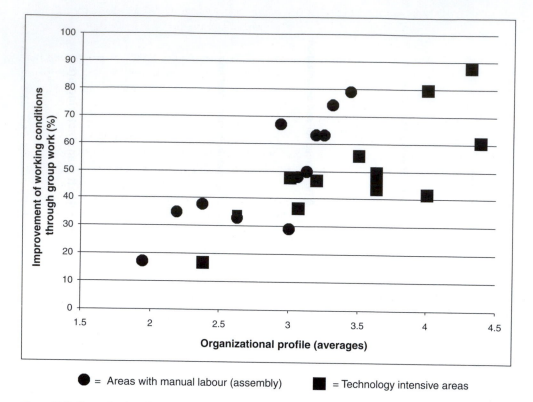

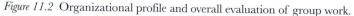

Figure 11.2 Organizational profile and overall evaluation of group work.

Note: For computing the organizational profiles, the means of eight aspects were selected on the scale '1' (low) to '5' (high): the four task-related and the four self-organizational dimensions from Figure 11.1. The value of 5 corresponds to the model of self-organized, task integrated group work.

The *medium level of development* of self-organized group work is plagued by problems result-ing from half-hearted solutions. In these cases, most workers are trying to live up to the ideal of self-organization, and the majority of the workers see at least some improvements in working conditions as well. However, the team situation remains precarious and is often experienced as a further imposition. In some of these cases organizational structures (super-visors, plant organization, tasks and organizational rules) are ill-suited to accommodate the new form of work organization. In terms of interaction within the groups, the medium level of development is often marked by confusion about the role of the group spokesperson as the mediator of group interests. They also experience routine failure of group discussions to yield solutions to internal problems or to negotiate consensus among group members. In contrast to the cases at a high level of development, a sense of self-directed group responsibility does not develop at a medium level of self-organization and task integration.

The *low level of development* is generally characterized by only minor changes in the work organization compared to the Taylorist past. Work organization remains largely the same, and the flexibility of individual employees or job rotation is only slightly developed so that the character of individual work remains dominant in most groups. Group-level regulation (in assignment of tasks, compensation issues, the organization of daily tasks, etc.) had been introduced but it remained ineffective. In many cases supervisors influence both the election of group spokespersons and the profile of their tasks to such an extent that they resemble sub-foremen in practice, while indirect functions remained the responsibility of a few employees in charge. Group meetings either do not take place at all, or are dominated by supervisors, who use them to convey enterprise directives. As the ordinary group members have neither a broadened range of tasks nor a wider scope of decision-making authority (on issues such as task assignment or vacation planning), the level of self-organization remains very limited. In some teams, feelings of betrayal and open cynicism have led to particularly strong negative reactions of the group members towards the supervisors who act exclusively along hierarchical lines. In the end, workload, stress and strain are highest in these cases.

In traditional settings, mutual support and at times even co-operative practices that counter management are important ways of coping with workload and the subordinate status of production workers. Therefore, several authors argue that the main problem with group work is that it does not lead to a more co-operative work situation. It often triggers conflict and elements of social exclusion within the groups generated by a form of team sur-veillance and continuous stress through peer pressure (Barker 1993; Ezzamel and Willmott 1998; Sewell 1998). Case studies of North American plants with a form of work organiza-tion based on 'lean production' team concepts often confirm this picture of a forced co-operation leading towards higher levels of intensity and less workplace solidarity among the workers (Parker and Slaughter 1988; Graham 1995). Does this picture of a new system of self-exploitation and exclusion hold for the examples of self-organized group work in our sample, too? Indeed the combination of a broader scope for decision-making, more respon-sibility and more external pressure on the workers arising out of intensified pressure on costs and performance does pose new dangers for the production units in the form of internal competition within the teams and extended self-exploitation. Teams may degenerate into vehicles of rigid monitoring of performance standards and heightened pressure to per-form. In the end the step beyond Taylorism might lead to higher workloads, more pressure on production workers and cause a much more intensive work situation with more stress and fewer possibilities to cope.

Our empirical findings offer no simple answer to the question of how group work relates to the problem of intensity. Advances in the areas of decision-making capabilities and more rewarding work are partly offset by rising performance standards. Group work can open up opportunities for co-operation and mutual support but at the same time provide the possibil-ity for mutual control and may lead to competition and an increase of internal conflict. In our sample, the effects and dynamics depend to a large extent on the type of teamwork and the level of development of group self-organization. However, in the case of all workers, their ambivalent attitude towards new work organization is heightened by the challenge presented by group work of having to negotiate balanced solutions for the different interests across vari-ous different interest spheres themselves. The firm's demand for high performance is to some extent at odds with the individual worker's own desire for a favourable work situation; group responsibilities can come at the expense of personal autonomy, and work-related concerns can conflict with concerns from other areas of life. Thus, the relationship between company objectives, team affairs and individual interests is often full of tensions. This calls for a high degree of social competence and problem solving capability on the part of the employees and points towards the importance of having enough resources to deal with the various conflicts. A detailed analysis of our empirical findings shows that the level of development of group work is of particular importance in determining whether workplace reorganization promotes experiences of practical solidarity instead of internal conflicts and social exclusion.

Considering social aspects of group work, there is a positive relation between the level of

development in the work situation and the perceived improvements in co-operation with colleagues, the level of camaraderie and solidarity and the consideration shown to less efficient
co-workers. However a higher percentage of the workers in conditions of low development
experienced improvements in solidarity, camaraderie, understanding and tolerance than
those in situations that had changed to reasonable conditions.

Apparently a high level of group-based self-organization and task integration does not only
lead towards an improved work situation: it also provides employees with much better chances
of generating a co-operative group climate. Workplace reorganization towards self-organized,
task integrated group work also produces a positive change in collegial attitudes and solidarity among employees. First, negative dynamics are less likely since the increased performance
standards are seen to be more attainable by the employees. Where group work is highly
developed, the workers themselves participate in the process of negotiating workloads.
Second, group discussions and the election of spokespersons to mediate group interests
change the social relations within the groups and enable them to handle conflicts more effectively so that their overall problem solving capacities are higher. Here, resources not only
include time and/or financial support but also the level of implementation of democratic procedures like elections and group meetings which make group-oriented solutions more likely.
The omnipresent micro-hierarchies of Taylorist production structures are partly suspended,
and in the context of self-organized discussions the groups have the opportunity to seek
compromise and consensus and address problems in a spirit of co-operation. The election of
group spokespersons by the groups' members institutionalizes democratic principles to some
degree. Groups that exhibit a high degree of self-organization and also have adequate
resources at their disposal pursue consensus-oriented and discursive strategies of problem
solving more frequently than teams that operate under restrictive conditions. Examples of
such resources are time resources and room for manoeuvre, variety in the tasks to be fulfilled
by the group, institutionalized rules about how to 'run the group' and negotiated performance
standards.

Fairness in rewarding performance remains a central concern in group work, too.
Performance comparisons inside the groups play an important role. As a result of the high
flexibility of self-organized group work, the contribution of each individual group member is
much more transparent for the co-workers in the new work organization than in systems relying on a more strict division of labour. The combination of higher performance standards
and greater transparency within the teams increases the risk of group pressure resulting in
social exclusion. Yet, central elements of self-organized group work make rigid forms of conflict resolution less likely. For instance, groups can compensate for deficits in skills relatively
easily, as a result of the team's own capacities for training people on the job. In particular,
competition for easy or highly qualified tasks, which is typical of individual work structures,
plays a considerably smaller role in self-organized group work. The culture of consensus in the
groups and the enlarged room for manoeuvre facilitate developments in which a balance
between individual and group interests is sought.

When the level of development of the group work organization is less than 'high', the work
climate may be affected negatively. Forms of group work defined as the 'medium' level of
development often contain contradictory elements in their practical implementation.
Problems like group pressure or a lack of consideration for colleagues' concerns are even
more difficult to resolve under the conditions of this intermediate level of development than
they are under the conditions of low levels of implementation of group work. Under the latter
conditions the traditional solidarity of workers and hidden practices of mutual support based
on a feeling of belonging in opposition to Taylorist work structures re-emerges, because the

introduction of group work is easily and mainly seen as reaffirming the hierarchical structures of fragmented work. In groups at the medium level of development self-organization remains precarious primarily because not all employees in the group benefit from the favourable results of enhanced self-direction to the same extent. While employees continue to work side by side without much interference in groups at the low level of development, internal conflicts tend to increase in groups at the medium level, as several group members at least try to achieve more self-direction in their groups. Compared with Taylorism this leads to a work situation and forms of intensity that are even worse.

Further research is required into the specific context, conditions and mechanisms that produce the differences between the various forms of group work that we observed.[2] However, it should be emphasized that self-organized group work can facilitate an improved and more sustainable work situation characterized by a more co-operative and cohesive problem solving climate, provided that certain resources are made available. These include the development of greater autonomy in decision-making and the establishment of democratic and discursive institutions like the elected group spokesperson or self-organized team meetings.

Self-organized group work is accompanied by enhanced collective and individual self-confidence and by increasing assertiveness on the part of production workers. Where it is implemented in its developed form, one can indeed identify democratic problem solving processes within the teams. As far as our sample is concerned, work solidarity improves at least in certain forms of group work. Considering our results within an international perspective, we also conclude that the activities of unions and works councils play an important role in relation to enterprise work organization strategies (see Chapter 7). Our results lend support to the argument made by André Gorz that where workplace innovation is part of a negotiated solution – with independent labour unions or works councils providing crucial inputs in the process of expanding self-organization – then there is a chance that post-Taylorist structures of work will not result in a progressive co-option and subjection under corporate goals (Gorz 1999). However, the influence and the policies of unions differ widely and, overall, do not give rise to an optimistic perspective on future developments.

Conclusion: group work and the problem of sustainability

In previous chapters of this book we have mentioned that new forms of work organization, even if they are stepping beyond Taylorism, do not automatically improve the work situation. Now, by comparing the experiences of production workers, we can make some general comments. From the very beginning socio-technical authors focused very much on the concept of (semi-) autonomous or self-directed work groups, where autonomy may be assessed from what and how much a work group is allowed to decide by itself (Gulowsen 1972). On the whole our results also point towards the importance of decision-making power. Furthermore, our results also indicate the need for at least some form of job enrichment. A closer look at the experience of the groups in our study shows, however, that focusing on the job itself is not enough to ensure that group work leads to a more sustainable work situation (Table 11.1). The benefit is even greater if it is linked to a higher level of group self-organization in the sense of group-based self-direction as well as resources for self-organization backed by the institutionalization of democratic procedures. The main results of our case studies about group work and sustainable work systems can be summarized in four steps:

Table 11.1 Comparing the effects of self-organization and task integration on the work situation

Extent of task integration (job enrichment)		Group-based self-organization (scope and resources)		
		low	*medium*	*high*
Low				
Number of cases		2	3	1
	has improved	28%	46%	48%
The work situation:	*is unchanged*	36%	43%	28%
	has deteriorated	38%	11%	24%
Medium				
Number of cases		2	6	4
	has improved	26%	48%	64%
The work situation:	*is unchanged*	53%	34%	32%
	has deteriorated	21%	18%	4%
High				
Number of cases			1	8
	has improved		44%	67%
The work situation:	*is unchanged*		49%	23%
	has deteriorated		7%	10%

1   *Job enrichment* and *task integration* which lead towards more variety and more rewarding work roles based on an extended integration of planning and execution are important features of sustainable work systems. Not only do they improve the work situation of production workers, but they also make the work systems more flexible and strengthen the capacities for problem solving and the improvement of production procedures. On tasks, our results confirm the basic principles of socio-technical job design (Cherns 1987; Pasmore 1988; Adler and Docherty 1998; Molleman and Broekhuis 2001). Task integration leads to more holistic job descriptions, a wider scope for action and decision-making and is a prerequisite of both the individual development of competences as well as work-based co-operation and mutual support in work groups. From the perspective of performance, task integration not only improves the possibilities of coping with a higher workload, but also leads to better bottom-up processes of improving the production system.

2   *Group-based self-organization* seems to be the cornerstone of a more sustainable work system. The most important aspect of group self-organization is not autonomy in the classical sense (Gulowsen 1972) but the extent of resources that are at the disposal of the groups, and whether the groups really establish new group-oriented working rules like mutual support or consensual decision-making. In those cases of our sample which scored highest in the workers' evaluation of their work situation, self-organization means more than self-direction and can best be understood in terms of rules and resources allocated by management and established by the group itself. Additional tasks were not allocated to specialists but distributed widely throughout the group so that the group as a whole becomes responsible for the work system. Time is made available for group meetings, which are used not only for the mutual exchange of information, but also to facilitate discussions, problem solving and consensus finding. A central principle of self-organization is that not only are decisions and responsibilities transferred to the group but resources are also provided (such as time, money, training, decision and participation rights,

institutions like group meetings or elected spokespersons, co-operative work structures). Of course, this depends not only on what happens inside the group, but also on the overall management systems, the role of supervisors and the extent of organizational decentralization. Since the group takes on the role of planning and improving its daily work, then the co-operation between the shop floor and the different planning departments has to be more intensive and less hierarchical. Overall our results point towards the importance of a resource-based perspective on sustainability (see Chapter 5), and we would like to add that rules like consensus-oriented decision-making and institutions like the elected group spokesperson and self-organized group discussions have to be seen as very important resources.

3   A big difference between the groups at a high level of development and those at lower levels of group self-organization is that the former were successful in establishing *democratic procedures*, at least on the internal level. The third aspect of sustainability in the organization of group work, therefore, contains the election – and sometimes rotation – of the group spokesperson but is even more evident in how the team meetings are organized and what really happens there. Problems are confronted openly. Intensive discussions take place based on the principles of dialogue (see Chapter 16). This means everyone has an opportunity to influence the outcome, to listen to their colleagues' views and to invite supervisors or other experts (especially those who are dealing with planning) from time to time to explain and justify what they are doing. Everything that affects the work group is seen as a 'public affair' and can be discussed in detail. Normally the group tries to reach a consensus, which makes its decisions more sustainable. When a real consensus cannot be reached, the groups normally agree on the principle that any burden has to be shared and nobody should be repeatedly disadvantaged. Of special importance are democratic principles like public discussion before a decision is made, protection of minorities or a fair balance between rights and duties which also takes into consideration what each person is able to accomplish. Here, our results are very much in line with the basic assumptions of the idea of transferring the concept of democratic dialogue into work life (Gustavsen 1992). The research on collective action and common pool resources, how they develop and how they are maintained, puts the question of self-organization and communicative democratic procedures into the forefront, too (Ostrom 1990, 2000). But democratic procedures do not only promote group self-organization and build a more sustainable work situation from the perspective of the workers. We even observed that those groups which organized themselves in a more co-operative and democratic way on internal matters were also more active and goal-oriented *vis-à-vis* management. Managers and planning experts told us that these groups are tough negotiators and sometimes not easy to handle but in the process of problem solving and negotiation better solutions are emerging even from the perspective of the firm.

4   Last but not least, another aspect of a more sustainable work organization is the question of how workloads, staffing levels and other targets or rates are set. Traditionally this has been done by management alone or in negotiations with worker representatives. The problems and conflicts that arise out of this are widely known. Therefore, in some of the cases we observed, a more sustainable way of dealing with the issue of workload and targets had been put into action. This new system was based on a combination of self-organized group work and direct *negotiations* between the groups and the foreman (*Meister*). Industrial engineering experts and worker representatives are not completely out of the game but they have a more supportive or advisory role and step in only when the foreman and the workers cannot agree. More research has to be done on the question of

how exactly these processes of direct negotiation are working and on their preconditions and long-term effects. But as it looks now, negotiations on the local level, the level where the work actually has to be done, are at least one way to reach a more sustainable work system when it is connected to a high level of group self-organization. The results of these negotiations are not only viewed as more fair, more balanced and more in line with local conditions, the process of negotiation itself can be organized as an attempt at continuous improvement and learning which strengthens problem solving capabilities even more.

All in all, our results are not a complete revision of the common wisdom of socio-technical thinking, but from the perspective of sustainability, we could get a more comprehensive perspective on the problems of workplace reform. On the individual, the group as well as the organizational levels our aspects (1) to (3) are examples that human and social resources are used in a productive way and that they are growing instead of being exploited. Our third and fourth aspects point towards the importance of organizational practices that make it more likely that there is a balance between different interests and demands. When the pressure on the workforce is becoming both boundless and more complex because of much more intensive and complex competition, the traditional way of dealing with setting workloads needs to be supplemented by other more decentralized and localized forms of negotiation. Our main conclusion is that how teamwork or group work affects sustainability depends very much on how work is organized. By comparing different groups, we can point out that there are more intensive *and* more sustainable ways of doing this. Finally, most workers we talked to felt that self-organized group work means that they are working both harder *and* smarter, and that they give a clear preference to it over their traditional work organization.

Notes

1 The number of case studies on which data are presented here is 27 from 6 plants. The data file of the survey consists all in all of 1,017 workers. But as not all of the questions were asked in every case study, since we modified the survey in each plant a little bit according to the specific problems in each case and the basic questions of the overall studies, the questionnaire data sometimes consist of a smaller number of workers. The most important questions about the assessment of the work situation by the workers, however, were asked in the same way everywhere.
2 Co-operative strategies of problem solving in manufacturing units are likely to feed on the high esteem for comradeship, which is still widespread among production workers. The still relevant experience of corporate interests prevailing at the cost of the employees' concerns facilitates co-operative and cohesive attitudes on the workplace level. In the firms that we studied this is further amplified by high unionization rates and the positive stance of works councils. In some cases some of the components of self-organized group work mentioned above were realized under the pressure of works councils and against the resistance of the firms' management or the resistance of individual managers.

References

Adler, P. and Cole, R. (1993) 'Designed for learning. A tale of two auto-plants', *Sloan Management Review*, 35, 1, 85–94.

Adler, N. and Docherty, P. (1998) 'Bringing business into sociotechnical theory and practice', *Human Relations*, 51, 3, 319–45.

Appelbaum, E. and Batt, R. (1994) *The New American Workplace*, Ithaca, NY: Cornell University Press.

Babson, S. (ed.) (1995*) Lean Work. Empowerment and Exploitation in the Global Auto Industry*, Detroit: Wayne State University Press.

Barker, J. (1993) 'Tightening the iron cage. Concertive control in self-managing teams', *Administrative Science Quarterly*, 38, 3, 408–37.

Benders, J., Huijgen, F., Pekruhl, U. and O'Kelly, K. (1999) *Useful but Unused. Group Work in Europe*, Dublin: European Foundation for Living and Working Conditions.

Benders, J. and Van Hootegem, G. (1999) 'Teams and their context. Moving the team discussion beyond existing dichotomies', *Journal of Management Studies*, 36, 5, 609–28.

Berggren, C. (1990) *Det nya bilarbetet* (Modern Car Works), Lund: Archiv. See also *The Volvo Experience*, Basingstoke: Macmillan, 1994.

Brödner, P. (1985) *Fabrik 2000. Alternative Entwicklungspfade in der Zukunft der Fabrik* (Factory 2000. Alternative Paths into the Factory of the Future), Berlin: Sigma. See also *The Shape of Future Technology. The Anthropocentric Alternative*, Berlin: Springer, 1990.

Camuffo, A. and Micelli, S. (1997) 'Mediterranean lean production. Supervisors, teamwork and new forms of work organization in three european car makers', *Journal of Management and Governance*, 1, 1, 123–40.

Cherns, A. (1987) 'Principles of sociotechnical design revisited', *Human Relations*, 40, 2, 153–62.

Cutcher-Gershenfeld, J., Nitta, M., Barrett, B., Belhedi, N., Bullard, J., Coutie, C., Inaba, T., Ishino, I., Lee, S., Lin, W., Mothersell, W., Rabine, S., Ramanand, S., Strolle, M. and Wheaton, A. (1994) 'Japanese team-based work systems in North America. Explaining the diversity', *California Management Review*, 37, 1, 42–63.

Durand, J.P., Stewart, P. and Castillo, J.J. (eds) (1999) *Teamwork in the Automobile Industry*, Basingstoke: Macmillan.

Ezzamel, M. and Willmott, H. (1998) 'Accounting for teamwork. A critical study of group-based systems of organizational control', *Administrative Science Quarterly*, 43, 3, 358–96.

Forslin, J. (1990) *Det klippta bandet – en Volvo-industri byter kultur* (Broken Line. Cultural Change at Volvo), Stockholm: Norstedt.

Freeman, R. and Rogers, J. (1999) *What Workers Want*, Ithaca, NY: ILR Press.

Gerst, D., Hardwig, T., Kuhlmann, M. and Schumann, M. (1995) 'Gruppenarbeit in den 90ern. Zwischen strukturkonservativer und strukturinnovativer Gestaltungsvariante' (Group work in the 90s), *SOFI-Mitteilungen*, 22, 39–65.

Gerst, D., Hardwig, T., Kuhlmann, M. and Schumann, M. (1999) 'Group work in the German automobile industry. The case of Mercedes-Benz', in J.-P. Durand, P. Stewart and J.J. Castillo (eds) *Teamwork in the Automobile Industry*, Basingstoke: Macmillan, pp. 366 94.

Gorz, A. (1999) *Reclaiming Work. Beyond the Wage-Based Society*, Oxford: Polity Press.

Graham, L. (1995) *On the Line at Subaru-Isuzu. The Japanese Model and the American Worker*, Ithaca, NY: ILR Press.

Gulowsen, J. (1972) 'A measure of work group autonomy', in L. Davis and J. Taylor (eds) *Design of Jobs*, Harmondsworth: Penguin, 374–90.

Gustavsen, B. (1992) *Dialogue and Development*, Assen: van Gorcum.

Jürgens, U., Malsch, T. and Dohse, K. (1993) *Breaking from Taylorism. Changing Forms of Work in the Automobile Industry*, Cambridge: Cambridge University Press.

Kenney, M. and Florida, R. (1993) *Beyond Mass Production. The Japanese System and its Transfer to the US*, Oxford: Oxford University Press.

Kern, H. and Schumann, M. (1984) *Das Ende der Arbeitsteilung? Rationalisierung in der industriellen Produktion* (The End of the Division of Labour? Rationalization in Production), Munich: Beck.

Kochan, T., Lansbury, R. and MacDuffie, J.P. (eds) (1997) *After Lean Production. Evolving Employment Practices in the World Auto Industry*, Ithaca, NY: Cornell University Press.

Kuhlmann, M. (1996) 'Erfahrungen mit neuen Arbeitsformen in der Automobilindustrie' (Experiences with new forms of work organization in the automobile industry), in R. Bahnmüller and R. Salm (eds) *Intelligenter, nicht härter arbeiten? Gruppenarbeit und betriebliche Gestaltungspolitik* (Working Smarter, Not Harder?), Hamburg: VSA, pp. 112–39.

Kuhlmann, M. and Schumann, M. (1997) 'Patterns of work organization in the German automobile industry', in K. Shimokawa, U. Jürgens and T. Fujimoto (eds) *Transforming Automobile Assembly*, Berlin: Springer, 289–304.

Landsbergis, P., Cahill, J. and Schnall, P. (1999) 'The impact of lean production and related new systems of work organization on worker health', *Journal of Occupational Health Psychology*, 4, 2, 108–30.

Lewchuk, W. and Robertson, D. (1997) 'Production without empowerment. Work reorganization from the perspective of motor vehicle workers', *Capital & Class*, 63, 37–65.

MacDuffie, J.P. and Pil, F. (1997) 'Changes in auto industry employment practices. An international overview', in T. Kochan, R. Lansbury and J.P. MacDuffie (eds) *After Lean Production. Evolving Employment Practices in the World Auto Industry*, Ithaca, NY: Cornell University Press, pp. 9–42.

Molleman, E. and Broekhuis, M. (2001) 'Sociotechnical systems. Towards an organizational learning approach', *Journal of Engineering and Technology Management*, 17, in press (Special Issue: Beyond Sociotechnical Systems).

Osterman, P. (1999) *Securing Prosperity*, Princeton, NJ: Princeton University Press.

Ostrom, E. (1990) *Governing the Commons. The Evolution of Institutions for Collective Action*, Cambridge: Cambridge University Press.

Ostrom, E. (2000) 'Collective action and the evolution of social norms', *Journal of Economic Perspectives*, 14, 3, 137–58.

Parker, M. and Slaughter, J. (1988) *Choosing Sides. Unions and the Team Concept*, Boston: South End Press.

Pasmore, W. (1988) *Designing Effective Organizations. The Socio-technical Perspective*, New York: Wiley.

Roth, S. (1997) 'Germany. Labor's perspective on lean production', in T. Kochan, R. Lansbury and J.P. MacDuffie (eds) *After Lean Production. Evolving Employment Practices in the World Auto Industry*, Ithaca, NY: Cornell University Press, pp. 117–36.

Sandberg, Å. (ed.) (1995) *Enriching Production*, Aldershot: Avebury.

Schumann, M., Baethge-Kinsky, V., Kuhlmann, M., Kurz, C. and Neumann, U. (1992) 'Neue Arbeitseinsatzkonzepte in der deutschen Automobilindustrie. Hat Lean Production eine Chance?' (New forms of work organization in the German car industry. Does lean production have a chance?), *SOFI-Mitteilungen*, 19, 15–27.

Sewell, G. (1998) 'The discipline of teams. The control of team-based industrial work through electronic and peer surveillance', *Administrative Science Quarterly*, 43, June, 397–428.

Shaiken, H., Lopez, S. and Mankita, I. (1997) 'Two routes to team production. Saturn and Chrysler compared', *Industrial Relations*, 36, 1, 17–45.

Wickens, P. (1987) *The Road to Nissan. Flexibility, Quality, Teamwork*, Basingstoke: Macmillan.

Womack, J., Jones, D. and Roos, D. (1990) *The Machine that Changed the World*, New York: Rawson Associates/Macmillan.

12 Institutional support for developing SMEs

Palle Banke and Annemarie Holsbo

Introduction

Creating networks to enhance competitiveness and sustain the performance of small and medium-sized enterprises (SMEs) is at the heart of this chapter. 'Network' is used to describe a new form of arrangements between entities. Network, as we understand it, represents a highly elaborated, but flexible system of interrelationships among associates in different geographical locations, held together by personal connections and with the help of communication technology. Associates are any external individual, group, organization, institution or nation that can contribute to the firm's success (Kilmann and Kilmann 1991).

The literature on the evolution of the network form reveals that many researchers have examined how networks operate within small groups, within a formal organization and across organizational boundaries (e.g. Tichy 1981). The first group of researchers to study networks within groups carried out their work in the early 1930s (Moreno 1934). Bavelas (1951) later developed a method to examine communication nets in small work groups. Mackenzie (1966, 1976) developed an elaborated model of small-group networks as the foundation for design and redesign of the firm. Kilmann (1977) extended the network approach from small group to informal organizations and then to formal organizational structures. During the last two decades, researchers advanced the need to explore a 'new' organizational form that better meets the strategic needs of the firm – the network organization (e.g. Miles and Snow 1984 1997).

At the core of the network perspective, one can find that instead of the monolithic hierarchical management structures that created vertically integrated empires, an alternative form, based on economic activities managed through flexible, often temporary, arrangements between suppliers, customers and even competitors, was advanced. Thus, according to Galbraith (1991), the network organization results from two basic strategic sources. First, the search for cheaper sources of supply or support and better quality causes companies to look outside their organizations. The trend seems to be that SMEs focus on fewer activities at which they excel and subcontract the rest. Second, national or global growth strategy seems to require a presence in key locations or countries. Thus, the trend to easy entry into a new location or country is via some strategic alliance with a local firm. As the number of joint ventures and/or alliances increases, the network size increases. In the context of SMEs, networks seem to emerge as a viable form that can help in the continuous need for change and reorganization and to sustain success.

The situation today is different. Many enterprises have tested elements of new work organization that is based on network forms. One of the experiences is that network-based projects often generate positive results quickly, but then the development comes to a standstill and sometimes reverts. Earlier in this book it was argued that in many situations, changes in work organization towards what is referred to as 'good work' can actually cause intensity and a waste of resources instead of a build-up of resources. If new goals are not formulated continuously the development process will stop. As it is sometimes expressed: if you think you are through – you are through! It is, among other things, in relation to this problem that development networks can make a difference.

Involving employees in change processes

In a society with a market economy, a decision to reorganize an enterprise in the direction of sustainable work systems (SWS) has to be based on an economic rationale, if not brought about by legislation. This is what is behind the much used expression 'win–win'.

The process can then start with one 'win' or the other. Either the employees can begin by looking into the possibilities of improving job quality, or management can begin by identifying development potential by asking the question: 'are there more profitable products or market segments we can target, or can we become more productive if we get rid of some of the constraints caused by traditional organization of work?'

However, the road to a permanent change of the organization of work is long and winding. Even when an enterprise acknowledges that its way of organizing work is inexpedient in relation to production and sales opportunities, there will be a considerable degree of inertia curbing innovation. The Tayloristic system in force has established a production paradigm balanced throughout decades of development. Elements such as products, markets, machinery, layout, buildings, corporate culture, the qualifications of managers and operators, planning systems, software, pay systems, productivity objectives, supplier networks, etc., have been so adapted to each other, that upgrading of individual elements to support a flexible strategy will have no permanent results (Banke *et al.* 1999). A parallel can be drawn to an organism, in which a disruption of an established balance is offset by a co-ordinated reaction by the individual parts of the system.

However, the Tayloristic character of many of these elements has become so common and self-evident that we have become blind to it as described in detail earlier in this book (see Chapter 2). To bring these hidden Tayloristic traits out in the open, it is an absolute necessity to involve all layers in the organization – and, not least, the operators. They must contribute to the identification of the locking elements in their working situation and participate in the reorganization process. At the time when production workers are involved in the process, they will normally be quite unprepared. An unequal information level in the starting position results in a need for the employees to gain insight in the basic conceptual framework behind the plans to change work organization and job content. However, the information work of the unions in Scandinavia over the last ten years is beginning to change this situation.

Experience shows that it is insufficient only to inform of the job quality related improvements that will be generated. The employees will never commit themselves or believe in a change, if they do not fully comprehend the economic rationale that must be the motivating force of the enterprise. This can be illustrated by the reaction of a supervisor who in the reorganization had to change his traditional role of giving orders and controlling to the role of coach. In an interview, he expressed his lack of acceptance and motivation in regard to this radical change: 'I have been here for 15 years. Does this mean that for all that time the enterprise has been dissatisfied with my work or have they simply not been aware of what I was doing?'

In relation to the problem of commitment, networks between enterprises, where employees at all levels gain the opportunity to exchange experiences, can be of great importance.

Managers may have a number of preconceived opinions about what they could get the employees to take an interest in. Many managers conclude that all discussion about delegation of responsibility is an impossibility. Operators often display reaction patterns that make managers conclude that there is little potential of workers taking part in a new work organization as it implies broader and more responsible jobs. They have even less potential to take part in a change process. Change implies grappling with numerous issues, ranging from supplies to customer relationships, via product development, production, planning and much more. The problem, then, is to design a learning strategy for a multilevel and complex situation.

Since change cannot be organized along one single axis, there is no single result dimension that success can be measured against. Rather, success demands success with numerous issues simultaneously. To achieve this, there is a need for the involvement of many people. Although they are not all to work with 'the same', they need to synchronize their efforts.

This all leads up to what is actually the core point: the need to get a large number of people to work out new patterns, but to do it together and in a way that leads to an improved overall situation; to start the process towards SWS. Each person must be brought into a process that stimulates new ideas and perspectives, but in such a way that what each person brings forth fits into a larger whole. Furthermore, the whole process has to have an element of innovation, and not be a replication of a previous pattern. The following provides an example of a network project in which the operators' role in change processes was enhanced.

MOVE: a network project on job development

MOVE is a Danish acronym for Employee Training and Involvement in Organizational Change in Business Networks. The aim of the project was to trace and cultivate alternative methods for integration of training and employee development in the development of the workplace and the enterprise as a whole. The purpose was to seek a practice that, on the one hand, uses experiences and knowledge of employees in the planning and carrying out of a training period. On the other hand, the training was to be arranged so that it contributes to the motivation of employees to participate in the development of their workplace.

Simultaneously, the management was committed to developing the work organization, so that the experience and knowledge of employees benefited the enterprise as a whole. A network of three enterprises, Maersk Medical, Union Pak and Scan-Globe, has been the centre of activities in the MOVE project. The creation of the network was facilitated by the decision to develop an application for a grant to the EU Network Development Programme. All three enterprises are SMEs and operating in market segments where they are exposed to tough price competition. This means that they are in a situation where they might have to move production to low wage countries. As an alternative, they regarded themselves as ready for initiating change processes.

All three enterprises had introduced group-based work organization in the beginning of the 1990s. It had happened rather accidentally – as if these enterprises just wanted to try out the new management 'thing': autonomous groups. In retrospect, it had thus far been insufficiently prepared, and the work of implementing the new work method had not been sufficiently thorough. Especially, clear goals and frames for the groups had been missing.

In all three enterprises, the process quickly came to a standstill and the enterprises had group organization more in name than in fact. In the mid-1990s, AOF (Workers' Educational Association), a training provider for enterprises, encouraged them to form a network with representation of production managers and shop stewards. It was a relatively loose forum for the exchange of experiences, primarily focusing on qualification issues. The Danish Technological

Institute was invited to participate in the network to add additional weight on the work organizational aspect. The network commissioned AOF in co-operation with the Danish Technological Institute to describe a project in which an extensive training effort should be integrated with a serious attempt to change work organization in a SWS direction.

An action learning project in a network of SMEs in Sweden and with a similar ambition is described by Forslin and Thulestedt (1993). Also, Brulin (1998) discusses networking among SMEs in a Swedish industrial district, as part of the EU Social Fund activity Objective 4. This activity, however also involves local universities and has its focus on regional development.

The objective and working methods of the network

MOVE was planned to be a development network, and it was meant to function as a development catalyst. Problems, solutions and strategies in one enterprise could inspire the other enterprises with corresponding problems. No one believed that the enterprises could merely imitate each other; they would have to tailor a solution for their own specific enterprise.

Within the common idea of employee participation and job development, different degrees of the vision exist, or rather different parallel interests. This illustrates that the work of implementing SWS has to be pragmatic in relation to the individual enterprise, and to its current situation. Therefore, the network ended up consisting of three enterprises that are similar in some areas and different in others.

Setting goals and limits

Furthermore, AOF and the Danish Technological Institute have participated as process consultants and teachers, and have functioned as facilitators in the network. The EU application served as a contract between the involved parties, since the enterprises were co-signers on the application. Whereas the objective and framework were clearly stated, the description of the operational level was more open-ended. This is normal practice in EU programmes. Enterprises can see that they have a need to develop their employees and work organization. Often, they also have a sense of the direction in which the solution is to be found, but few enterprises realize from the beginning what solution is needed.

Therefore, consultants have to balance how much information about the possible consequences of a project and unexpected needs for adaptation of the action plans should and could be given at the beginning of the project. At the outset of the project, management will have difficulty believing that its employees possess other resources than the ones they use on the job. Consequently, management is not very likely to be able to see its employees as capable of taking on a lot of responsibility, living up to trust shown in them, and willing to commit themselves deeply to the enterprise. An example: one year into the project, one of the enterprises had big problems meeting delivery times. A group of operators offered to work overtime on Sundays. They got a key to the factory and extended in that way the operation time of the machine that formed the bottleneck in the production flow. This event gave a new platform for discussing delegation of authority and responsibility in the new structure. But before the project started, it would never have been possible to be specific in discussing this kind of outcome of the project, either with management or with the employees. It would simply have been too far away from daily life and the enterprise culture at that time.

It is therefore unrealistic to expect management to be able to define clear, visionary goals for delegation and employee involvement in advance, just as it is utopian to imagine top management committing itself to a demanding and expensive project with no guarantee of results. Consequently, the consultants should inform about the project, its expected results and consequences, but should not necessarily work out the kinds of problems that can occur during the project. Modest but visible successes are key words here. Implementing SWS has to be an open-ended process.

In this way, the nature of the MOVE project became more like 'clinical research' as described by Schein, where activities and the gathering of data are based in terms of people seeking advice and guidance. This is to be seen in relation to an original definition of action research where, according to Schein (2001), the research process will be more rigid in pursuing originally determined targets of the research process.

Network activities

A number of specific methods to release the potential in network learning have been developed and tested in the course of the MOVE project.

Cross-enterprise courses – exchange of job and learning experiences

The operators from the three companies in the network participated in joint courses, where they exchanged experiences from their working life. They visited each other's job sites and discovered alternatives to the work organization in their own company. The working method was a combination of traditional lecturing and class discussion, creative work and project work. The central themes covered in the course were: the historical development of work and technology, the history of female unskilled workers (most of the operators being women), the psycho-dynamics in the process of change, communication and creativity. And last, but not least, there were discussions on possible improvements in the daily work situation, and what possibilities there are for finding 'win–win' situations to finance the change.

The training procedure was to challenge and commit the participants and had to be planned democratically. One could suggest that the ambition was to provide training on common ground. Teachers and participants had to enjoy equal status in order to demonstrate the preconditions for development-oriented dialogue. The involvement of other employee groups and management was to take place in compliance with the same principles.

The learning situation

Training should contribute to broadening the employees' perspective to come up with solutions for the problems they encounter in their daily work. Training should build up the employees' self-confidence in expressing suggestions for remedial action or change. Training is thus more than acquiring new knowledge and skills because the job content has been enlarged. In the MOVE project the learning was aimed at creating a company culture which supports and furthers learning as suggested by Argyris and Schön (1992). Something is required in the training room to significantly rupture traditional perspectives and to introduce the participants to new ways of thinking.

Particularly favourable experiences have come from bringing in the Danish training tradition, the so-called General Information, specifically aimed at innovating the job situation of the individual employee. Experience indicates that production workers have no difficulty in identifying areas for innovation, implying improvement of the enterprises' results as well as workers' job quality. The achieved effects proved very favourable, in that the employees from

Network seminars – learning labs on a large scale

Representatives of the participating enterprises have regularly met in network seminars to exchange ideas and support the processes of change. At the start of the project, a theatre group called Dacapo was engaged to perform the play *Change – the Spice of Life* for all employees at the enterprises. It was a so-called forum theatre group and the play was designed to engage blue and white collar workers in discussing problems and misunderstandings that typically capsize a change project, e.g. when introducing autonomous groups. Some of the employees participated when the play was performed at one of the other enterprises. That promoted a common language on autonomous groups and change processes between the enterprises.

The videos also proved to be a strong lever for change. The presentation of the videos took place in an atmosphere of opening night anticipation and celebration. The participants' work was commemorated with combined big screen showings and dining arrangements, for example in the conference hall of the Danish Technological Institute.

When the video was presented to management and colleagues, a process was included involving prioritization of the presented ideas and wishes for change. The result of the process was included in the minutes of the management meeting and areas for both short- and long-term change were outlined. The process implied a comparison of the individual group's suggestions with ideas from other groups, taking into account the plans and possibilities of management. The joint preparation of the priority list, also including specification of long-term development targets, was important in giving both employees and management concrete experience of change as a constantly ongoing activity. According to Gustavsen *et al.* (1996), this was the very source of ABB's success with T50 (see below).

For the first time, the operators felt that they had been setting the agenda for a discussion on how the enterprise should be developed. Management and white collar workers were finally convinced that the operators were committed to the process of developing the company, which many of them had doubted before.

The video activity comprises favourable possibilities of discussing subjects otherwise difficult to address. In the video, situations of conflict may be described using role-playing and various solutions may be tried out. For the employees, it has proved quite inspiring to be able to illustrate, for example, problems related to co-operation by acting out the situations in other enterprises. The possibility of applying fiction in working with inter-human relations is a method also applied by the Dacapo Theatre in their forum work at enterprises. Among other sources, inspiration has been gained from Keith Johnstone (1999).

This method of illustrating typical conflicts can also be used at the network level. Some of the videos – for instance those welcoming new employees – were considered too critical and unrealistic for the enterprise where it was recorded. However, they proved suitable for raising constructive discussions at other enterprises in the network and only later were the problems taken up at the enterprise where the video had been made.

A manager in one of the enterprises said:

> Video is a strong medium; frightening, but good. Frightening because each employee has a copy as evidence of what we are enthusiastic about and what we want to change. You can't run away from it, which is good because it makes us all stick to what it really is we want to do something about. We can see that employees have a sincere desire for changes and they see what daily life is all about – they are the ones with the everyday problems.

The employees involved feel pride about having produced the videos. Management and white collar employees at the companies saw the videos and were surprised about the enthusiasm and commitment of the operators. Some departments finally realized how constructively the operators viewed the problems that they also face in other areas of the enterprise. Today, it is generally agreed by management in the network enterprises that video production leads to a broader acknowledgement of common problems, and that the operators have a lot to offer and must be consulted in the transition process.

Employee swapping within networks

Inspired by the strong effect of employees visiting each other's workplaces, activities on this theme have developed within another network. This network consists of the enterprises Bang & Olufsen, Carlsberg Breweries and Grundfos, which all experienced a standstill in their group-based organization at the time when new goals for development were to be outlined.

In order to regain energy and vision, they decided to initiate an employee swapping project with the Danish Technological Institute as project manager. Eight middle managers and thirteen production staff participated in the project. For one week, the employees acted as spies for their own production groups during the visit to the other enterprises, and as ambassadors promoting their own models and results when they entertained visitors. The middle managers completed visits in two other enterprises.

During the visits, the production staff obtained a thorough insight into the daily production processes by participating in the daily work. All groups had prepared questions in advance with the consultants on issues they wanted exposed during the visit. The questions focused on organization, management and distribution of responsibility and competence.

Following the visits, the 'spies' reported back to their group. Employees and management subsequently gave an account in the company newsletter. The evaluation of the activity was very positive, the conclusion being that even though the enterprises manufacture entirely different products, the employees may obtain valuable knowledge of organizational and job development. The participants expressed, for instance, the view that the physical or psychological working environment at the visited enterprises could provide inspiration for changes in their own production groups. Also, it had positive consequences when they thought that they were practising group organization in the best way. This produced a focusing that motivated further development.

Conclusion

Networking offers some practical advantages. For instance, SMEs can have easier access to employee training, because in a network it is easier to meet requirements of training institutions regarding the number of participants. The problem for SMEs is that they cannot do without more than a few employees at a time. Being a network means that a group of companies can together tailor training that fits with the needs of the companies.

However, far more important in relation to implementation of SWS is that networks have a substantial potential for working as a facilitator for an ongoing renewal of the work organization.

One of the most important preconditions for networking in the SWS process is that the activities include all layers in the organizations. In many enterprises, this dictates a radical change away from the established model of implementing top-down control and initiation of new measures. Use of theatre, video and other methods for stimulation of creativity has turned out to be of great significance for achieving a broad commitment in the development work.

Among several issues, Gustavsen *et al.* (1996) point to the importance of achieving a critical mass for obtaining a continuous development of the work organization. They are critical of the ability of the individual paradigmatic cases in generating change in other enterprises and emphasize that development in a given enterprise depends on whether other enterprises develop too. As an example they mention ABB's project T50, where a large number of projects were run in parallel, giving all of them an opportunity for encouragement and to learn from each other. For single enterprises, and especially for SMEs, recognition of the need for a critical mass will bring into focus the opportunities with development networks.

In the networks in this chapter, the enterprises have very different production facilities, products and customers. However, this has not been an obstacle to the exchange of experiences. Both management and employees have reported the significance of inspiration from others. Perhaps the significance has almost been intensified by the fact that the lack of similarities has clarified the organization theme. In the same way, another enterprise's choice of model will not necessarily form the basis of similar solutions for others. But the differences provide a basis for discussion and consideration at a given enterprise. Thus, if an enterprise chooses another solution, this solution will be ensured a more solid base. Gustavsen, Finne and Oscarsson (2001) report, on the basis of Norwegian network experiences, that the core element in interactive learning actually seems to be *difference*.

The special characteristic of the two development networks is the total lack of joint business interests between the enterprises. What is lacking is the economic force that traditionally has been the glue that ties networks together, for example the networks in the industrial district as described by Piore and Sabel (1984) and Chisholm (1998). Still, there is great interest among enterprises in development networks – an indication that this form of exchange of experiences on equal terms pays off.

Initiatives in establishing development networks seem to have focused little on the dynamics that networks between operators from different enterprises can give to the development of the work organization. SMEs, in particular, which seldom have the resources to carry out a top-down change process, could have great development potential by using a network with the active involvement of operators. The MOVE project has shown that it is possible to give operators a head start that qualifies them to an active role in the process, partly due to cross-enterprise activities. For the first time, they felt that they had been setting the agenda for change.

In many of the change processes carried out in single companies by implementing socio-technical principles, including delegation of decision-making and responsibilities, there are SWS-related models to build upon. When it comes to using networking for such development, the examples are much more limited. In this chapter, there has been a description of some approaches building upon an SWS perspective. They have been very successful in the test situation, and the conclusion must be that development networks deserve much more effort in regard to method development.

References

Argyris, C. and Schön, D.A. (1996) *Organizational Learning II. Theory, Method and Practice*, Reading, MA: Addison-Wesley.

Banke, P., Holsbo, A. and Madesen, A.M. (1999) *New Organisation of Work. Not as Easy as You Might Think*, Copenhagen: ACIU.

Banke, P. and Nørskov, E.C. (1998) *Taking Bottom-up Seriously. Employee Videos set the Agenda for Change*, Taastrup: Danish Technological Institute (video).

Bavelas, A. (1951) 'Communication patterns in task oriented groups', in H. Lasswell and D. Lerner (eds) *The Policy Sciences*, Stanford, CA: Stanford University Press.

Brulin, G. (1998) 'How to shape creative territorial energy. The case of the Gnosjö region', *International Journal of Action Research and Organizational Renewal*, 3.

Brulin, G. (2001) 'The third task of universities or how to get universities to serve their communities', in P. Reason and H. Bradbury (eds) *Handbook of Action Research. Participative Inquiry and Practice*, London: Sage.

Chisholm, R.F. (1998) *Developing Network Organizations. Learning from Practice and Theory*, Reading, MA: Addison-Wesley.

Forslin, J. and Thulestedt, B.-M. (1993) *Lärande organisation. Att utveckla kompetens tillsammans* (Learning Organization. Developing Competence Together), Stockholm: Publica.

Galbraith, J. (1991) 'Structural responses to competitive strategies', in R. Kilmann, I. Kilmann and Associates (eds) *Making Organizations Competitive. Enhancing Networks and Relationships Across Traditional Boundaries*, San Francisco: Jossey-Bass.

Gustavsen, B. (2001) 'Theory and practice. The mediating discourse', in P. Reason and H. Bradbury (eds) *Handbook of Action Research. Participative Inquiry and Practice*, London: Sage.

Gustavsen, B., Hofmaier, B., Ekman Philips, M. and Wikman, A. (1996) *Concept-driven Development and the Organization of the Process of Change. An Evaluation of the Swedish Working Life Fund*, Amsterdam: John Benjamins.

Gustavsen, B., Finne, H. and Oscarsson, B. (2001) *Creating Connectedness. The Role of Social Research in Innovation Policy*, Amsterdam: John Benjamins.

Johnstone, K. (1999) *Impro for Storytellers. Theatresports and the Art of Making Things Happen*, London: Faber & Faber.

Kilmann, R. (1977) *Social Systems Design. Normative Theory and the MAPS Design Technology*, New York: Elsevier North-Holland.

Kilmann, R. and Kilmann, I. (1991) 'Creating perfectly competitive organization', in R. Kilmann, I. Kilmann and Associates (eds) *Making Organizations Competitive. Enhancing Networks and Relationships Across Traditional Boundaries*, San Francisco: Jossey-Bass.

Mackenzie, K.D. (1966) 'Structural centrality in communication networks', *Psychometrika*, 31, 1, 17–25.

Mackenzie, K.D. (1976) *A Theory of Group Structures*, New York: Gordon & Breach.

Miles, R.E. and Snow, C.C. (1984) 'Fit, failure, and the hall of fame', *California Management Review*, 26, 3, 10–28.

Miles, R.E. and Snow, C.C. (1997) 'Organizing in the knowledge age. Anticipating the cellular form', *Academy of Management Executive*, 11, 4, 7–24.

Moreno, J.L. (1934) *Who Shall Survive?* Washington, DC: Nervous and Mental Disease Publishing.

Piore, M.J. and Sabel, C. (1984) *The Second Industrial Divide. Possibilities for Prosperity*, New York: Basic Books.

Schein, Edgar H. (2001) 'Clinical inquiry/research', in P. Reason and H. Bradbury (eds) *Handbook of Action Research. Participative Inquiry and Practice*, London: Sage.

Tichy, N.M. (1981) 'Networks in organizations', in P.C. Nystrom and W.H. Starbuck (eds) *Handbook of Organization Design*, Oxford: Oxford University Press.

13 An innovative coalition succumbs to bureaucracy

Peter Docherty

Introduction

How should we think about the interaction between IWS and SWS? Only a decade ago, there was a tendency in the comparative sociology and political economy literature to link positive economic and social outcomes with the 'correct' mix of institutions. For example, neo-corporatism (i.e. strong labour unions, wage equality, etc.) predicted lower inflation and unemployment in OECD countries. While naïve ideas about the role of institutional frameworks have gradually been replaced by more complex ideas about the interaction between institutions and economic organizations, they still inform, at least initially, many of the debates.

The Regional Competence Development Coalition (RCDC) is a Swedish case that illustrates the interaction between institutions and companies in efforts to further sustainability.[1] The aims were: at the individual level, to maintain sustainability through 'employability', re-skilling and resettling potentially redundant workers in new jobs within the company or in other companies; at the company level, to ensure competence quality assurance by upgrading workers' skills in original equipment manufacturers (OEMs) and their suppliers; and at the regional level, proactively to avoid redundancies and ensure the availability of qualified personnel to the manufacturing industry. This chapter traces the development initiated by a major manufacturing company or OEM in forming a very broad and innovative coalition between a wide range of companies within the manufacturing sector. The coalition included private companies, regional authorities and government agencies, practitioners and university researchers, and employers and unions.

The coalition's lifecycle also illustrates the sensitivity of such coalitions to their institutional context. Changes in the coalition's institutional relations led to internal decisions which altered its structure, processes and fortunes. Its development is described in two stages. Stage one describes the coalition as an egalitarian network that made an amazing start to the issue of the upskilling and re-skilling of experienced workers. Stage two of the coalition's development work was funded by an external body on the condition that two specific parties in the coalition should be responsible for the administration of the funds for the development effort. This led to the coalition rapidly becoming a bureaucracy and a loss of its innovative character.

The coalition

Its composition

Several major manufacturing companies, or OEMs, were initially members of the coalition. One of them had a policy of employability towards its production personnel. It was anxious to extend this in two directions, towards the re-skilling of personnel and to competence quality assurance of the personnel employed by its suppliers. The National Employment Board's (NEB) regional office was anxious to participate to test new ways of working with companies to forestall redundancies for risk groups and to participate in the development of tools and methods for competence development. The Municipal Education Authority and major training consultants were interested in the development aspects of new methods, tools and courses for training and the Trade and Industry Office was interested in change and development in companies in the region. The trade union was interested to test new ways of meeting its members' needs for jobs, employability and competence development. The local employers' association was interested for similar reasons. The university departments dealing with adult learning and work organization were also very keen members. Competitive development was the common denominator.

The broad development

Stage one was characterized by leadership from a key OEM, joint funding by the OEM and the NEB and a clear egalitarian culture in the steering committee which included all the key constituencies. Competence development was focused at three levels: individual, group and company. The establishment of a competence culture and 'change competence' were two key issues in Stage one. Change competence, regarding structure, resources, commitment and knowledge on people and change, was a key issue at company level. Job enrichment in teams and a general raising of the competence level for those with few qualifications were the main issues at the group and individual levels.

A key aspect of the innovation was the focus on continual competence development for people *already* in the labour market – a group that was previously 'outside the field of vision' for government interest. The RCDC broached the issue of *employability* as distinct from employment, of complementing the goal of attaining a place in the labour market with retaining a place in the labour market. The programme underlined the coupling between knowledge management and organizational change and development.

A basic idea behind the coalition was to develop tools and methods to strengthen the skills of the personnel in manufacturing companies in the region. The idea was to arrive at a competence profile that would hold for production workers in a manufacturing sector and would enable the establishment of a common practice in a supplier chain (Thång and Wärvik 2001). This in its turn would improve the companies' competitiveness and create jobs in the region. The core strategy was to start development projects and build networks between companies and personnel. The project started in 1994. The first review of analysis methods in Stage one covered five such methods for the competence analysis of production workers. A computer-based method was chosen for use in the programme. The important factor in this context was not the use of a sophisticated method but a conscious, goal-oriented, long-term process to handle the analysis of workers' competences and the competences demanded by the production teams and the gaps between 'supply' and 'demand'.

The costs of work in Stage one were largely defrayed by the major OEM and the NEB. Considerable professional support was also provided by the public sector authorities and agencies involved. For the last six months in Stage one the programme had no external financier, and allotted specific resources to formulating grant applications to different national and European bodies.

Stage one: the egalitarian network

Developments

In the 1990s management at the leading OEM in the coalition gave priority to projects aiming at developing and utilizing workers' knowledge and skills. This was attained by creating 'teams along the line' that have responsibility for goal fulfilment and problem solving, and for taking part in the development of processes and products, often via their own personal initiatives. This organization is aimed at facilitating and enhancing on-the-job learning. The vision for the production teams is to be able to achieve world class performance with a good plant environment and to utilize the workers' full competence. Goals for the teams are very clear, for example 'to reduce their costs by 10 per cent per year'. As can be seen from Figure 13.1, there is a strong interdependence between organizational and individual development. As tasks and decision-making are integrated in teams, the skills and knowledge required by the workers increase.

The early 1990s saw a fall in the demand for the OEM's products. Its main factory was forced to cut a shift. This meant that nearly 1,000 workers were potentially redundant. The situation was delicate. The labour market legislation on security of employment prevented management from choosing which workers to retain. Furthermore company experts estimated that the demand for the products, and thus labour, would rise again within one or two years. The company contacted the regional office of the NEB and negotiated a broad educational programme which would be subsidized by the NEB and entail keeping on personnel while participating in the programme. Some of the people would be retrained to 're-enter' the

Work group's level of development		*Group's organizational context*	*Main meaning of the competence concept*	
Extensive admin./planning tasks	Development and improvement	*Learning group* with responsibility for the group's task and development. A central actor in the business process.	Social competence: support co-operation, acceptance of shared vision	Theoretical competence: reflection and learning
Execute and maintain operative tasks			Practical competence: assignment oriented	
Few admin./planning tasks		*Goal-steered group* with group tasks and joint responsibility. Decentralized flow-oriented organization.	Social competence: support, co-operation	
Execute and maintain operative tasks			Practical competence: support, assignment oriented	
Execute and maintain operative tasks		*Administrative group* with individual tasks, physical proximity and job rotation. Functional, centralized and hierarchical organization.	Social competence: support	
			Practical competence: assignment oriented	

Figure 13.1 The work group development in terms of organizational contact and competence context.

Source: Hart, Berger and Lindberg 1996, p. 17.

company in 'new' jobs. The others would be helped to find jobs outside the company. The programme covered subjects outside the company's specific competence. It also entailed building up relationships with external educational organizations – both private and public. The main goal of the project was *improved employability*.

A second project arose in a one year gap between two products. The changes in the product meant that 1,100 people had nothing to do for twelve months. A new significant negotiation took place between the main OEM and the NEB on a second jointly financed training programme. This time the focus was on skills required to build products in a highly developed technical environment. The educational authority of the local municipality joined the network to help design the programme to meet the company's needs. After the programme the majority of the participants returned to the plant. The others either went to new jobs/occupations outside the company or continued their studies.

Launching the Regional Competence Development Coalition (RCDC) was 'the next logical step'. This was a joint venture between all the partners listed earlier. The aim of the programme was to improve the region's possibilities of successfully developing the competence and employability of people in the manufacturing industry. One aspect of the project was to produce tools and methods concerning:

- competence demands then and in 2000+;
- models for the learning organization;
- pedagogics for adult learning, e.g. utilizing multimedia;
- prerequisites for competence development;
- models for co-operation between actors on the labour market.

One important lesson from the previous projects was that training alone is insufficient for improving work and efficiency. Participants, who returned from training to the same working situation they had left a year earlier, benefited little from the training. On the other hand, participants who joined a new team based on the principles of job enlargement and job enrichment benefited a lot. Thus the project entails a shift from the training as such to the learning organization and the learning society. Another very important lesson was that individuals must take responsibility for their own future, must participate in designing their own educational programme and must be motivated to participate. This entails personnel having a clear idea of what comes after their training programme.

The fourth project was the first one within the RCDC framework, addressing all five of the issues bulleted above. Some 2,400 workers were retrained for re-entry into the company. Cost reduction necessitated the reschooling and outplacement of 600 workers from the OEM. The project was occasioned by a decline in the market. After negotiations with the unions the parties agreed on yet another competence development programme. The education was broad and basic with subjects such as Swedish, English and mathematics. These were combined with specific technical subjects and an extensive programme in skills of working in teams. The project used the RCDC analysis tools and developed individual development plans for each worker involved in the retraining programme. The OEM introduced this practice in factory production as a whole. Each participant in the retraining programme was aware that the programme would lead either to a new job in the OEM, their current employer, or to a job in another company in the region. Thus one stream in the programme addressed a broad orientation on possibilities in the labour market.

The fifth project primarily addressed the competence development of employees in the manufacturing industry in the region. The main innovation in the project was to focus on developments in competence and work organization through co-operation in that sector between SMEs and the large companies. High priority was given to participants with little or dated formal training. One of the main aims of the project was to develop methods for custom-designed change-oriented training for suppliers and subcontractors. The project utilized a radically new method for the analysis of production systems. This was developed following the insight that the formal training available from the public educational system did not meet the current demands for renewing the knowledge and skills of workers in industry. This was related to the increasing rate of change in the sector and to the decline in the numbers of young, well-educated workers entering the sector. Change and renewal must therefore be focused to a greater extent on those already employed in the industry.

Lessons

The main lesson of the coalition from its first efforts was that training is an excellent alternative to laying people off and that training can be much broader than simply vocational training for those people outside the labour market.

A clear lesson from the fourth project was the importance of individual development plans based on matching competence analyses with personal needs, expectations and aspirations. Another was the importance of conducting a joint venture between different actors. It was clear that some participants would re-enter their current employer and that others would leave, but it was not clear who would choose which. People made their choice gradually during the programme. In a sense the programme was process-oriented rather than goal-oriented.

The first phase of such a programme, six to eight months, should include: an environmental analysis, a review of learning at work and learning organizations, pedagogical developments, required developments in competences and forms for co-operation between the various stakeholders on the labour market. The environmental analysis indicated that customers would be playing a more active and demanding role. Process flow models would be more important in production. Demands on competences in production in terms of breadth and level would continue to increase regarding administrative, IT, planning, maintenance and social skills.

Stage two: a hierarchy

In 1997 the security council formed between the national employer and union organizations took over the role of main financier from the NEB. The council gave the RCDC programme a grant of 4 million Euros for the period 1997–2000. Stage two was characterized by 'new management' in the steering committee appointed by the external financing institution as a condition for its support. The roles of all members in the steering committee were affected. Previous professional relations and consultative capacities received less recognition in this second stage of the development.

The reorganization of the RCDC

A number of important changes were made in the organization and management of the programme when the RCDC received substantial finances from the security council. According to the standard terms of the contract with the council, the decisions on the use of the grant were to be made by the regional representatives for the manufacturing employers' confederation and the metalworkers' union. These bodies were already members of the egalitarian network managing the programme, but now they alone had control of the major external resources. Their management of the programme entailed changes in: (a) the criteria for the eligibility of specific companies and personnel categories to participate in the programme; (b) the priority given to different themes in the programme; (c) the attention and resources allocated to different themes and different constituencies in the programme; and (d) the routines and work practices adopted in the programme. The new 'owners' felt a need to adhere closely to the routines and perspectives of the financing body may have reinforced the administrative perspective that came to characterize this stage of the programme.

Thus the employers' association stipulated that only companies that were members of its organization would receive financial support. The union made a similar restriction with the condition that the financial support should be restricted to activities involving its members as distinct from non-unionized personnel or members of other unions. This led to companies either not joining the projects or dropping out.

Sixty-seven companies and about 7,400 people participated in or came into contact with the programme in the four year period of Stage two. The RCDC steering committee controlled a group of development projects in the manufacturing industry in a region. The activities in this period were grouped around four parallel themes:

- knowledge management (competence development of production workers);
- learning organizations (forms of learning);
- networks (for learning);
- renewed work organization (for competence utilization).

The RCDC management has worked to instil a sense of urgency into employers and unions on the need for major efforts to ensure the sustainability of the region on the national and international scene.

The main fields of activity in Stage two

The RCDC programme operated with four themes as named above. These constituted parts of a whole in the following way:

1   The development work in the participating companies started from personal planning meetings between individual employees and their immediate superiors based on the company's goals and strategy and the individuals' needs and ambitions. Development plans were drawn up for the individuals and teams (knowledge management).
2   These plans were then carried out in different ways (forms of learning).
3   These measures were followed up and evaluated (knowledge management) and experiences shared with other companies (networks).
4   The centre for these activities was the work organization. The development of the work organization and of the infrastructure for the skills and knowledge development processes formed a key element in the process.

Methods and tools for measuring competence and for learning

The development of tools and methods for competence analysis and competence management was a central task for RCDC from the outset. The development of methods and forms for learning was the other goal, which in this context took the form of IT-based or IT-supported pedagogical programmes. The idea was to develop forms for learning that could be integrated in the workplace. Present production requirements are no longer generally compatible with releasing groups or even individuals from production to participate in extended training programmes. The programme was also to provide opportunities for joint discussions, problem solving and exchanges of experiences in different networks between companies, union clubs and professions. The external financing body was especially interested in the innovation of creating networks of production workers as a means of developing their skills and qualifications.

The new regime: bureaucratization

Developments

The conditions for the prolonged existence of the programme were that 'all the partners were equal, but some were more equal than others', in George Orwell's words from *Animal Farm*. There was never any open discussion of the impact of this power shift in the programme and a general uncertainty spread through the other established members of the steering committee or 'network'. The allocation of resources to the different programme areas in the RCDC had previously been preceded by discussions on what was to be done in the areas. In some cases such joint discussions no longer took place. This resulted in some of the members of the 'network' knowing little about their scope for action in the continuation of the programme. Contracts were not drawn up with the members in the individual work groups. At least several members of RCDC perceived the allocation of money between activities as non-transparent. These events were of great import for the further development of the programme (Thång and Wärvick 2001, p. 42).

Two factors contributed to the changing of the formal organization and informal ways of working in the RCDC programme. The first was the conditions attached to the council's financing; the second was the turnover in the individuals holding positions in both the steering committee and in project groups, especially project managers. There were also certain difficulties in establishing the programme in the participating mentor companies, the OEMs.

As the programme grew, the RCDC steering committee had more difficulty both in overviewing the programme and its separate activities and in following the individual projects. Thång and Wärvik (2001, p. 59) pose the question whether the original network idea of the RCDC had collapsed. The work and management organization had become increasingly formalized and, at the same rate, the internal network idea had become weaker. The flexibility that characterized Stage one was weakened. The new organization strengthened the impression that this was basically a competence development programme, rather than a broader and more integrated enterprise. The steering committee became predominantly an administrative body as distinct from a policy body. Many felt there was no integrating policy, little discussion of ideas and practically no co-ordination of the separate themes or activities in the programme. There was neither a meta-theme to pull together the four areas of activity or themes, nor an overall vision of the future working life for small and medium-sized companies. There had been a distinct effort to make such an analysis at the outset of the programme. The work done in Stage two is presented under the thematic headings presented earlier.

Knowledge management (or competence development for production workers)

In the four year period, eighteen companies were involved in ten projects concerning knowledge management. The leading 'mentor' company was an OEM. Competence was defined as the ability to carry out allotted tasks and realize allotted goals. A major activity was the development of methods and tools for competence analysis and assessment. In Stage two a second sweep of the market regarding competence analysis methods and tools was conducted. A further fifty tools for competence analysis of jobs and individuals were identified on the market. The tool used in Stage one was designed to be used primarily in large companies. The programme had hoped to develop a method and tool that could be used over a broad spectrum of company sizes, for example by an OEM and its suppliers as part of a quality competence assurance programme. However, the results were disappointing, as the smaller companies, with less than fifty employees, did not have the time or energy to make such efforts to use the tool chosen at that time.

The competence analysis phase turned out to be the most demanding task in these projects. In general the process took far longer than expected. The competence gap analysis of a worker took between ten and fifteen hours. It required patience, commitment, farsightedness and involvement by management. Companies were, however, difficult to recruit to the programme and their interest was sporadic and coupled to their acute needs. The workers' participation and responsibility were regarded as a very positive part of the exercise. They became personally involved in the formulation of competence areas and levels.

The important aspects of the knowledge management projects were: the focus on competence, the pedagogical method, the user friendliness of methods and tools, their adaptability to the needs of the situation and reasonable costs. Some basic lessons drawn from this theme in the programme were:

- Management's insight, understanding and long-term commitment to knowledge management is essential to success.
- The task requires one or more dedicated champions to succeed.
- The entire competence development cycle must be implemented. Ignoring any particular step in the process will radically reduce or eliminate the results obtained.
- The process functions excellently as a practical exercise in developing leadership in groups.
- The planning horizon of the participants was extended.

Learning organization (forms of learning)

In the same period, twenty-six companies were involved in fifteen projects concerning forms of learning. The leading 'mentor' companies were two OEMs. The main aim of the projects was to develop new forms of learning integrated into daily work activities. Different models would be identified, developed and tested with respect to the specific needs and goals of the participating companies. These projects focused primarily on the 'how to learn' issue and not on the 'what to learn' or 'who learns' questions. There was no explicit strategy regarding the selection of participants. Each project should contain 'something new' without closer specification. Factors that have been shown to influence learning in formal training situations include: action control (Aronsson 1990), individual expectations and motivation (Ellström and Koch 1993), training possibilities, career development, opportunities to apply the training in the job and feedback, both in the training and on the job.

The projects had a clear focus on the utilization of information and communication technologies (ICT). The majority of participants reported that they had not acquired sufficient proficiency in the use of computers in the introductory courses to be able to work as independently as they had expected in the later courses. The majority wanted more follow up and continued tutoring. Thus much of the potential of ICT-mediated learning was not realized. The interaction between the technology and learning needs to be highlighted. Proficient educational professionals were a very scarce resource in the programme.

Learning centres were very dependent on the involvement of management and unions. The majority of learning centres were closed down following the completion of the projects (Thång and Wärvik 2001, p. 106). The success of the learning centres was very much dependent on their champions. It is unclear what role the RCDC played in the projects. The majority of the projects were very short, up to ten months at the most. This proved to be too short a time, even for companies with considerable experience of in-company training. It should be added that it was difficult, generally speaking, to involve companies in such training. It is usually allotted times when people are not engaged in productive work.

Experiences from these projects showed that:

*   It takes up to six months to sell the learning centre idea to management and personnel.
*   They require an extended, regular and systematized period for the participants to define their problems and form groups.
*   Learning centres should be in or directly adjacent to the production facilities and workers should not need to change clothing when moving between their work and 'learning places'.
*   Problem-based learning is an excellent method for the teachers and tutors involved.

Distance between the learning centre and a company's production facilities and the host company's price-setting for its use were serious obstacles to their utilization by SMEs. In fact learning centres in or adjacent to production facilities do not appear to be a viable solution for small companies.

Networks for learning

During the four year period between fifty and seventy networks were established to support development processes. A network may be defined in this context as a means for collective value creation regarding the development and renewal of competence through the exchange of ideas, thoughts, experiences and knowledge. Examples are: a network between personnel departments in different companies, networks between SMEs wishing to form 'complete system' suppliers to OEMs, training programme networks, learning centre networks and a personnel development network.

In general, the management of a network organization is distinctly different from a traditional hierarchy. The mandate for management is different. This became evident already in the early stages of the programme when project managers working with network project groups had a tendency to demand greater commitment and efforts from their project members from the participating companies than the latter had been granted by their primary employers.

The networks experienced companies successively dropping out. The focus of many networks was the courses they were giving – they were more 'a series of seminars' than a network. This tendency was reinforced by the short time frames. The purpose of the network was unclear in many cases. It was more or less assumed that if a few meetings were held a network would emerge. The RCDC had no long-term strategy regarding the networks.

Renewing work organization

In the same period, twenty-one companies were involved in ten projects concerning work organization in which the development of the business was coupled to the development of the work organization and the workers' competence and decision discretion. The leading 'mentor' company was a third OEM. About ten companies coupled organizational development to the development of the knowledge management system with its methods and organizational infrastructure. Others were more directly coupled to structuring work and developing information management.

Some lessons

The RCDC programme spanned several areas from research-oriented studies of learning processes to consultation-oriented company development. There was a continual shift in the focus of the work in the programme. The network view of the steering committee, which had prevailed more in Stage one, was severely challenged later in the programme and was not maintained. In Stage two the steering committee became two factions – the 'owners' and the 'others'. The presence of 'ownership' limited the programme's freedom of action. The owners determined the conditions for investments, which investments were made, which companies and personnel categories could or could not participate.

In Stage one the steering committee functioned as a network formed on the basis of previous professional experience and relations. The power shift had occurred so that a holistic or multi-constituency perspective of the issues addressed was changed to a stakeholder perspective. An effect of this change in power and priorities was that there was an increased turnover in the representation of different constituencies and a gradual dropping out of different constituencies. The programme itself is not really sustainable, nor are many of the project networks.

The programme's economy was good, which meant that the steering committee was not forced to choose between programme themes. The members of the steering committee and the project managers shared an involvement in and a commitment to the 'experimental workshop' dealing with methods and tools, and to the long-term development of competence. There were naturally different weightings on research/consultation orientation and individual/company/region orientation. There was a certain tension between the large companies and the small companies.

The companies participating regarded the programme as a source of inspiration, a push in the right direction. It afforded them the insight into the need for training and developing personnel.

The union representatives felt that the programme was too management-oriented and that personnel had not been sufficiently involved. Management support for a union role in the projects was weak in many companies. The union had not been able to support the work at project level. The latter was critical as union members in many small companies do not have a club organization. In fact the programme steering committee had been very distant from the personnel working in the projects. It was simply perceived as a distributor of money.

There were only weak ties between the research and development elements in the RCDC. This meant that relevant positive opportunities for certain activities were not taken, e.g. studies of learning processes. The focus was on techniques and models whereas 'irrational' perceptual and value dimensions were ignored.

The activities in Stage two were characterized by a general and serious misjudgement of the time factor in the processes involved, irrespective of company size. The programme underestimated the need to explain thoroughly to the companies what they would be letting themselves in for. The experience proved an eye-opener for many production personnel.

Consultants played very important roles. Although the companies became dependent on them, they ensured that the development work continued when the demands on production were high. The consultants, in their turn, needed high involvement and, preferably, previous experience of development work on the part of management and the unions.

In summary

Sustainability in the context of this illustration is tightly coupled to competence, its availability, its development and its utilization. For the individual this meant personal development and high value on the labour market (employability), for OEMs it meant their own workers were of high quality as were those of their suppliers (quality assurance: competence). For the (SME) suppliers, they got access to qualified labour which fulfilled the OEMs' demands. For the region it meant an attractive labour force and less unemployment.

The programme addressed the issue of competence development. Its efforts were, however, limited to achieving results in the short term. The creation of the coalition was occasioned by pressing and serious skill development problems in the manufacturing industry in the region concerned. It was natural and fortuitous that the major OEMs in the region activated their network with the public sector to involve them in attaining a solution. The really interesting development in this case is that the original construction of the coalition managed to bring together representatives from so many different constituencies with different perspectives and priorities, but whose values, interests and resources complemented each other. Here were to be found interest in the individual worker, teams, companies, unions and the region, as well as resources from staff, line management, unions, consultation, education and training and research. Even if a major OEM provided key resources and was the driving force at the outset, an egalitarian climate was established which benefited the motivation and commitment of all the members of the steering committee. Perhaps the most innovative aspect was the temporary alliance between an experienced development-oriented private company and an experienced development-oriented government agency.

The primary innovation was to involve the National Employment Board which at the regional level widened marginally, but highly significantly, the envelope of its mission, by involving itself in the issue of employability, of supporting the skills development of people presently employed but seriously under the shadow of dismissal. Such support in a 'grey zone' is, at least periodically, very controversial. Economically the situation offered a clear 'win–win' situation. The company refrained from dismissing personnel (who it really did not want to lose) and shifting the responsibility and full costs for the dismissed workers to society (the NEB) (loss 1 and step 1 in 'normal practice' in the labour market). The normal training supplied by the NEB does not always match that needed by the OEM or match jobs available for the dismissed individuals (loss 2 and step 2 in 'normal practice'.) The parties in the RCDC took the win–win alternative of sharing the costs, matching the supply and demand of the training and avoiding redundancies. (People not being retained by the OEM after reschooling were outplaced in jobs in other companies.)

The benefits of this joint action in Stage one differed significantly from those in Stage two. The key actor shouldering the financial role in Stage one, namely the NEB, had a keen professional interest in the structures and processes entailed in realizing the competence development of the workers. It was actively represented in the coalition steering committee by experts whose work at the NEB consisted in running development and consultation projects on these issues.

The NEB had made clear that its financial role in the programme was of limited duration and another (traditional) financier was to be found. In this context, its successor, the security council, was basically responsible for managing and controlling the distribution of funds to projects. The RCDC programme became a case in a bureaucracy: it was simply subject to the conditions and routines holding for all other cases. It was not accorded any 'special treatment'. The council's standing operating procedures required that the project be 'owned'.

The owners in this case were very conscious of their rights and duties as owners, principally regarding the management and control of the financial resources in relation to the council and their constituencies. Unfortunately an opportunity was missed. The adopted management role could well have been combined with an active role in the professional development issues forming the basis of the programme. These were, for example, clearly related to the central union's ambitions to play a more active role for its members in employment, employability and competence development issues (Berggren and Brulin 1998).

Such an interest could have maintained the egalitarian climate in the steering committee and utilized the considerable professional resources available from the OEMs, NEB and the universities. These were, however, underutilized, allotted very few assignments or resources and gradually withdrew from the programme. In addition, the union members and companies participating, the programme owners' constituencies, expressed disappointment at the level of support they had received when wrestling with difficult development issues. It is not clear if the owners' failure to utilize the professional resources available in the programme was due to (a) insufficient knowledge and experience of development work; (b) insufficient trust in and understanding of the potential contributions of these professionals; (c) insufficient resources to be able to work with these professionals; or (d) the active assignment of low priority to these tasks.

The RCDC programme was envisaged as a temporary organization and must be evaluated as such. The programme as such is finished. A government R&D agency has the task of spreading the experiences from the programme and designing a suitable next step. A positive precondition may be that this agency was responsible for the evaluation of the national work life development programme in the early 1990s, which included experiments in 24,000 workplaces (Gustavsen *et al.* 1996). Some of the main lessons from that programme were that key elements for development are: the formal processes designed by top management, the project-oriented work forms at the participating workplaces and the co-ordinating functions between projects. Shortcomings on these points have already been noted in this case. The absence of a structure and processes for continual reflection, analysis and the re-evaluation of the programme's context and goals were probably the most serious.

The issue of sustainability, coupled to the issues of the forms and arrangements for learning at different levels and in different contexts, were clearly addressed in the RCDC programme in Stage one, but they were left aside in Stage two. Thus the case illustrates the vulnerability of processes working with and for sustainability in temporary coalitions in which the parties are unclear about each other's goals and priorities and the resources available. From a development viewpoint, the programme constituted an innovative experiment but the organizational structure of the programme was not robust. The two main disappointments from Stage one are first, that the positive results of its first stage have not been publicly reported, and second, that this type of innovative alliance or coalition to explore and develop structures and processes for sustainability across the levels (individual, organizational and regional) has not received more attention. New innovative experiments are required.

Note

1 This case study is based on interviews with people involved in the coalition during Stage one and the beginning of Stage two. It is also based on the analysis of secondary data in the form of internal documents from the coalition during this time. The description and analysis of the later developments in Stage two are based heavily in the first instance on two reports: the final report from the programme to the security council and an academic evaluation conducted by P.O. Thång and G.B. Wärvik at the Department of Education at the University of Gothenburg (Thång and Wärvik 2001).

References

Aronsson, G. (1990) 'Handling och Kontroll' (Action and control), in G. Aronsson and H. Berglind (eds) *Handling och Handlingsutrymme*, Lund: Studentlitteratur, pp. 69–93.

Arvedson, L. (1998) *Downsizing: När företag bantar* (Downsizing: When Companies Slim), Stockholm: Trygghetsrådet.

Berggren, C. and Brulin, G. (1998) *Goda arbeten och utvecklande regioner. Metall på två ben* (Rewarding Work and Developing Regions. Metall on Two Feet), Stockholm: Svenska Metallarbetareförbundet.

Ellström, P.E. and Koch, G. (1993) *Kompetensutveckling i den offentliga sektorn. En kunskapsöversikt*, Stockholm: Civildepartementet Ds.: 65 Allmänna förlaget.

Gustavsen, B., Ekman Philips, M. and Hoffmaier, B. (1996) *Concept-driven Development and the Organization of the Process of Change. An Evaluation of the Swedish Working Life Fund*, Amsterdam: John Benjamins.

Hart, H., Berger, A. and Lindberg, P. (1996) *Ständig förbättring – ännu ett verktyg eller en del av arbetet i målstyrda grupper* (Continuous Improvement), Stockholm: Arbetslivsinstitutet.

Österlund, L. and Alverå, L. (2001) *Tillsammans skapar vi större värde* (Together We Create Greater Value), Göteborg: Sveriges Verkstadsindustrier och Svenska Metallarbetarförbundet.

Thång, P.O. and Wärvick, G.B. (2001) *Kompetensutveckling för yrkesverksamma inom den västsvenska verkstadsindustrin: är det möjligt?* (Competence Development for Skilled Workers in the Manufacturing Industry in the West of Sweden. Is it possible?), Göteborg: Göteborg University report: 4.

Part 4

Attaining sustainability and sustainable change

Part 3 provided some illustrations of work systems in different contexts nationally and industrially. The examples were practices that emerged in the interplay between intensity and sustainable work and were examined to varied degrees from different theoretical frameworks. We looked at sustainable work systems through different lenses, or from different perspectives, chosen to respond to and respect the characteristics of each system or analysis level in question. However, what unites our lenses is their focus towards work, towards individuals and organizations at work.

This section of the book – *Attaining sustainability and sustainable change* – attempts to suggest some roadmaps and mechanisms for achieving sustainability. A common denominator in this section is the focus on developmental mechanisms that can aid in developing and attaining sustainable work systems. Furthermore, sustainability is not a state, it is a process; and in order to attain and maintain these processes expertocratic approaches have to be re-examined. Scientists, consultants and managers do have important roles also in the more sustainable futures, probably not as creators, but rather as contributors and facilitators. Their task is to support the process of sustainability and to facilitate the continuous common search for balance in working lives and firms' efficiency.

Chapter 14, 'Feedback, intangibles and sustainable performance', provides a focus on measurement and feedback mechanisms. Creating a balance between the legitimate needs and goals of different stakeholders in organizations and at the same time reflecting on the results of actions taken to attain sustainability, both in working and business life, require systematic feedback in management systems that encompass much more than is usual today. Quantitative information needs to be complemented with qualitative data on intangibles. This also entails a re-evaluation of the centrality and importance of human reflexivity, collective and organizational learning. This is strongly coupled to the role and nature of dialogue and participative communication and the crucial part played by knowledge creation and application in new products.

Chapter 15, 'A reflexive methodology of intervention', outlines a methodology of intervention in organizations that is compatible with the idea of sustainable work systems. It presents reflexive methodology as an alternative to the dominant paradigms of organizational intervention. The proposed alternative builds upon epistemological principles of reflexivity. The intervening person here is conceptualized as part of the analysed system; furthermore, the person is seen as embedded in a broader social context that shapes their ways of understanding; attention is centred around the concept of unintended side effects of action in both organizational and intervention practice. Thus, evaluation as reflection-on-action is viewed as a critical dimension of the intervention.

Chapter 16, 'Deutero-learning and sustainable change', provides a focus on deutero-learning mechanisms. This chapter contains a reflection on and discussion of the need for sense-making and learning processes that go beyond the single individual and the single task. We are all involved in sense-making and learning processes in everyday work. The predominant working ingredient in these processes is often some sort of oral communication such as conversations and dialogues. Of special interest here is the focus on work task-based communication as a bridge between different individuals and their experiential knowledge about the work, to reach a deutero-learning that constitutes sustainable learning and change processes. Sustainability is, in this context, directly dependent upon the possibilities of developing space for experiential knowledge formation processes that support deutero-learning.

Chapter 17, 'Eclectic design for change', focuses on design mechanisms and process. This chapter addresses the issue of SWS design and change. Anchored in action research, socio-technical systems, self-design and reflexive methodological foundations, this chapter advances an eclectic change methodology for sustainable work systems. The eclectic methodology is viewed as an alternative approach that integrates design process requirements, design criteria and work-based learning. The methodology transcends existing design and change models and highlights the importance of design choices.

Chapter 18, 'Sustainable work systems: lessons and challenges', recaptures the different parts and chapters. A comprehensive reflection on the perspectives, illustrations and attainment provides the foundation for the appreciation of the current state of knowledge and practice. The last section focuses on challenges for future practice and research.

14 Feedback, intangibles and sustainable performance

Peter Cressey and Peter Docherty

Introduction

What type of follow-up system is appropriate to manage sustainable work systems? What regular and systematic feedback do the various parties concerned need to support their joint learning and planning? The general purpose of accounting is to determine the value and outcomes of various forms of economic activity. The basic metric for determining value in economic institutions is money. In business assets are everything owned by a company that has value. Assets may be broadly categorized into tangible and intangible assets. The main differences between these two categories are shown in Table 14.1. The dominance of the metrics of money has emerged historically partly through the joint interests of the owners of capital and of society's institutions and partly from the broad acceptance of quantification by economists and engineers, expressing things in numbers. As the physicist Lord Kelvin stated: 'If you can't express something in numbers, you don't know anything about it.' This reduces accounts and calculations principally to the sphere of tangible assets. Intangibles are included to the extent that they may be expressed in economic numbers. However, tangible assets often make up a minor part of an organization's value. Trends in US equity markets reflect the growing importance of organizational capabilities and intangible assets. There is a consistent widening of the ratio of the *market* value of the firm (i.e. the shareholders' assessment of the firm's value) to its *book* value (the shareholders' initial investment). This ratio has more than doubled in the last ten years alone (Becker *et al.* 2001, p. 8).

The role of societal institutions in exercising their legitimate tasks of protecting and ensuring the welfare of citizens is so accepted that their impact on organizational accounting is

Table 14.1 Tangible versus intangible assets

Tangible assets	*Intangible assets*
Readily visible	Invisible
Rigorously quantified	Difficult to quantify
Part of the balance sheet	Not tracked through accounting
Investment produces known returns	Assessment based on assumptions
Can be easily duplicated	Cannot be bought or imitated
Depreciates with use	Appreciates with purposeful use
Has finite applications	Has multiple applications without value reduction
Best managed with 'scarcity' mentality	Best managed by 'abundance' mentality
Best leveraged through control	Best leverage through alignment
Can be accumulated and stored	Dynamic, short shelf life when not in use

Source: Becker *et al.* 2001, p. 7.

seldom questioned by non-professionals. However, the public reporting of value and value creation in organizations is, for the majority of organizations, steered by legal regulations and constraints. This information is simply historical. In the 1970s and probably in many organizations today the figures and statistics reported to government authorities are collected by systems designed solely for this purpose and which lack the flexibility necessary to utilize the information for the organizations' own purposes (Persson 1974).

Chapter 1 outlined the rapid changes that have taken place in the global economy at the end of the last century. These have changed the 'rules of the game' for most organizations. Naturally many organizations have difficulties in adjusting. Two-thirds of the companies listed on the inaugural *Fortune 500* list in 1954 had either vanished or were no longer big enough to make the list on its fortieth anniversary. The marked increases in the complexities and interdependencies in spheres of activity and difficulties in managing the time dimension demand organizations formulating multiple goals to a greater extent than previously. These must relate to a broader spectrum of constituencies or stakeholders than simply their owners. This is coupled to a societal and organizational interest in 'corporate social responsibility', which was the main development theme for the European Union in the year 2001. In the context of sustainability we quote:

> Without the acceptance on the part of business of a wider notion of accountability and its underpinning concepts of auditing, accounting and public reporting, the advancement of the holistic sustainable development agenda will suffer.
>
> (Sillanpää 1999, p. 537)

This acceptance will also lead to the reconsideration of practices whereby costs have been transferred from enterprises to the individual, the region and the state – in a number of ways, for instance unemployment, poor working conditions, health and stress problems for individuals and the issues of pollution and job insecurity (Zadek 1993).

In the following sections we will address the questions of what is to be measured and why, measuring for whom and the way forward to monitor and develop sustainability primarily at the individual and organizational levels.

Measurement issues

What should management be measuring? The various interpretations of the term 'efficiency' are shown in Table 14.2. The rows in the table show the classic management concepts of internal and external efficiency, and the columns describe the concepts *static* and *dynamic* efficiency. The terms static and dynamic efficiency focus attention on the kinds of performance important in different corporate environments: those regarded as stable or static and those characterized by change and turbulence. In the car industry, managers in the US and Europe have traditionally regarded the environment as static, and its typical perspective has been called 'Fordism'. In Japan, management, as distinct from the politicians, has long regarded the world as dynamic, and their typical perspective has been called 'Toyotism'.

Discussions of internal efficiency focus on the effective use of the company's resources, which is usually expressed as productivity. The health and well-being of the employees is another important aspect of internal efficiency, reflected in such concepts as 'quality of working life'.

A focus on the turbulence and mutability of the business environment means that priority must be given to internal efficiency in yet another area, namely learning and competence

Table 14.2 Performance concepts

Performance concept	Characteristics	
	Static	*Dynamic*
Internal efficiency	Rational use of resources Productivity 'Quality of working life'	Learning and competence development
External efficiency	Customer value Profitability Competitive strength	Adaptability Flexibility Innovation ability Competitive strength
Societal frameworks	Ethics, laws and regulations, best practice, societal values (e.g. environmental concerns)	

Source: Docherty 1996.

development. The usual goals of external efficiency are customer value, profitability and competitive strength. Considering the instability of the environment, learning and competence development must be supplemented by flexibility and ability to adapt and innovate. Dynamic efficiency also contributes to competitive strength.

The job of management is becoming more difficult, partly because the areas where it is important for management to formulate goals are multiplying and partly because it is necessary to create a sensitive balance among these goals. For example, if too much attention is focused on productivity the intensity of work may increase to the point that it becomes both detrimental to the health and well-being of the employees and destructive to the conditions critical for competence development and learning at work. This approach forms the basis of many multi-goal follow-up models of the 'balanced score card' type that are discussed later in the chapter.

'Societal frameworks' dictate the conditions that limit management's ability to realize its goals. These frameworks are made up of ethics, laws, regulations, 'best practice' for various sectors and the values of society. The environmental impact of production processes and products, for example, is becoming increasingly important to increasing numbers of people.

For whom are measurements being made and for what purpose? The traditional answer to these questions is management and control. It is management that defines what is to be reported, how, when and by whom. This is basically necessary for the business planning cycle with its four steps: plan, execute, obtain feedback and evaluate. The information generated is evaluated by management in its control and command functions. The steps in this cycle also constitute the steps in the learning cycle: action, experience, reflection and conceptualization (Kolb 1984). The business planning process is the basis of management's learning.

A number of key developments are taking place with the introduction of group work, not least the development and implementation of 'local planning systems', i.e. systems which are designed for the workers' self-management and learning processes. These and other systems are also important tools for management and learning *dialogues* between individuals and/or groups on different levels or in different parts of the organization or between unions and management (Bengtsson *et al.* 2000).

The sustainable work system (SWS) approach reverses much of the Taylorist model and picks up on notable and incipient changes in production and work systems, emphasizing:

- The combining of quality with quantity in production and service settings.
- The centrality and importance of human reflexivity, human learning, organizational learning (Chapters 15 and 16).
- The role and nature of dialogue and participatory communication (Chapter 16).
- The central role of subject (employee) co-ordination in the design and application of new knowledge and products (Chapter 17).

The emergence of the new stakeholders

The customers

The customers have always been with us, but until the mid-1970s they were very much taken for granted. Nevertheless the disciplines of economic psychology and marketing have invested heavily in the study of customer behaviour. A number of both national and international customer satisfaction barometers have been introduced in the last decade, for example for Europe, Germany, Norway, Sweden and the United States. The models differ slightly in the different countries but they cover such areas as customer satisfaction, customer loyalty, customer expectations, customer complaints, perceived performance (value), quality and price. Typical service branches participating in these surveys include airlines, banks, bus companies, petrol stations and railways. The impact of price on attractiveness and loyalty varies strongly among branches. Commitment and trust between service and customer are also important in the relationship and affect switching propensity (Johnson *et al.* 2001). Thus, though systematic and regular monitoring of customer satisfaction is only conducted by a few companies, there is a steady diffusion of this practice. The results are used as material for discussions in management and also for discussion by all personnel, for example in bank branch offices, to develop their treatment of customers (see Chapter 10).

The 'associates', personnel

Human resource costing and accounting

In the early 1960s personnel staff in organizations started developing behavioural accounting, human resource costing and accounting, ratio analysis, human resource audits, utility analysis and now core competence analysis to capture the financial dimension of their activities (Boudreau 1996). These aimed at facilitating more rational and productive choices in personnel management and at being a persuasive means of pursuing a dialogue with management. These covered, for example, costing the flow of personnel through the organization and different human resource interventions. With time there was a certain shift from a focus on separate HR activities to estimating the impacts, for example, of training expenditures and the percentage of personnel receiving training on company performance (Bassi *et al.* 1997) to competence stock (Eliasson and Braunerhjelm 1998) and financial results (Ulrich 1997).

An indicator of the power of a business function is 'the extent to which its role is taken for granted and is not (independently) assessed using a variety of micro-measures' (Pfeffer 1997, p. 262). Human resources accounting inadvertently highlights costs in the short term, while the value generated by the outcomes accrues in the uncertain future. However, the fundamental question in HR measurement is not 'how do we construct the best HR measures?' but 'how do we induce change through the HR measurement systems?' In this context it is critical to get a better understanding of management's responses to these HR measurement systems.

Organizational climate

From the early 1970s there has been a steady growth in the utilization of survey methods for the regular, often every other year, and systematic measurement of employees' attitudes and perceptions in organizations. The survey results are fed back to groups or departments, together with reference data, either from other groups or from previous measurements. These results are usually used as the basis for joint discussions on organizational and business development in the units concerned in the immediate future.

The generic concept of 'climate' is amorphous. Schneider (1975) proposed that climate studies should have a focus – a climate for something. Two examples will be given here. The first is from the Swedish insurance company Skandia. It has been conducting such surveys for decades with a special focus on leadership and empowerment with the aim of developing a 'high trust culture'. The area 'leadership' includes indices on trust, effectiveness and leadership profile. The area 'empowerment' covers the issues motivation, social support, decision discretion, responsibility and competence seen from a management and associate perspective.

A second example is taken from a telecommunications company in which the focus was on learning in the workplace. In this case the survey included questions on such dimensions as openness, readiness for change, tolerance of conflicts and risk taking, factors that facilitate reflection on and discussion of joint experiences. Organizational climate barometers have been used mainly in dialogue situations to arrive at common positions on necessary action.

Competences

The political and business debates on skills and competence development, life-long learning, e-learning, knowledge management and the learning organization have in fact convinced many organizations that the competence of their personnel and its organization is indeed their most effective and viable means of competition (see Chapter 10). The marketplace is not only demanding a far broader range and level of competences of personnel, it is also demanding a much more rapid rate of learning (Lundgren 1999). As companies strive to become learning organizations or knowledge intensive organizations, their investments in learning and competence development are increasing. Planned and systematic competence development is not only expected by young academics in the 'fast lane', but by all personnel even on the shop and office floor. And such developments are being reported more and more often. Co-operation between management and unions is resulting in the competence development of all factory workers in major plants, based on annual personal interviews and tests and discussions in work teams to ensure that the needs of the team are matched to those of its members (see Chapter 13). Similar developments are seen in the service sector. In the bank case presented earlier, each employee had a personal development plan for the year (see Chapter 10). In these cases the companies have a clear picture of their competence resources and their development in relation to the market.

It would seem that a feature of the current economic development is that corporate flexibility to meet market demands entails companies shedding personnel. It has been, and in many contexts still is, the established practice to simply fire personnel with no feeling of responsibility for their future. There are reports, however, of an emerging practice of 'employability' in which companies, alone or in co-operation with other organizations, retrain and outplace workers to jobs in other companies. This is understood by management and unions to be a 'win–win' situation for individual and corporate sustainability (Docherty and Ullstad 1999).

The emergence of concepts and models

The concept of capital

In an effort to redress the existing imbalance between the attention directed to the tangible assets to the neglect of intangible assets in companies, practitioners and researchers have coined new concepts regarding 'intangible capital'. Examples are intellectual, human and structural capital.

Intellectual capital is the possession of the knowledge, applied experience, organizational technology, customer relationships and professional skills that provide a company with a competitive edge in the market (Edvinsson and Malone 1997, p. 44). Intellectual capital is the sum of human capital and structural capital.

Human capital is the combined knowledge, skill, innovativeness, experience and ability of the company's individual employees to meet the task in hand. It also includes the company's values, culture and philosophy. Human capital cannot be owned by the company (Edvinsson and Malone 1997, p. 11)

Structural capital is the embodiment, empowerment and supportive infrastructure of human capital. It is the hardware, software, databases, organizational structure, patents, trademarks, goodwill and everything else of organizational capability that supports those employees' productivity. It is sometimes summarized as 'everything that is left at the workplace when the employees go home'. Structural capital also includes customer capital, relationships developed with key customers. Some models represent customer capital separately from structural and human capital. Unlike human capital, structural capital can be owned and thereby traded. See Figure 14.1

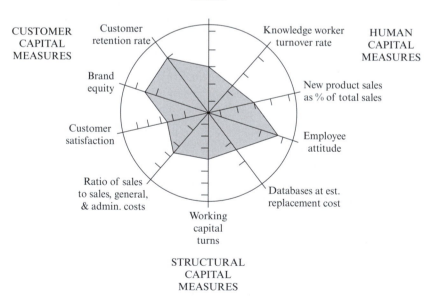

Figure 14.1 Visualizing structural capital measures.

The Skandia 1994 Intellectual Audit was an important innovation as the first of the company's biannual 'forward-looking' reports to the general public. Edvinsson calculated that for most organizations the ratio of the intellectual capital to the value of physical and financial capital is between 5:1 and 16:1 (in Stewart 1997, p. 63).

Sveiby (1997) defines three types of intangible asset: employee competence, internal structure and external structure. Employee competence involves the capacity to act in a wide variety of situations to create both tangible and intangible assets. Internal structure includes patents, concepts, models and computer and administrative systems. These are created by the employees and are generally owned by the organizations. The external structure includes the relationships with customers and suppliers. It also encompasses brand names, trademarks and the company's reputation or image. Investments in external structure cannot be made with the same degree of confidence as investments in internal structure (Sveiby 1997, pp. 10–11). Sveiby defines indicators in these three areas with respect to their stability, efficiency and their growth and renewal.

Multidimensional models

Balanced score cards (BSC) include financial and non-financial elements. The original model presented by Kaplan and Norton (1996) had four basic dimensions: financial, customers, processes and renewal and development. They are based on the strategic plan and are a management tool. Two early and pedagogic examples based on the Harvard researchers' model are Skandia (1995) and DOW chemicals (Edvinsson and Malone 1997, pp. 139–45). Balanced score cards are primarily designed for internal management processes related to strategic management. Human resources BSC are not widespread, though one prominent example of their use is in professional football clubs. It is difficult for BSC models to satisfy all legal accounting criteria regarding the assets declaration in the balance sheet.

Skandia AFS produced a 'navigator' model, which incorporated about thirty indicators, covering five main areas: a *financial* focus (e.g. premium income, result of operations); a *customer* focus (telephone accessibility, policies without surrender); a *process* focus (processing time, applications without error); a *human* focus (empowerment index); and a *development/renewal* focus (R&D expense/administrative expense). Human focus, process focus and customer focus are equivalent to Sveiby's three forms of intangible asset. Each focus area has its key indicators (Sveiby 1997, pp. 186–90)

For use in enterprises Kaplan and Norton suggest that each of these main categories are broken down further in the assessment procedure. The specification of the sub-categories depends upon the precise goals set by the organization considering the circumstances they face. Even though these can be detailed they are still nominalistic and rarely stray into the more difficult intangible areas of constitution of quality, the form and process of learning, the impact of dialogue and participation and the organization and application of creativity. Instead the new measurements and their subsequent communication become a critical strategic point in an improvement process in relation to long-term output targets. Sveiby (1997) has developed the 'intangible assets monitor' (IAM). He notes the similarities between the two theories of BSC and IAM. However, there are also some important theoretical differences. The IAM model:

- is based on the notion that people are an organization's only added-value creators;
- assumes a set of three intangible assets, and that we should try and find metrics indicating the growth, renewal, efficiency and stability of these assets;
- goes to the core of organizations by asking 'what constitutes a firm?', something the BSC

fails to do. Kaplan and Norton regard the firm as given by its strategy and simply want managers to take a more 'balanced view'.

The French researchers Bourguigon *et al.* (2001) point out that French companies have no need of BSC as support for the management hierarchy and refer to an equivalent French model of fifty years' standing, *tableau de bord*. This differs from BSC in that it does not couple rewards to performance measurement, nor is it confined to metrics but includes qualitative descriptions, and its reference points are reference norms rather than standards. Its main use is to support learning through dialogue and discourse. The *tableau de bord* has been criticized from a theoretical standpoint as being more complicated to use than BSC, and as being solely internally oriented having no focus on external benchmarks. It is regarded as being 'too local' and not an interactive management process.

Ongoing developments

Thus the past twenty years have seen considerable efforts and progress in developing and providing regular and systematic feedback on all vital processes and outcomes in organizations. There are good examples of how this feedback may be tailored to the prioritized needs of an organization's different stakeholders. This feedback has not simply been used for management control but has also been used for joint learning and planning through dialogue. However, there are still many issues that require further effort. The complexity and subtlety of processes, outcomes and the interactions defy simple reduction and quantification. Some of the issues that are broached here are:

- experiential learning, tacit knowledge and communities of practice;
- industrial relations, partnership and tacit co-operation among the social partners;
- work organization;
- quality;
- creativity, research and development;
- culture, values and their impacts; and
- corporate social responsibility.

Experiential learning, tacit knowledge and communities of practice

Stahl *et al.* (1993) offer a catalogue of twenty-one normative conditions for the learning organization. All of these in one way or another discuss the enablement of the individual, the creation of the necessary context for reflexivity, for dialogue and participation. Sattelberger (1991) in particular makes this point, as the overall objective of learning is to create the capacity for survival in turbulent conditions by 'transforming intentionally the ability of the organization to face the future successfully'. Sattelberger (1991, p. 130) distinguishes three immediate learning objectives connected to sustainability:

- Gaining organizational responsiveness to the needs of all the stakeholders.
- Establishing the ability to apprehend and apply valid knowledge about oneself, the context and the wider social environment.
- Achieving competence, defined as the ability to act with the aim of satisfying given and perceived needs.

These three objectives illustrate clearly the difficulty of applying nominalistic measurement indicators of knowledge in use and notions of competence when we are talking about a process of deconstructing views of reality, meaning creating processes, appropriations embedded in changing contexts.

In addition current learning research is deeply involved in the study of adult learning in the workplace regarding such topics as tacit knowledge at the individual and group level in communities of practice, and essential processes for the level of performance in organizations.

Industrial relations, partnership and tacit co-operation among the social partners

There is a body of work that seeks to pin down the relationship between partnership/participation and performance by using available industrial relations (IR) data. Fernie and Metcalf (1995) sought to test the relationship between employee participation and positive organizational outcomes. They conducted a review of previous research and extensive workplace data. They used a number of performance measures including relative productivity growth, changes in employment levels and IR climate. Their results show that employee involvement is positively related to relative productivity and employment increases.

Sako (1995) conducted a large-scale survey in car component plants across Europe on the relation between employee participation and product quality. She focused on different combinations of (a) direct participation at the workplace and (b) representational participation in policy bodies. The results are again positive in companies where a range of employee participation is present. The quality defect rate was lowest in firms that had both quality circle-style groups *and* representational participation and was appreciably worse in low participation plants.

The partnership developments at the company level are a clear feature of management–union developments in countries such as The Netherlands, Sweden and the United Kingdom. These have covered such issues as continuous improvement, organizational and product development, and employability and competence development. These are basically win–win solutions for both the social partners in terms of sustainability.

Work organization

There is growing evidence that organizational success is correlated to the combination of 'high performance' works designs and 'high performance' HR practices (Buchanan and McCalman 1989; Lawler 1992). These organizations rely upon employee self-management and participatory management regimes that transcend representation and become active in the workplace and work tasks. They devolve decision-making to groups or operators, develop routes for individual development and organizational learning and change its human resource policies in order to sustain commitment and active participation. The more advanced developments entail grouping numbers of workers into what are, in practice, small companies that may perform all business functions. The learning and work processes in these contexts are still poorly understood.

Quality

In many respects the interest in total quality management (TQM) did try to reinstate quality on a different footing where quality was woven into the process of production rather than being a separate area. It also linked with continuous improvement mechanisms that mobilize the tacit and acquired knowledge of workers. Once again, however, the issue of measurement of quality came to be dominated by the tools, statistical packages and rule-based systems for more general application. However, there are institutional demands for a metric of quality in many commercial transactions regarding the physical characteristics and outcomes of products and services, for example as covered by product liability legislation.

Creativity, research and development (R&D)

The knowledge creation processes in R&D activities are also very poorly understood. The efforts to measure and evaluate these activities have to date mainly focused on the software development industry, using sophisticated mathematical models including key variables in individual projects (Moore 1999).

Culture, values and their impacts

In a sustainability context, values are very important in determining the decisions taken by management. Evidence shows that giving priority to social goals, e.g. concerning personnel, is quite compatible with good company performance, i.e. gives win–win situations. Thus Collins and Porras (1994) found that a key to success for eighteen US corporations over a hundred years in business was their strong commitment to developing people and an unfailing ability to capture and share knowledge. They also outperformed the US stock markets by a factor of 70. Similarly, Kotter and Heskett (1992) compared the performance of businesses with a 'shareholder first' philosophy with others with a balanced stakeholder policy over an eleven year period. The growth of the 'balanced' group surpassed the former by a factor of 4 for sales and a factor of 8 for employment growth. A key issue here is to study the factors influencing management's reluctance to adopt a more balanced strategy.

Corporate social responsibility: social auditing

Corporate social responsibility has economic, social and environmental dimensions. Social and economic justice are needed if sustainable development is to be achieved in any of the dimensions. The accelerated fragmentation of social cohesion in the industrialized world where a 'culture of contentment' for some means dispossession and depression for many must be addressed (Galbraith 1992).

There are clear signs of a convergence of standards and the emergence of consensus regarding what constitutes 'good practice'. Key principles for social audits have been listed, namely completeness, comparability, inclusivity, regularity and evolution, embeddedness, disclosure, external verification and continuous improvement (Gonella *et al.*1998 in Sillanpää 1999).

Gray *et al.* (1995) surveyed shareholders' demand for information and found that shareholders feel it more important to stop pollution and improve product safety than to pay higher dividends. Epstein and Freedman (1994) found similar results in that shareholders requested more information about product safety and quality, environmental activities, ethics, employee relations and community involvement.

Shifts in perspective for progress

The 'sustainability' concept remains abstract and difficult to materialize. Some observers predict that it will remain fuzzy, elusive, contestable and controversial for some time to come:

Sustainability and sustainable development remain elusive concepts. They have been variously referred to as 'vision expression', 'value change', 'moral development' or 'transformational process' (Gladwin *et al.* 1995).

In our current turbulent and changing work organization environment a one-dimensional approach is insufficient and possibly damaging. The key issues for organizational performance in both manufacturing and services industries are diverging from simple Taylorist strategies. The dominant and active elements in that paradigm had to do with control, fragmentation, routinization, stability and replicability of performance. Contrast this with core issues now dominating work organizational discussions – creativity, commitment, reflexivity, learning, chaos, quality and dialogue. When talking about what is active in the value-creating process now it is the nature of design processes, forms of dialogue and the input of the subject that are at the centre of the discussion: how to apply reflexivity in design processes, how to maximize competence and learning, how to organize inter-subjectivity whether it be in R&D, project groups or in production teams, how to minimize uncertainty by increasing the subject's or group's adaptive response. In general this calls for perspective shifts that, on a number of dimensions, involve abandoning a simple narrow perspective for a broader more complex one (Table 14.3).

Table 14.3 Perspective shifts for the evaluation of sustainable work systems

Perspective shifts	
From	*To*
A choice of 'either, or'	A choice of 'both, and'
Simple jobs, complex organizations	Complex jobs, integrated organizations
Evaluation of simply a financial dimension	An holistic, multidimensional evaluation
A shareholder perspective	Perspectives of all stakeholders and constituencies
Only outcome-oriented	Both outcome- and process-oriented
Only a management function	Management, dialogue, partnership and learning functions
Only focusing on the organization	Focusing on the organization and its context
Including only static effectiveness	Including static and dynamic effectiveness

In the debates initiated by the environmental movement the issue of appropriate indicators for organizational performance has often been discussed. MacGillivary and Zadek (1995) recognize the reductive exercise inherent in most measurement processes but also accept the need for them in the absence of other ways of representing complex information. However, they do see the need for new indicators, echoing J.K. Galbraith's warning that 'if it is not counted it tends not to be noticed'. (We would prefer the formulation 'that which is not explicitly addressed tends to be forgotten'.) The act of measurement they see as having three elements – simplification, quantification and communication – and all of them are tied to quantitative approaches. However, a more sophisticated designation of stakeholders and an extended notion of corporate impact does not get to the methodological root of the problem about how we account for internal processes underpinning sustainability and the impact of intangibles on short- and long-term corporate performance.

The approach necessary for sustainability and ethical business tends to widen out the areas for scrutiny. Social auditing is a clear step in this direction (Zadek 1993, 2001). At the heart of this is the idea of a stakeholder dialogue that precludes the privileging of any one interest above the rest. To date the social and ethical accounting approach has concentrated upon improving company reporting by incorporating social, environmental and employee reports in their annual reports. Hence corporate social responsibility now figures large on the agenda of some major companies.

The positivistic approach seeks to isolate variables, measure a given effect and offer a quantitative result in relation to a single outcome. Organizational reality, however, is an arena of human activity, of commitment, expectation and mutual interdependence. Hence there is need for both a structured system of measurement together with a perspective that values quantitative and qualitative aspects, explicit and tacit skills. The latter areas involve a host of crucial processes and policies in the human resource and organizational governance areas. Such processes or management regimes of co-operation have powerful effects on a range of matters that can be of enormous long-term importance to organization outcomes.

The cumulative evidence indicates that adopting a partnership or participative orientation with its associated shift from short-term thinking and the reification of the bottom line can be decisive. The reordering of the corporate culture, psychological contract or social/governance approach towards mutuality and co-operation is a vital first step towards greater 'holistic efficiency'. Following this is the need to align and have consistency of human resource policies as the partial introduction of policies can lead to internal tensions and contradictions. Hence the introduction of a partnership forum or agreement in itself does not necessarily have an effect if a range of other and supportive policies are left unchanged, for instance the matter of employment security, employee development, rewards, appraisal and so on.

Following directly on from this, the work organizational approach emphasizing the role of dialogue is not restricted to strategic matters or issues for representational discussion but has to be *ingrained* within decision-making structures across the organization, in the strategic, planning, operational and implementation phases. The range of factors that affect performance as identified in the work organization approaches illustrates the opportunity and scope for dialogue, mutuality and partnership.

What this chapter has shown is a range of approaches that collectively point to the need for a perspective shift across the board when evaluating 'efficiency'. The BSC and IAM approaches, whilst still framed within a nominalistic context, are trying to extend the range of active factors. The social audit approach builds upon that with its notions of extended stakeholding, scrutiny and environmental context. But it is when we look at the learning organization concept that we see the sharpest debate. The learning organization cannot be viewed as a prescriptive model with a checklist of defined policies. Rather it can be seen as an emancipatory concept enabling organizations to struggle with the increasingly rapid nature of change and its consequences. In this body of thought, more humanistic and people-centred values emerge, which view humans as the source of value creation in organizations (Cressey and Kelleher 2002).

The overall conclusions reached are that we need to shift from a simple evaluatory perspective that focuses narrowly on goals and outcomes to one that also concentrates on processes. The approach of sustainability lies more firmly rooted in this humanist tradition where reflexivity is an active element in organizational renewal. To approach performance with a reconstituted set of standards for universal applicability is wrong. But the chapter does offer a starting point to review which factors need consideration and what perspective shift this implies within the organization. It is the start of a long road rather than its finish.

References

Bassi, L., Benson, G., van Buren, M. and Bugarin, A. (1997) *Human Performance Practices Report*, New York: American Society for Training and Development.

Becker, B.E., Huselid, M.A. and Ulrich, D. (2001) *The HR Scorecard. Linking People, Strategy and Performance*, Cambridge, MA: Harvard Business School Press.

Bengtsson, L., Lind, J. and Samuelson, L.A. (2000) *Styrning av team och processer. Teoretiska perspektiv och fall-studier* (Managing Teams and Processes), Stockholm: EFI vid Handelshögskolan i Stockholm.

Boudreau, J. (1996) 'The motivational impact of utility analysis and HR measurement', *Journal of Human Resource Costing and Accounting*, 1, 2, 73–84.

Bourguigon, A., Malleret, V. and Nørreklit, H. (2001) *American Management Theory and French Acts of Resistance*, Barcelona: EURAM Inaugural Conference, April 19–21.

Buchanan, D. and McCalman, J. (1989) *High Performance Work Systems. The Digital Experience*, London: Routledge.

Cable, J. and Fitzroy, F. (1979) 'Co-operation and productivity. Some evidence from West German experience', University of Warwick Economic Research Paper no. 153, University of Warwick, Coventry.

Collins, J.C. and Porras, J.I. (1994) *Built to Last. Successful Habits of Visionary Companies*, London: Century/Random House.

Cressey, P. and Kelleher, M. (2002) 'The conundrum of the learning organisation. Instrumental and emancipatory theories of learning?' in B. Nyhan, P. Cressey, M. Kelleher and R. Poell (eds) *Learning Organisations. European Perspectives, Theories and Practices*, Thessaloniki: CEDEFOP.

Docherty, P. (1996) *Läroriket. Vägar och vägval i den lärande organisationen* (The World of Learning. Ways and Crossroads in the Learning Organisation). Stockholm: Arbetslivsinstitutet.

Docherty, P. and Ullstad, C. (1999) 'Partnership for employability. A win–win strategy.' Paper to the Human Development and Productivity Conference, Manchester University, UK, July.

Eccles, R. and Mavrinac, S. (1995) 'Improving the Corporate Disclosure Process', *Sloan Management Review*, 36, 4, 11–25.

Edvinsson, L. and Malone, M.S. (1997) *Intellectual Capital*, New York: Harper Business.

Eijnatten, F.M. van (1993) *The Paradigm that Changed the Work Place*, Assen: Van Gorcum.

Eliasson, G. and Braunerhjelm, P. (1998) 'Intangible, human-embodied capital and firm performance', in G. Eliasson and J. Green (eds) *The Microfoundations of Economic Growth*, Ann Arbor: University of Michigan Press.

Epstein, M.J. and Freedman, M. (1994) 'Social disclosure and the individual investor', *Accounting, Auditing and Accountability Journal*, 7, 4, 94–109.

Fernie, S. and Metcalf, D. (1995) 'Participation, contingent pay, representation and workplace performance. Evidence from Great Britain', *British Journal of Industrial Relations*, 33, 3, 379–415.

Galbraith, J.K. (1992) *The Culture of Contentment*, London: Sinclair-Stevenson.

Gladwin, T.N., Kennelly, J.J. and Krause, T.S. (1995) 'Shifting paradigms for sustainable development. Implications for management theory and research', *Academy of Management Review*, 20, 4.

Gonella, C., Pilling, A. and Zadek, S. (1998) *Making Values Count. Contemporary Experience in Social and Ethical Accounting*, London: Association of Chartered Certified Accountants/The New Economic Foundation Research Report 57.

Gray, R., Kouhy, R. and Lavers, S. (1995) 'Corporate Social and environmental reporting. A review of the literature and a longitudinal study of UK disclosure', *Accounting, Auditing and Accountability Journal*, 8, 2, 47–77.

Hackston, D. and Milne, M.J. (1996) 'Some determinants of social and environmental disclosures in New Zealand companies', *Accounting, Auditing and Accountability Journal*, 9, 1, 77–108.

Johnson, M.D., Gustafsson, A., Andreassen, T.W., Lervik, L. and Cha, J. (2001) 'The evolution and future of national customer satisfaction index models', *Journal of Economic Psychology*, 22, 217–45.

Kaplan, R.S. and Norton, D.P. (1996) *The Balanced Scorecard. Translating Strategy into Action*, Boston: Harvard Business School Press.

Kolb, D.A. (1984) *Experiential Learning. Experience as the Source of Learning and Development*, Englewood Cliffs, NJ: Prentice-Hall.

Kotter, J. and Heskett, J. (1992) *Corporate Culture and Performance*, New York: Free Press.

Lawler, E.E. (1992) *The Ultimate Advantage. Creating the High Involvement Organisation*, San Francisco: Jossey-Bass.

Lundgren, K. (1999) 'Kortare lärotider och ett nytt lärandesystem' (Shorter learning time and a new learning system), *Arbetsmarknad Arbetsliv*, 5, 4, 287–302.

MacGillivary, A. and Zadek, S. (1995) *Accounting for Change. Indicators for Sustainable Development*, London: New Economics Foundation.

Marchington, M., Goodman, J., Wilkinson, A. and Ackers, P. (1992) *New Developments in Employee Involvement*, Sheffield: British Employment Department, Research Series no. 2, May.

Moore, C.R. (1999) 'Performance measures for knowledge management', in J. Liebowitz (ed.) *Knowledge Management Handbook*, Boca Raton, FA: CRC Press, pp. 6.1–6.29.

Persson, S. (1974) *Apropå myndigheternas uppgiftskrav*, Stockholm: Svenska Arbetsgivareföreningen (Talking about the Authorities' Demands for Information).

Pfeffer, J. (1997) 'Pitfalls on the road to measurement. The dangerous liaison of human resources with the ideas of accounting and finance', *Human Resource Management*, 36, 3, 357–65.

Sako, M. (1998) 'The nature and impact of the employee's voice in the European car components industry', *Human Resource Management* 8, 2.

Sattelberger, T. (1991) (ed.) *The Learning Organisation*, Wiesbaden: Gabler.

Schneider, B. (1975) 'Organizational climates. An essay', *Personnel Psychology*, 28, 447–79.

Sillanpää, M. (1999) 'Taking the social dimension seriously', in M. Bennett and P. James (eds) *Sustainable Measures. Evaluation and Reporting of Environmental and Social Performance*, Sheffield: Greenleaf Publishing, pp. 535–68.

Skandia (1995) *Value Creating Processes*. Supplement to 1995 Skandia Annual Report.

Stahl, T., Nyhan, B. and D'Aloja, P. (1993) *The Learning Organisation. A Vision for Human Resource Development*, Brussels: European Interuniversity Press.

Stewart, T.A. (1997) *Intellectual Capital. The New Wealth of Organisations*, New York: Doubleday/Currency.

Sveiby, K.E. (1997) *The New Organizational Wealth. Managing and Measuring Knowledge-based Assets*, San Francisco: Berrett-Koehler.

Ulrich, D. (1997) 'Measuring human resources. An overview of practice and a prescription for results', *Human Resource Management*, 36, 3, 303–20.

Zadek, S. (1993) *An Economics of Utopia*, London: Avebury.

Zadek, S. (2001) *The Civil Corporation. The New Economy of Corporate Citizenship*, London: Earthscan Publications.

Zadek, S. and Evans, R. (eds) (1993) *Auditing the Market. A Practical Approach to Social Auditing*, Gateshead: Traidcraft/New Economics Foundation.

Internet source: www.sveiby.com.au/IntangAss/MeasureIntangibleAssets

15 A reflexive methodology of intervention

Manfred F. Moldaschl and Peter Brödner

Introduction

Previous chapters in this book have explored new ways to understand work, organization and reorganization in terms of sustainability. Criteria to evaluate the sustainability of work systems were proposed, some company specific illustrations were provided and some principles that should characterize what we call sustainable work systems were identified and discussed. A possible next logical question to address is how SWS can be realized in practice, that is, how can we *implement* those principles? Some might argue that in the context of sustainability this might be the wrong question to address. A reflexive-based perspective requires 'letting go' of the idea that work and organizational structures can be comprehensively designed and total systems can be implemented as initially planned.

At the most generic level, intervention is viewed as a purposeful and comprehensive attempt to change the status quo of an organization (Cummings and Worely 2000). Thus, from a design perspective intervention is the process of creating artefacts by intentionally and purposefully changing a given environment. This definition implies that we posit a distinction between making technical artefacts or modifying things, i.e. design, and attempts to change social relations or systems, i.e. intervention.

Too often the transfer of such approaches to the living and the social has nurtured the belief in universal regularities, and, where failing, just the opposite belief, that purposeful intervention in social systems is impossible. Of course, organizational structures and procedures can be designed, in the sense of 'planned', but this should be strictly distinguished from the real process, from organizational change, and the activities of external experts involved. What can be expected from a reflexive methodology of intervention and designing artefacts will be described in the next section of this chapter. There, our second main thesis will be elaborated, namely that the reflexive approach provides an alternative beyond, not between, the two dominating paradigms of organizational change. In the third and fourth parts of this chapter we will sketch some heuristic principles of how a reflexive methodology could work in practice.

Intervention: expertocracy versus proceduralism

The discussion about problems and adequate forms of intervention by social scientists is presently dominated by two paradigms. The first is the model of knowledge transfer from science into practice. The roles of subject and object of intervention and research are well defined, with the researcher or consultant as the subject, and the organization members as the object of change, even if their participation is allowed or desired. We call this model expert-centred or prescriptive, or 'expertocratic'. It starts from the assumption that scientific knowledge is superior to the practitioner's knowledge, and allows the deduction of unambiguous, empirically provable design criteria. The task of the scientist – or the scientifically legitimated practitioner – is conceptualized as analysing the fit between external requirements and internal conditions, deducing a diagnosis, and recommending an optimal solution and a redesign concept. The repertoire of methods for change is underdeveloped because this approach assumes that the intended effects will be achieved when the recommendations are detailed enough and their application is precisely controlled.

The second model dispenses with the idea of an optimal solution, or generally with the idea of clear causalities between an external context and requirements for organizational solutions. Instead, it is assumed that the relevant knowledge is already present in the organization, and it only has to be mobilized by stimulating and moderating organizational communication. In this view, organizations and groups should be supported only in processes of self-organization by communicative procedures. There is no claim of superior expert knowledge, except the communicative aspects. Thus, we could call the interventionists of this model procedural experts, and the paradigm proceduralistic or discursive, because it restricts itself to procedural methods, and claims to refrain from inducing external goals, models, norms and values. The social scientist or consultant understands himself as a mediator of self-change, as a communicator who helps people to develop a common view on an organizational problem, and to achieve a consensual definition of a goal.

This second paradigm can be found as represented in the consulting process of Schein (1969) and the 'transformative' branch of organizational development (French and Bell 1998), or in the systemic intervention approach, based on the new (constructivist) systems theory of Luhmann (1990) and Willke (1999). Other approaches where we can find some of these ideas are in the field of action research. For example, Whyte's (1992) concept of participatory action research, Gustavsen's (1992) concept of democratic dialogue, and Copperrider and Srivastva's (1987) concept of appreciative inquiry. The egalitarian, emancipatory and democratic orientations of these approaches seem to have shortcomings – due to the fact that organizational reality is not always democratic, or free from domination and ideology.

Of course, we have neglected many relevant differences between the approaches within the two paradigms, as well as intermediate expressions. What we find in practice are just accentuations of these approaches, mixed up more or less with elements of the other paradigm. This should be kept in mind when we discuss the different approaches in 'ideal-types' mode. Furthermore, we distinguish between two general types of intervention, an analytical and conceptual type on the one hand, and a processual and communicative one on the other, classically called 'change management'. See Table 15.1.

Inherent problems of both approaches

The prescriptive or *expertocratic* paradigm is based upon an understanding in which organizational change is mainly seen as a socio-technical problem solving task (instrumental rationality). It ignores the role of actor strategies, subsumes individual or group interests under a virtual interest of the organization (or under a one-best-way of organization design which is represented by the expert), overlooks social dynamics, and takes problems as givens. But: 'In real-world practice, problems do not present themselves as givens. They must be constructed from the materials of problematic situations which are puzzling, troubling, and uncertain' (Schön 1983, p. 40). Addressing the same issue, Habermas discusses the 'double

Table 15.1 Paradigms and types of organizational intervention

	(1) Expert-driven approach *Functionalism*	*(2) Procedural approach* *Participationism*
Concept of intervention	*Goals and tools* • Application of best practice model • Deductive process • Work design criteria • Participation (casually) as means	• No preconceived solution • Open process • Process design criteria • Participation as (the only legitimate) goal
Methods of change management	*Phases and cycles* • Analysis, diagnosis • Deduction of concept • Implementation, execution • Success control	• Orientation • Establishing and developing groups • Moderation, conflict management • Iterative evaluation

hermeneutics' of social sciences and argues that they have to deal with socially constructed facts, and they have to reconstruct these constructions. The 'espoused theory' of social scientists and their 'theory-in-use' (in the sense of Argyris and Schön 1978) often show the same big discrepancy in scientific practice as we observe in the practice of other practitioners.

The problems in the purely discursive or *procedural* approaches are not smaller. A first main problem is that they normally pay a high price for accepting a plurality of perspectives: power and domination in the actor relations are weakly addressed or ignored. Neither the relation between the practitioners nor the relation between scientists and practitioners is free of unequal power. Second, in exchange for avoiding the normative problems of an expert-centred approach they must accept a responsibility problem. If the intervention does not introduce 'external' values, norms, models and concepts, the outcome of a change process is always the responsibility of the organization members, never that of the scientific or commercial consultants. As we know from empirical studies, a 'criteria-free' application of the participation principles creates possible risks for the employees. They might participate in decisions, perhaps, without being able to consider the preconditions, consequences and alternatives. Therefore, participation assessment is needed.

Furthermore it has to be questioned whether it is possible to interact as a change agent without introducing any values, any preconceived notions of what a good society looks like, or what people's needs are. A fourth concern is related to the previously mentioned problem of local theories or, more accurately, of local 'theories in use'. Why, if all relevant knowledge is present in the organization, should there be a need for intervention? And how does a 'procedural intervention' deal with the problem of implicit theories? Because all experience is embedded, the ability to imagine alternatives to daily practices is always limited. Thus, proceduralism is even less adequate in a knowledge society, where knowledge is so separated and cultures of practice are so segmented. The change agent needs content knowledge that is about different applicable forms of group work and their preconditions, about proved measures and criteria.

Reflexivity and reflexive action

This chapter proposes an alternative to the normative and procedural paradigms. The alternative is inspired by anti-rationalistic epistemological positions, which understand science as one practice among others and practice as situated action. When we apply this kind of thinking to a reflexive methodology of intervention, we must leap over the necessary steps of mediation. Basically, we understand such a methodology as an alternative beyond, not between, the expertocratic and the procedural paradigms of interventions.

What does reflexivity mean?

Reflexivity as a concept within human and social sciences has been developed in a variety of disciplines: anthropology (e.g. Marous 1994), sociology (e.g. Holland 1977; Giddens 1984), political theory (e.g. Landau 1972), family therapy (e.g. Tomm 1987), personal psychology (e.g. Kelly 1955), and organization and management theorists (e.g. Willmott 1993; Hardy, Phillips and Clegg 2001), to mention a few. As a consequence, we face a large variety of meanings in the definition and the use of the term. The orientations can be reduced to two general clusters of meaning. The first has no recourse to mental categories, as in the mathematical definition of recursivity in fractal geometry, which describes the application of operations or transformations on themselves. In his socio-historical theory about self-modernizing modernization (reflexive modernization), Ulrich Beck (1994) uses the category mainly in this sense of a systematic reflection process based in a general systems theory perspective.

The second is based on categories of reflection and reason, with a consciousness that presupposes the division of object and subject. In the most simple case, reflexivity means nothing more than 'thoughtfulness', 'pensiveness' or reflectiveness, a cognitive state or style. This use is common for instance in psychology. Here, reflectiveness is frequently conceptualized as the semantic differential to impulsivity (Baron 1985). Other authors claim self-reflexivity as a characteristic of the human species, e.g. Lefebvre (1992, p. 1): 'the subject possesses a specific quality which we call reflexivity: he has an image of the self, which, in turn, also has an image of the self.' West (1996) defines reflexivity as a continuous questioning of group tasks, co-operative rules, etc. Referring to the tradition of enlightenment, Giddens puts forth a societal criterion: justification. In this version, the necessity to justify each action arises from social embeddedness and the existence of alternative options. These definitions can be subsumed under the subjects' or actors' perspective.

From the organizational studies perspective, Alvesson and Sköldberg (2000, p. 5f.) identify two 'basic characteristics': first, the assumption that all 'empirical data are results of interpretation' and, second, reflexive thinking 'turns attention "inwards" towards the person of the researcher'. Ray Holland (1999) proposes a distinction between types or understandings of reflexivity. His reflexivity one encompasses Alvesson and Sköldberg's first characteristic: the beliefs of persons investigated by a scientist's beliefs (referring to George Kelly's theory of personal constructs). To be reflexive means in this case to be aware of the fact. What he calls reflexivity two finds its initial example in Alvin Gouldner's concept of a reflexive sociology, which claims to apply sociological analysis to ourselves, our actions, beliefs and ideologies.

It seems useful, therefore, to explicitly put forward a third definition. Here, the use of the word reflexivity only makes sense if it makes a difference to recursiveness and reflectiveness individually – and integrates them as necessary complements of one another. As a term that integrates a system perspective and a subject perspective, reflexivity means an insight of actors into their social or contextual embeddedness and of the difference between strategic action and systemic results. From there, self-reflexivity seems to be a tautological term because the actor is, in a sense, always part of the system. As a consequence, research has to apply theories about social reality on itself – very important for a conception of reflexive intervention. If an action researcher wants to intervene in a social system, being reflexive means that she is aware that she can neither be value-free nor control the effects of her intervention; she knows that her own categories, concepts, ideas and interpretations are always situated; her activity is based on numerous undiscovered conditions; her intervention will cause 'side effects'; and finally, she would replace substantialist categories by a relational thinking (see Chapter 5).

Reflexive design of technology and working conditions

The acting person, normally in co-operation with others, where a reflective generation of meaning is mutually confirmed, partly shared or slightly changed, creates technical means and mental constructs. Concepts enable us to 'act' within our minds, and they can be objectified as symbols (language) or tools (technology). Thus, formation of symbols and construction of tools are closely related characteristics of human activity that are both rooted in mental concept formation and reflection. In this way, technical artefacts emerge as objectified explicit knowledge about human work. Technology, thus, is a constant concomitant of work, out of which it emerges through reflection and objectification of knowledge and that, in turn, is in itself changed through appropriation (Brödner 1997).

Consequently, usefulness and usability of technical artefacts are determined by appropriate form, i.e. by adapting their forms and functions to the acting context as well as by satisfying their action requirements. Since technical artefacts are often derived from abstract, de-contextualized knowledge, they have to be interpreted and re-contextualized. As a consequence, their use-value is constituted in application, which is open for diverse use. Users learn to express or to articulate their action plans in the technical language of the artefacts' forms and functions and to internalize them as new action patterns. The effective and efficient use of technical artefacts requires that they are designed appropriately for the tasks at hand, and that the users learn to use them for accomplishing the tasks (see Figure 15.1).

According to this dialectic of form and process, the interaction with technical artefacts to accomplish a given task can be understood as a process of social construction of reality. Consequently, design is the activity of conceptualizing and determining new, unknown forms and functionality that satisfy a given set of requirements based on known cause-and-effect

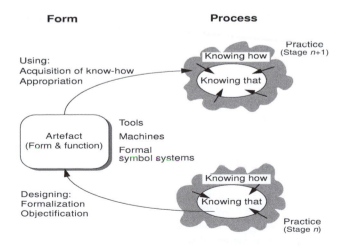

Figure 15.1 The spiral of competence development through practice.

relationships. Design of work and technology is a process by which artefacts are created. By their very nature, the dynamics among the artefacts change the course of acting or the working process they are designed for. Thus, design is viewed as inherently a reflexive concept (see Chapter 17).

Reasons for a reflexive design

Human acting is basically intentional and goal-oriented. Acting then always has a range of intended and unintended effects that, simultaneously, form new conditions for further acting. If the effects of acting correspond to a person's intentions or expectations, the internalized action schemes will be confirmed and stabilized. In this way, they are a basis for a continuous flow of acting, which is taken for granted. This process of fluent acting may be disturbed, however, if the used flow of activity produces surprising or unexpected effects, if things in acting attract attention rather than being ready at hand; in short, if there is irritation about the difference between anticipated and actual results of acting. This irritation or 'breakdown' gives rise to reflection as a different, a conscious, mode of acting. Reflection takes into account and reviews given conditions and means of acting as well as the expectations linked to it. It creates consciousness about acting ('reflection-in-action', Schön 1983).

These basic considerations on human acting and design have consequences for the design of sustainable work systems. Design inevitably has a number of unperceived conditions and unintended effects. Explicit knowledge used in design is limited and incomplete in principle. Designers are neither aware of all conditions for the design process, nor do they know all of the cause–effect relationships of the artefacts they create. Moreover, the nature of the design process inevitably produces unexpected side effects. This also applies to the design of work and technology as well as to organizational interventions for achieving sustainable work systems.

In accordance with these considerations, the methodology of reflexive design and intervention in organizational change calls for 'reflexive loops' as procedural building-stones. The procedure normally starts with a collective reflection of the present situation that the organization is in, and an agreement on necessary goals and requirements for further business. This shared strategy provides the actors with the orientation needed to derive first tentative steps of design and intervention for change that can then be made subject to reflection in recurring reflexive loops. After some time, provided that enough room is left for collective learning, shared views and action schemes will emerge that make sense of the new forms of work envisaged and that establish a new collective practice in the organization. This can be viewed as a modified orientation to 'organizational learning' (Argyris and Schön 1978; see Chapters 16 and 17).

Reflexive intervention for sustainable change – some heuristics

The idea that the creation of technical artefacts and new operating procedures is a negotiation of commitments between working persons – as we define reflexive design – meets with our understanding of intervention as a social medium for renegotiation and self-reflection of organization members and external experts (e.g. action researchers, consultants). The heuristics for the reflexive methodology of organizational intervention that we are proposing can be used to observe one's own practice as well as the intervention practices of others. Since we reject the idea that social systems can be 'designed' through a single intentionality, however powerful, we do not call them 'principles' or 'design principles'. Heuristics, instead, are more open to and dependent on a reflective use; they provide an idea, an orientation or a general path. They have nothing to do with the popular lists of necessary competences of change agents. These epistemological heuristics could be presented in a more generalized mode, or more operationalized as descriptions of interventional roles and methods. We prefer the first mode, in order to stimulate the reader's ideas of how to make use of them in his or her own interventional practice.

1   *Legitimacy (and) power of an intervention.* In the expertocratic as well as in the procedural paradigm, we identified as a weakness the lack of consideration of the role of power, which has a central place in our approach. The first question we have to answer is: who is legitimated to 'design' work? And the second: what gives anyone the legitimacy to intervene? Expert-centred approaches do not worry much about these questions since management is normally the customer. Consultants adhering to democratically inspired procedural approaches tend(ed) to side with the workers regardless of the customer. We assume that it is necessary to think in two categories of contract: a formal one, constituting a legal and an economic commitment, and a social one, constituting trust relations and mutual commitment between the external expert and each social group he or she works with. The latter is difficult to establish since it requires evaluating whether and what the 'objects' of change would like to change. That the relation between these contracts can be conflictual or contradictory is obvious, and will be addressed below, along with the question of which of our unquestioned and unconditioned values are adequate and legitimate in practice.

2   *Focus on side effects.* Since reflexivity means being aware of the contextual embeddedness of one's activity, the focus on unintended consequences of action is in the centre of a reflexive methodology of intervention. It focuses on side effects on both levels of strategy-in-practice: the practitioner's and the scientist's. That means, reflexive change agents are aware that even 'good design' can have negative effects. For example, if an organization (the management, a coalition) plans to autonomize departments and persons, they would understand that as a walk on the ridge, not as a summit conquest. Careful with language, they would take the use of the term 'implementation' as a semantic indicator for the inability to disengage from rationalistic thinking. Thus, the iterative evaluation of strategies with respect to the actual outcomes of interventions is a central practice of reflexive methodology. This requires an open process model with iterative evaluation loops instead of linear phase models.

3   *Conceptualization.* A main 'principle' is to reject context-free principles. To follow a reflexive methodology of intervention means to remain sceptical of any universalism, any recommendation of 'one-best-way' or 'best practice'. It means accepting that any social 'system' has its history, culture and context (e.g. Bourdieu 1990), and must be 'treated' according to that specificity. Instead of simply recommending or transferring knowledge and solutions from other organizations to a present one, the reflexive researcher or consultant would see his or her main task in the contextualization of experiences for the specific case. Instead of offering general problem solving models, the researcher would prefer a thinking in dilemmas – such as between stability and change, autonomy and responsibility, involvement and relief.

4   *Reflexivity through expert knowledge.* In contrast to procedural approaches, reflexive scientists or consultants assume that not all necessary knowledge is given in the respective organization, and that knowledge transfer makes sense. They will make use of scientific knowledge in a reflective way. Hence, they draw the attention of the practitioners to

alternatives, or offer them the opportunity for a co-construction of alternatives (Raeithel 1998). This implies mistrusting former reasoning, and opening mentally closed spaces of action. This is the core of increasing the reflexivity in practice. Scenario techniques are adequate methods. If the scientific consultant does not only use them as a method of intervention, but recommends using reflexive methods, he or she pleads for an institutional reflexivity instead of rule-following behaviour. However, this requires from the external expert a deep contextual knowledge of models and practices in the specific branch or industry, as well as the specific organization in order to assess their applicability.

5   *Decentring – the power of questioning.*[1] To increase the reflexivity of a practice is not a reflexive activity *per se*. Opening spaces for action becomes reflexive if the researcher or consultant is aware that he or she inevitably introduces values and norms into the organization. Only if we are aware that not only the practitioners but also researchers are 'loaded' of implicit theories can we be open to discover and question these implicit values and intentions. Reciprocal openness – and observation – between researcher and practitioner is a central element for the legitimacy of intervention. Thus, the category 'reflexive' applies not only to the cognitive style of the researcher, but to the relation between the researcher and the research-partner. How else can researchers or consultants receive support to decentre themselves from their actor's perspective? What can a reflexive methodology offer as help to reflect on our own paradigmatic bonds, a priori ends, value ties and implicit moral commitments? An adequate method is the self-application of recommended methods, particularly of evaluation. A reflexive approach would use such methods regularly.

6   *Confinement of identities.* A methodology of reflexive intervention inspired by social science will only be able to increase the reflexivity of practice if it is aware of, and care for its particular identity, its relative autonomy. This is an idea from systems theory in Luhmann's tradition (Willke 1999). It is one of the biggest and most popular errors of many practice-oriented scientific approaches that tend to adopt the view and logic of the practice they refer to. A reflexive methodology of intervention implies accepting the legitimacy of the practitioner's rationalities, and does not claim a superior scientific rationality. It has the latter in common with 'procedural thinking'. At the same time, it encourages the researcher to insist on a difference in perspectives, and to use this difference as a means of productive puzzling of implicit everyday assumptions; just as the above mentioned systemic approaches argue. This also applies to the people involved: there must be a productive difference between the *person* and the *role* of the researcher in order to allow for more incisive questions of value and sense. This is also true for the employed people of an organization. Cultures of consulting, as well as corporate cultures, can be differentiated by the scope which they allow for a particular identity, distance and reflexivity.

7   *Recentring.* If 'decentring' emphasizes reflection, and 'confinement' distance, then 'recentring' emphasizes action. This is a common mode of action research. In contrast to the systemic approach, and according to the other stream of proceduralism (organization development (OD) movement and dialogue approach), reflexive researchers will not assume that they could succeed in remaining 'independent'. They are aware that there is no presence in the field without effects; that they intervene merely by observing, asking or answering. Of course, they can attempt to be 'inside' and 'outside' the organization, while being aware that they are always and inescapably a part of the interaction system. Hence, they gather experience through participating in practice, try to apply what they have learned by decentring, and utilize the effects of being actors among actors. Since it

is difficult to be an observer and actor at the same time, it makes sense to explicitly decide on the adequate mode within a cyclical phase model.

8   *Politics and organizational change.* As mentioned previously, the idea of reflexive intervention accepts that there is a difference between perspectives or interests between science and practice. But this is only the special case of a social constructionist view which assumes that different social practices – with science as one of them – create different perspectives and interests. It is necessary, therefore, to refer to adequate organization theories (Holland 1999; Alvesson and Sköldberg 2000; Kühl and Moldaschl 2001). First, theories that can feed a reflexive intervention theory should understand structures as 'negotiated orders', where interests, power and domination play crucial roles in the negotiation processes. That means they do not understand organization as an 'independent variable' as is common in organizational psychology. Consequently, they would never assume a uniform organizational purpose or goal, as strategic management theories or the systemic consulting approach do. Instead, attention would be focused on the structuring interplay of these interests. Third, the organization framework needed should not work with a concept of interests that is reduced to material goals. Instead, it should deliver an interpretive understanding that is capable of capturing social and symbolic interests.

Conclusion

Taking all these aspects together, the process of organizational transformation towards sustainable work systems turns out to be a risky endeavour with a moving target, insufficient knowledge, partially conflicting interests and, hence, with wide ranges of uncertainty and unexpected side effects. Thus, our heuristics of reflexive design and intervention for sustainable change are not a toolbox for 'how to build' SWS. They propose procedures that help to cope with insufficient knowledge, uncertainty, unforeseen side effects, contradictions and conflicting interests. Together, they insist on the necessity to introduce knowledge and values, models and strategies. These can be reflected by the practitioners, selected or singled out, rejected or processed into proper options. Sustainability, as a multi-level measure, is a compass in this regard.

Even if in modern organizations there is no real master of the process, power plays a crucial role in all selections, and a reflexive methodology has to reflect this. Experts must expect that their best-meaning proposals, which try to balance all stakeholder interests on all levels, will be filtered through the existing web of power relations; and they must always count on being instrumentalized by particular interests. Keeping this in mind, we can still maintain that procedures of reflexive design and intervention deliberately make more, and more sustainable, use of reflective skills, of individual and collective expertise; also they force actors and external experts systematically to evaluate the consequences of their activity in relation to the measures and goals they had agreed on.

Again, this requires another reflexive loop, concerning the limits of reflexivity. As a form of institutionalized critique, reflexivity is not smoothly compatible with some practical interests. Managers and other practitioners are not interested in continuously questioning every aspect of their activity or co-ordinative solutions: 'Excessive reflection can paralyse the individual', as Sternberg (1984, p. 13) states. Even if this addresses only the reflection side of reflexivity, the conclusion is still the same: practitioners under pressure do not want to check numerous options, nor hear how complex and contradictory the world is. They normally want to hear: that is the way; go for it; you will get it! This need is the economic basis of subsistence for the mainstream consultancy business. For intervening actors with a social science backpack a permanent tightrope walk remains – balancing rationality and reflexivity, goal-oriented rational action and systematic questioning, advice and critique, self-confident action and self-critique.

Note

1　We borrow the categories *decentring* and *recentring* from Arne Raeithel (e.g. 1998), an action theorist, who describes them (referring to Piaget's concept of egocentrical thinking, and to Hegel's phenomenology) as fundamental modes of perceiving and acting, that is, of being in the world.

References

Alvesson, M. and Sköldberg, K. (2000) *Reflexive Methodology*, London: Sage.

Argyris, C. and Schön, D.A. (1978) *Organizational Learning. A Theory of Action Perspective*, Reading, MA: Addison-Wesley.

Argyris, A., Putnam, R. and Smith, D.M. (1985) *Action Science*, San Francisco: Jossey-Bass.

Baron, J. (1985) *Rationality and Intelligence*, Cambridge, MA: Harvard University Press.

Beck, U. (1994) 'The reinvention of politics. Towards a theory of reflexive modernization', in U. Beck *et al.* (eds) *Reflexive Modernization*, Oxford: Blackwell, pp. 1–56.

Bourdieu, P. (1990) *In Other Words. Essays Towards a Reflexive Sociology*, Cambridge: Polity Press.

Brödner, P. (1997) *Der überlistete Odysseus. Über das zerrüttete Verhältnis von Menschen und Maschinen*, Berlin: Sigma.

Buchanan, D. and Boddy, D. (1992) *The Expertise of the Change Agent*, New York: Prentice-Hall.

Copperrider, D. and Srivastva, S. (1987) 'Appreciative inquiry in organizational life', in R. Woodman and W. Pasmore (eds) *Research in Organisational Change and Development*, Vol. 1, Greenwich, CT: JAI, pp. 129–69.

Cummings, T. and Worely, C. (2000) *Organization Development and Change*, St Paul, MN: West Publications.

Foote Whyte, W. (ed.)(1991) *Social Theory for Action*, Newbury Park, CA: Sage.

French, W.L. and Bell, C.H. (1998) *Organization Development*, 6th edn, Englewood Cliffs, NJ: Prentice-Hall.

Gergen, K.J. (1985) 'The social constructionist movement in modern psychology', *American Psychologist*, 40, 266–75.

Giddens, A. (1984) *The Constitution of Society*, Cambridge: Polity Press.

Giddens, A. (1994) 'Risk, trust, reflexivity', in U. Beck *et al.* (eds) *Reflexive Modernization*, Oxford: Blackwell, pp. 184–97.

Gustavsen, B. (1992) *Dialogue and Development*, Vol. 1, Assen: Van Gorcum.

Hardy, C., Phillips, N. and Clegg, S. (2001) 'Reflexivity in organizations and management theory. A study of the production of the research subject', *Human Relations*, 54, 5, 531–60.

Holland, R. (1977) *Self and Social Context*, London: Macmillan.

Holland, R. (1999) 'Reflexivity', *Human Relations*, 52, 4, 519–56.

Kelly, G.A. (1955) *The Psychology of Personal Constructs*, New York: Norton.

Kühl, S. and Moldaschl, M. (eds) (2002) *Organisation und Intervention*, Munich: Mering, Hampp (forthcoming).

Landau, M. (1972) *Political Theory and Political Science*, New York: Macmillan.

Lefebvre, V.A. (1992) *A Psychological Theory of Bipolarity and Reflexivity*, Lampeter: Edwin Mellen Press.

Luhmann, N. (1990) *Essays on Self-Reference*, New York: Columbia University Press.

Marous, G.E., (1994) 'What comes after "post". The case of ethnography', in N.K. Denzin and Y.S. Lincoln (eds) *Handbook of Qualitative Research*, London: Sage.

Moldaschl, M. (1998) 'Rationality, culture and politics of production', in E. Scherer (ed.) *Shop Floor Scheduling and Control. A Systems Perspective*, London, Berlin: Springer, pp. 67–90.

Moldaschl, M. and Weber, W.G. (1998) 'The "three waves" of industrial group work. Historical reflections on current research on group work', *Human Relations*, 51, 3, 347–88.

Raeithel, A. (1998) 'On the ethnography of cooperative work', in Y. Engeström and D. Middleton (eds) *Cognition and Communication at Work*, Cambridge, MA: Harvard University Press, pp. 319–39.

Schein, E. (1969) *Process Consultation*, Reading, MA: Addison-Wesley.

Schön, D.A. (1983) *The Reflective Practitioner*, New York: Basic Books.

Steier, F. (ed.) (1991) *Research and Reflexivity*, London: Sage.

Sternberg, R.J. (ed.) (1984) *Handbook of Human Intelligence*, Cambridge: Cambridge University Press.

Tomm, K. (1987) 'Reflective questioning as a means to enable self-healing', *Family Process*, 26, 167–84.

West, M. (1996) 'Reflexivity and work group effectiveness', in M. West (ed.) *Handbook of Work Group Psychology*, Chichester: Wiley, pp. 555–79.

Whyte, W.F. (1992) 'In defence of street corner society', *Journal of Contemporary Ethnography*, 21, 52–68.

Willke, H. (1999) *Systemtheorie II. Interventionstheorie*, Stuttgart: Fischer.

Willmott, H. (1993) 'Breaking the paradigm mentality', *Organization Studies*, 14, 5, 681–719.

Woolgar, S. (ed.)(1988) *Knowledge and Reflexivity*, London: Sage.

16 Deutero-learning and sustainable change

Monica Bjerlöv

The aim of this chapter is to suggest some basic considerations when developing sustainability in change processes with special attention to workplace learning. However, the vast issue of organizational learning is beyond the scope of this chapter.

It is a hopeful proposition made here, that ordinary workplace conversations, a most profound human expression, actually could be the vehicle for an advanced organizational learning. A conceptual framework for understanding the nature of such conversations is offered. The frame is based on a study of a Swedish governmental authority (Bjerlöv 1999) together with experiences from studies in the field of workplace development in a school, and several regional health care organizations. Despite being public institutions, they are examples of new dilemmas and demands associated with today's leaner organizations and decreasing resources, which put new pressures on organizations and individuals.

A neglected type of learning

Without venturing into a fixed definition of a sustainable work system, I argue here that learning is a vital element in such a system. Whether a work system is to survive and develop depends on its capacity to adjust to new situations, i.e. its capacity for learning. Research on learning in organizations has a long history with contributions from a number of scholars such as Chris Argyris, Donald Schön and Peter Senge. During the 1990s this issue again gained momentum as reflected among other things in the concept of knowledge management (e.g. Nonaka and Takeuchi 1995).

Even if nomenclature varies, major authors agree that there are several types of learning, as demonstrated by Pawlowsky (2001); see Table 16.1. Of these types, the third – *deutero-learning*, in the terminology of Argyris and Schön (1978) – appears as the most evasive but also the most intriguing. Argyris and Schön define deutero-learning as organizations' *ability* to learn and they emphasize the need for continuous learning as a way to exploit and adjust to changes in society. Deutero-learning represents a higher level of reflexivity and depends on the ability to reflect upon previous episodes of organizational learning, or failures to learn, and is thus linked to an organization's considering, facilitating or inhibiting learning. It also has to do with inventing and evaluating new strategies. The result becomes encoded in individual sense-making that could be used in and reflected upon in the learning practice in a workplace.

As is often pointed out, organizations live in a turbulent field of expectations, where increased pace and slimmed resources are often seen as the solution. Although one might have to accept change in work life as a permanent condition, there is a need to at least evaluate and learn from its effects. This has to do with creating conditions for a deutero-learning process

Table 16.1 Examples of different types of organizational learning

Authors	Learning types		
	Type 1	Type 2	Type 3
Bateson	Learning 0 Learning I	Learning II	Learning III
Starbuck and Hedberg	First order learning	Second order learning	
Argyris and Schön	Single-loop learning	Double-loop learning	Deutero-learning
Hedberg	Adjustment learning	Turnover learning	Turnaround learning
Shrivastra	Adaptive learning	Assumption learning	Development of knowledge base
Fiol and Lyles	Lower level learning	Higher level learning	
Morgan	Self-organization		Holographic learning
Lundberg	Learning as organizational change	Learning as organizational development	Learning as organizational transformation
Senge	Adaptive learning		Generative learning
Garratt	Operational learning cycle	The policy learning cycle	The integrated learning cycle

Source: Pawlowsky 2001, p. 77.

that develops a competence to define and solve problems. Deutero-learning is a problem solving learning, which requires collective reflection on governing rules and assumptions (Pawlowsky 2001, p. 77).

There are thus strong indications of a growing need for space to consolidate and to understand changes, and to find new solutions. A recent Swedish study (Härenstam *et al.* 2000) shows that continuous change in an organization tends to break down well-functioning social and professional networks. This may prove to be detrimental to the long-term survival of the organization. In a sense-making process a phenomenon needs to be put in a context that helps us to comprehend it. The effort at making things comprehensible and meaningful is an ongoing activity within as well as between individuals in the workplace. People are each other's context of meaning.

It is assumed here that in all work activities sense-making and learning are necessary for the members of an organization. It demands laborious cognitive and social processes, which have to start all over again, whenever goals or management philosophy change. Ironically, repeated reorganizations and changes can thus create conditions that are counter-productive to their primary aim. Therefore, it seems important to create an alternative agenda for discussing organizational changes, which allows the employees to regenerate their energy.

A theoretical and conceptual frame

Here an understanding of deutero-learning will be offered in the light of theories about human cognitive development and learning. The focus is on the step between the individual development processes and the collective. Some concepts are presented as threads in a web for developing a model for deutero-learning. The suggested concepts are seen as vital elements in a practical epistemology for sustainable change in everyday work. The ability to develop deutero-learning is about using experiences from what we thought and did last time, using the results in a new situation or context and further developing the experiences into an enlarged capacity for making choices.

According to Basseches (1994) changes must occur gradually through a dialectical process in which changes in individuals' cognitive structures lead to changes within the organization; which in turn lead to further development of the individuals. Development in organizational learning is to be recognized as 'lived through experiences' taking the gestalt of work-based knowledge.

The definitions below will be applied in the following reasoning:

- *Learning* implies a change or a development of a belief, or a change in an understanding of a phenomenon or a situation. This can be described as a series of perceptual reformulations that can result in changes of perspectives – a transformation of perspective.
- *Deutero-learning* is a learning process where single individuals, together, engage in learning about the previous contexts for learning (Bateson 1972, pp. 169–70; Argyris and Schön 1978, pp. 26–9). They reflect on and inquire into previous episodes of organizational learning, or the failure to learn. They consider facilitated or inhibited learning. They invent new strategies, test and evaluate them. The result becomes encoded in individual sense-making that could be used and reflected upon in the learning practice.
- *Sense-making* is, according to Weick (1995, p. 133), about the enlargement of small cues. It is a search for context within which small details fit together and make sense. It is people interacting to flesh out hunches. It is a continuous alternation between particulars and explanations, with each cycle giving added form and substance to the other. The process of sense-making implies actions of 'grasping' in relation to the specific context. It then comes close to 'contextualize' (Halldén 1994; Bjerlöv 1999, p. 34).
- *Decentring* is described by Piaget (1962, pp. 3–5) as a perceptual reformulation of previous points of view to shift the given cognitive perspective. This specific process of revision is what Piaget calls cognitive decentring.
- *Differentiation* means to consider what actually separates a particular way of understanding a phenomenon or situation from other ways; to investigate and realize wherein the differences lie between my own understanding and that of others, and carefully evaluate these differences.
- *Social decentring* is a process very close to cognitive decentring, here suggested as the ability to differentiate between one's own point of view and other possible ones, and from there to go further and act from the assumption that the way I understand a phenomenon is as true for me as another person's understanding is for her/him.
- *Social morale* is a mutual attitude and respect for each other's knowledge in dealing with work-related issues. This manifests itself in a mutual way of relating to each other's experiences. It also encompasses a mutual understanding of the modus needed in the conversation with regard to each other's knowledge about the work (Bjerlöv 1999, p. 156).
- *Dialogue or work-based conversations*. These are delimited here to oral, face to face communication.

Within this theoretical frame, all these concepts reflect aspects of ordinary human thinking and learning. The problem is, however, that organizations are designed and change managed in ways that are prohibitive to learning, sense-making and communication – and thus sustainable change, which requires a workplace-related epistemology.

Sense-making and learning

Besides our own history of experiences and knowledge, we use the nearest environment as a frame for interpretation when we try to understand. At the workplace this environment could be the group, the larger unit, the client relation, or a part of the production line. We also use the larger context such as the department, the plant, the entire production line, i.e. the whole system or workplace or maybe the whole society. This movement between the different levels of context and phenomenon is a complex ongoing cognitive and social activity in everyday work. With this perspective, work and organization are understood as social constructs.

When joining a new game, one feels at a loss and insecure until the rules and how to apply them have been learnt. It takes time to make sense of the rules and integrate them into one's own interpretations. When playing, the participants build a common understanding and knowledge of each other's ways of acting and thinking. The same can be said of the learning processes in occupational life. Time and space are needed to grasp new things, to assimilate and accommodate to make them fit our understanding. We also need to be able to act accordingly and adjust to them. These processes go on whether we are conscious of them or not. To acknowledge the dialectical frame (Basseches 1994) for individual and organizational learning, we have to accept the need for time and reflection, something that most researchers in the field agree upon.

Sense-making is about making the world comprehensible and injecting meaning into the world, for instance the work task, the work process, the way peer groups co-operate, the work unit and the whole enterprise. What stands out as important is the ability to relate to each other's knowledge and efforts at making sense of the workplace reality.

According to Weick (1995, p. 71), sense-making as a collective activity is a way of both generating an ability to communicate and establishing a frame of joint contextualization. Weick refers to the work of Linell and Markova (e.g. 1993) and Wiley's (1988) interpretation of inter- and intra-subjectivity.

Sense-making could be defined as learning. Sense-making and learning are prerequisites for each other. To change a subjective assumption or a perception there is a need for an ongoing process of intentionally investigating 'other possible assumptions or perceptions'.

To distance oneself and to differentiate

Reflection and sense-making for learning, both cognitive development and collective learning, are coupled with developing professionalism and work itself. According to Kegan (1982, p. 31) reflection contains basic elements, such as taking distance and separating ourselves cognitively from a context or situation. We cannot internalize anything new without distancing ourselves and differentiating. In doing so we open ourselves to investigate the content and the gap between our understanding and other possible ones. The Swedish philosopher Molander (1993, p. 127) describes this activity as an act of estrangement; a familiar phenomenon is turned into a strange one. In a good dialogue we participate in a process of shifting focus and comparing our actions with the actions of others. This, in turn, leads to an awareness of learning processes between people. This awareness has to do with the possibilities to develop thoughts and work-based problem solving learning – deutero-learning.

Dixon (1994, p. 13) comments on this: 'We must be able to hold the difference within our minds long enough to make sense of it.' We could benefit even more from our different understandings by highlighting the specifics of the difference. We then design a space, where the learning is free. In this gap between ways of understanding, a space can be created for individual, collective and organizational learning. Where is this arena or space to be found? Sometimes existing arenas and processes can be highlighted, for example workplace meetings or conferences. Where different interpretations and views meet, we need to look at what is said. We need to interpret the speaker not solely as if he or she talks only out of personal interest or for winning an argument, but according to her or his interpretation and experience. This may seem self-evident, but nevertheless makes a difference in the dialogue practice.

It is important for the design of transformation processes at the workplace to realize that individual cognitive structures are conservative by nature (Basseches 1984, pp. 361–2). It takes time to alter – both consciously and unconsciously – the structures and contents of our thoughts and to make the necessary perceptual reformulations. The steps in learning how to relate to other possible ways of viewing things, and of reformulation, are important for understanding a new phenomenon or situation or to create new knowledge under familiar conditions. This is thus one reason for devoting time and energy on work-related reflection. When a group of employees reflects together the system could be verified and developed in the same process. Importantly, it would be validated by those having the closest experience of everyday operations and work.

Learning as cognitive and social de-centring

To escape a cognitive egocentrism the individual has to decentre (Piaget 1962, pp. 1–5) both in thinking and in social activity. This is something that we do in interaction with others and it is one aspect of a learning process where the work-related dialogue becomes an active ingredient. A constructivist perspective on learning builds on the idea that the individual constructs his or her knowledge of the world in interaction with the environment. Learning is heavily influenced by contextual factors in the workplace: workplace system, division of labour, work organization, degree of autonomy and, not least, the culture, all of which determine how we relate to each other.

There is an iteration between individual and group. This movement can also be seen as an expression of the perspective constructivism. In constructivism the focus is on the cognitive development of the individual. When discussing the needs of and the content in collective learning, we talk about participating in something, in the social construction of knowledge.

Two aspects of decentring are of interest, when dealing with the step between individual learning processes and collective. The first is cognitive decentring according to Piaget. The second aspect is a social decentring (Bjerlöv 1999, p. 40), which, like cognitive decentring, concerns the ability to make perceptual reformulations. But it also concerns an extended ability to evaluate consequences for other persons and for larger parts of the work or, in other words, an ability to look further and to take in larger contexts. It encompasses a moral about relating to each other's knowledge about work and the workplace. Piaget (1962) sees the opposite of decentring 'cognitive egocentrism' as stemming from a lack of differentiation between one's own point of view and other possible ones.

Both cognitive and social decentring bring understanding to the step between the individual learning process and learning between individuals. When thinking together, the participants have to make their beliefs, their taken-for-granted premises and their interpretation, public. Employees who have been socialized during years in intensive work systems and hierarchy might find it hard to cope with more autonomy. This has a background in the need to create, interpret and manage work solely according to one's own competence. Basseches (1994, pp. 361–2) gives three examples of this problem. In the first case, individuals look for a new order or norms or opportunities to rest from required work. In the second, individuals assume that they lack the necessary experience to make decisions, and if something needs to be done someone else will make sure that they do it. This is what is called learnt helplessness. And finally they depend on either conformity or disobedience rather than taking constructive initiatives.

These descriptions may, however, not correspond to the self-understanding of those involved, if they have not had the opportunity to take the necessary distance from their own way of acting. And if someone else describes a behaviour in the above terms, it will just be felt as an intimidation. Learning and change are, in both an individual and organizational perspective, about transformation and reformulation. This is painful and has to be carefully elaborated (see Chapter 9).

Communication as an active ingredient

As reflexivity, dialogue in working life – work-related discourses – has become increasingly focused (see Chapter 15). This is in particular the case for research in organizational learning. Several of the researchers in Table 16.1 emphasize work-based talk, conversation, interaction or dialogue.

Obviously people have always talked with each other in the workplace and oral communication can be an active ingredient in sense-making and learning, if carefully elaborated. It can be a bridge between personal taken-for-granted premises and an arena where personal sense-making of different individuals could develop into a shared view. A carefully elaborated work-related conversation or dialogue could be a context in which employees and management develop their respective knowledge together into a joint understanding. This process can be understood as a cognitive and/or a social process of validation, built upon the possibilities and abilities for cognitive and social decentring. The work-based dialogue sets the tone for collaboration at the workplace. This tone also influences the way in which we relate to one another's experiential knowledge of work and work processes.

With a successful dialogue one of the most important opportunities for developing work-related learning and change processes is opened. This is not a striving for consensus; it rather concerns an inquiry-driven evaluation with the aim of learning from each other's interpretation.

As pointed out, dialogue has become an ordinary and often used term in work life, used for a variety of conversations, with widely shifting intentions. The delimitation here is the face to face talk closely related to the work. (We do understand that sometimes there are video and phone conferences approximating to the face to face group talks situation or context.) By studying how and about what people talk with each other in relation to work, something might be learnt about the prerequisites for development and change and suitable models for workplace development.

Bohm (1999, pp. 26–7) regards the dialogue process not as just any conversation, but talk with the aim of systematically questioning opinions and assumptions and, as a consequence, also questioning behaviour, i.e. the way we act. To be constructive this has to be done in a modus that does not intimidate. One possible starting point is to focus on what intention the words have and the need for us to be intentionally understood (von Wright 1971, pp. 99–102). Mezirow (1991, p. 65) sees dialogue as a critical validation process, which is closely related to the decentring process described above. To engage in a dialogue is a process that builds on the ability to decentre, to understand that there are other ways of understanding. Learning to learn in organizations is dependent on communicative competence and the ability to decentre. What is needed is an ability to shift focus and compare one's own actions with other possible ones (Graumann 1990, p. 113).

Shotter and Gustavsen (1999) propose what has been called a 'new constructivism'. One basic thought in this concept emphasizes that people create their orders and practices as they move through a social landscape, continuously engaging in dialogues with other people. The role of dialogue in the development of learning regions is, according to Shotter and Gustavsen, 'to do from within our lives together what we cannot do apart', which underlines the need for work-based talk among those who are closest to the task or the problem at hand.

Arenas for work-based talks

Most people have experienced boredom and frustration at work meetings. Such meetings are normally an established context for oral communication at work and might not always function well. Sometimes little is said; sometimes the whole meeting is just repetition of former meetings. Sometimes there is a fight with words. No concrete action follows. Maybe the most common situation in meetings is where everything is about whose version of reality is the true one (see Chapters 8 and 17).

This situation is more or less unnecessary in a constructivist perspective, as there is no such thing as one fixed truth. There are several different ways of understanding, each being true for the beholder. The work meeting is an example of an arena for an already ongoing dialogue (or maybe monologue) process that can be developed further.

To alter work procedures and use the force of the (face to face) dialogue as a working ingredient in everyday work is a long-term process, though. To realize that what you say is as true for you as what I say is true for me takes energy, time and space. There will also be periods when discord between old and new values turns out to be a disturbance that steals energy, by demanding new processes of sense-making in everyday practice. Norms and values which guide the procedures and organization of work live on in the organization, whether any individuals live by them or talk about them or not (Herbst 1972). The organization harbours old organizational and political ideals, sediments representing once successful problem solving (Danielson 1983).

In a deutero-learning process individuals engage in a work-based dialogue about the previous contexts for learning. They reflect upon and inquire into previous episodes of sense-making and learning opportunities or failures to learn. They also invent and evaluate new strategies, like a shared sense of how to relate to each other's experiential knowledge. The result is encoded in the individual sense-making and can be used in the following learning practice. These processes can start when something out of the ordinary happens. Then one has to reflect, differentiate, decentre and reorganize one's thinking as a process of perceptual reformulation.

It is a long-term process for a group to develop a way of learning from each other by oral encounters. Nor is it a shortcut to success and it is a work task in itself. What seems to be needed is the development of co-operative methods to facilitate participation and joint responsibility. One important contribution in this respect is the 'democratic dialogue' developed by Björn Gustavsen (1992, pp. 3–9). The entrance ticket to the democratic dialogue is the subjective work-related experiential knowledge. The aim is: 'doing from within our lives together what we cannot do apart' (Shotter and Gustavsen 1999). There is also a need to establish a common understanding or social morale for co-operation. This is probably related to trust, which is a problem the democratic dialogue partly tries to solve by a rather strict set of rules for the dialogue process.

A quiet dynamic with heated episodes

After this theoretical comment, there is a need for stating that life sometimes is about what can be seen as trivialities. A work-based conversation should start from where the participants are. By this I want to underline how important it is that those involved should identify the problem and find the solutions. Then the start needs to be in something that the persons concerned can recognize. This is also about acknowledging the complexity and importance of everyday trivialities. I would like to present an excerpt from a transcript which at first sight looks like trivial talk. Nevertheless this was an important episode for those involved. The excerpt is from a dialogue among a group of ten people trying out a local method for developing communication and co-operation in their work meetings. It is an example of an episode that later on changes the group's communication and understanding of their taken-for-granted premises about leadership and 'knowledge management' in a group. In the transcript some comments by the researcher are inserted.

Christina is the head of the department in which this group works. She starts by saying that she wants to be a part of the preparation of the applications the group is working on:

'I'd really like to tag along on this journey.'

Then Erik presents his understanding of the manager's role and the function of the workplace meeting for the work:

'It is not solely in my role as a manager of this unit. It is a co-ordination of other activities in the authority as a whole.'

Erik explains that he finds it important that

'people don't run different races. It is the full picture of the situation then that is needed.'

The researcher now asks: 'Isn't this part of a discussion about the work meeting as an opportunity for changeover (to a more elaborated communicative learning)?' Christina answers as if this was self-evident:

'That is the idea! That is what we have said. The whole idea with the project group is that we should have discussions like these.'

Later on she says:

'It is vital that I am present, but it is equally vital that others who possess supplementary skills are present.'

This can be looked upon as a way of legitimizing other participants – they all have skills that are important. This is further underlined when she comments on her own ability to uphold the skills necessary for the function as manager. She says:

'I cannot have this position if I don't also have access to other people's skills.'

Gunnar seems to agree with what has been said:

> 'I can learn a lot from the collective experience.'

Are all participants equally important then? Earlier we talked about whether everyone is equally competent. How do the participants look upon skills and competence? The researcher:

> 'Are all people's skills equally important?'

Margareta, an assistant and new to the group, answers:

> 'Yes! But only if everyone has participated equally long.'

The researcher, however, suggests that it seems as if it is primarily the manager's skills that are required by the group. Christina becomes irritated:

> 'I have to protest! That is what *you* say! But I need everyone's competence for sure! I cannot uphold this function if I don't also have access to other people's skills.'

Here some participants reached a point where they actually openly presented their individual taken-for-granted premises and at the same time their lack of joint sense-making. After this meeting they gave up (at least partly) their earlier assumptions and taken-for-granted premises, e.g. that the manager possesses all the answers and therefore is responsible for checking all the preparations and suggestions before a decision is made. At the same time the work-related knowledge of the others comes into focus. This talk not only develops the context of the meeting into a kind of shared contextualization but also illustrates from where a professional dialogue could depart. The suggestions elaborated in this text should start in the everyday reality and already ongoing processes in the specific workplace.

In this process a joint sense-making can give rise to something which is more than what the single individual possesses. It will also be more than the sum of each and everyone's knowledge and ability. This is due to a reciprocal dependency between the individuals and the organization.

Deutero-learning as a process

Work-based dialogue is a matter of sense-making. Sense-making can be achieved if we in practice, in actual conversations, develop our ability to understand and accept that others may have understood the same thing differently. After that we need to reflect further on what these differences consist of in order to develop a tool for understanding other parts of the work. This is to learn that what I do will have consequences for what others do. In this phase of the process there are opportunities for a workplace-based learning, through our own and others' experiences (see Chapter 17). If this takes place, an actual workplace development is set in motion, since an increasing number of people will learn more about the work and thus be able to act in a different way. This new perspective will come about within and through relating one's own knowledge to that of others, which becomes a method for problem solving learning, built on knowing how to relate and co-operate. The whole learning process depends on reflection, insight and maturation. The content as well as the results of the knowledge formation brought about in this learning process is about orchestrating knowledge within the organization. Deutero-learning is about orchestrating and the result is a local theory/epistemology and method on how to learn to learn. This method is to be understood and used as a sustainable element to hold on to in change processes.

Finally

Since the early research by Kurt Lewin on social groups, we have learnt that when people work together there is something created between the individuals, which is 'more' or 'goes beyond'. Trujillo (1983, p. 82) describes this as a parallel perspective, a meta-communicative function, where every message has both a content and a relationship aspect: 'The content dimension is presumed to carry information, whereas the relationship dimension refers to the meta-communicative aspect of the message by which interactants mutually define and display their relationship.' Deutero-learning is a joint sense-making process that goes beyond the single task and the single individual. Here this means that we engage in a social construction of our work life.

Oral communication is seen as the active ingredient in workplace development. The outcome could be an everyday task-oriented learning. When dialogue takes place at a specific workplace, it could develop into a deutero-learning process, a learning that goes beyond re-creation of knowledge as the participants develop knowledge about the prerequisites for contextualization and perceptual reformulation in their specific situation. This could generate a joint social morale – a praxis that contains important aspects of trust and how to relate to one another's knowledge about work. The latter is closely related to the joint feeling of professional and social trust, something that in the context of learning and sustainable change demands a chapter of its own.

The meta-function of the dialogue could be developed to create something beyond distributing information or making decisions. A way of securing the necessary trust in work-related dialogue is to decide from the very beginning, that all work experiences are equally valid. This is in itself an opportunity for reinvesting human resources in the work organization, which has to do with acknowledging social and professional networks within the organization. From that we may develop and elaborate and understand the organization as a complex social construct; to view the learning processes as an everyday ongoing phenomenon depending on and living in this construction. The point here is that learning processes and knowledge are distributed through social construction – the dialogue.

References

Argyris, C. and Schön, D. (1978) *Organizational Learning. A Theory of Action Perspective*, Reading, MA: Addison-Wesley.
Basseches, M. (1994) *Dialectical Thinking and Adult Development*, Norwood, NJ: Ablex Publishing.
Bateson, G. (1972) *Steps to an Ecology of Mind*, New York: Ballantine.
Bjerlöv, M. (1999) *Lärande i en arbetsplatsbaserad diskurs. En studie av samtal och lärande i arbetsplatsmöten* (Learning in Work-based Discourse. A Study of Talk and Learning in Meetings at a Workplace), Stockholm: Department of Education, Stockholm University.
Bohm, D. (1999) *On Dialogue*, ed. Lee Nichol, London and New York: Routledge.
Danielson, A. (1983) *Företagsekonomi – en översikt* (Business Economics. An Overview), Lund: Studentlitteratur.
Dixon, N. (1994) *The Organizational Learning Cycle. How We Can Learn Collectively*, London: McGraw-Hill.

Graumann, C. (1990) 'Perspective, structure and dynamics in dialogues', in I. Markova and K. Foppa (eds) *Dynamics of Dialogue*, New York: Harvester Wheatsheaf.

Gustavsen, B. (1992) *Dialogue and Development. Action Research and Restructuring of Working Life*, Stockholm: Swedish Centre for Working Life.

Halldén, O. (1994) 'Constructing learning tasks in history instructions', in M. Carreto and J.F. Voss (eds) *Cognitive and Instructional Processes in History and Social Sciences*, Hillsdale, NJ: Lawrence Erlbaum.

Härenstam, A., Westerberg, H., Karslquist, L., Leijon, O., Rydbeck, A., Waldenström, K., Wiklund, P., Nise, G. and Jansson, C. (2000) *Hur kan arbete och levnadsförhållanden förstås i ett könsperspektiv* (How Are Gender Differences in Work and Living Conditions Understood), Solna: National Institute for Working Life Report series *Arbete och hälsa* 15.

Herbst, P.G. (1972) 'The product of work is people'. Conference paper in *The Quality of Working Life*, New York: Harriman.

Kegan, R. (1982) *The Evolving Self. Problems and Processes in Human Development*, Cambridge, MA: Harvard University Press.

Linell, P. and Markova, I. (1993) 'Acts in discourse. From monological speech acts to dialogical inter-acts', *Journal for the Theory of Social Behavior*, 23.

Mezirow, J. (1991) *Transformative Dimensions of Adult Learning*, San Francisco: Jossey-Bass.

Molander, B. (1993) *Kunskap-i-Handling* (Knowledge-in-Action), Gothenburg: Daidalos.

Nonaka, I. and Takeuchi, H. (1995) *The Knowledge-creating Company. How Japanese Companies Create the Dynamics of Innovation*, New York: Oxford University Press.

Pawlowsky, P. (2001) 'The treatment of organizational learning in management science', in M. Dierkes, A. Berthoin Antal, J. Child and I. Nonaka (eds) *Organizational Learning and Knowledge*, Oxford and New York: Oxford University Press.

Piaget, J. (1962) *Comments on Vygotsky's Critical Remarks. Concerning: The Language and Thought of the Child and Judgement and Reasoning in the Child*, Cambridge, MA: MIT Press.

Shotter, J. and Gustavsen, B. (1999) *Doing Within Our Lives Together What We Cannot Do Apart. The Role of the 'Dialogue Conferences' in the Development of 'Learning Regions'*, Stockholm: Centre for Advanced Studies of Leadership, Stockholm School of Economics.

Trist, E. (1981) *The Evolution of Socio-technical Systems*, Ontario: Ministry of Labour.

Trujillo, N. (1983) 'Performing Mintzberg's roles. The nature of managerial communication', in L. Putnam and M. Pacanowsky (eds) *Communication and Organization. An Interpretive Approach*, London: Sage.

Weick, K. E. (1995) *Sense Making in Organizations*, London: Sage.

Wiley, N. (1988) 'The micro-problem in social theory', *Sociological Theory*, 6, 254–61.

Wright, G. H. von (1971) *Explanation and Understanding*, Ithaca, NY: Cornell University Press.

17 Eclectic design for change

Michael W. Stebbins and A.B. (Rami) Shani

Introduction

Sustainable work system (SWS) design theory is emerging, and therefore a chapter on this approach to change is necessarily preliminary. To date, the contributions have been mainly conceptual, with a limited number of applied design projects under way. Significant applied research on work intensity and sustainability is just beginning. This is in itself somewhat unique, as prior design theory has mainly evolved from practice. In this chapter, we cover foundations for an emerging theory: we provide brief coverage of action research, socio-technical systems and self-design theory on change. More recent theory on reflective design and work-based learning is also considered central to SWS design. Accordingly, we focus more on operational design in place of strategic organization design. There is a well-developed literature on strategic organization design (see, for example, Hanna 1988; Galbraith 1994) but it is beyond the scope of this chapter.

Our view is that SWS design builds upon and transcends prior organizational design approaches. *Design* is thought to be a blend of theory (organization science), knowledge embedded in the particular industry/sector and work situation, and the contributions of those who participate in the redesign process (Mackenzie 1986). It involves purposeful effort to design the organization as an integrated system, and is both a technical and a political process. Moreover, design is treated as a complex task that will align the people, resources and work. In mature organizations, design projects are conducted to unravel what has often been an unplanned evolution of the enterprise. In today's environment, the list of participants in redesign projects includes a cross-section of employees in the organization, key suppliers, union representatives and customers. Accordingly, there is potentially a wide separation between a science-based solution that a manager might hope to use and one that will meet the needs of different constituents and work well in practice.

SWS design has strong roots in action research theory. *Contemporary action research* (Reason and Bradbury 2001) is a participatory, democratic process concerned with developing practical knowing in the pursuit of worthwhile human purposes. The authors refer to action research as 'the whole family of approaches to inquiry which are participative, grounded in experience, and action oriented'. In keeping with action research theory, SWS design provides flexibility to deal with emergent goals and technology changes that occur in real time. There is considerable trial and error involved as people deliberate with others in the pursuit of change. The most recognized design approach that uses action research thinking is self-design (Weick 1977; Mohrman and Cummings 1989). SWS weaves together action research, socio-technical systems and self-design. We will summarize self-design, action research and socio-technical systems foundations to SWS below. Then we will examine a few early cases, propose an eclectic SWS change process and conclude with a section on research issues and planned redesign projects.

Core SWS values and concepts

SWS thinking stems from European and American scholars and practitioners and certain common values have emerged. The values relate to the context for initiating change, the change process and the desired outcomes. At a very macro level, SWS is somewhat different from prior design approaches in that it considers the country and institutional setting and potential constraints on redesign. Institutional frameworks such as training systems, forms of worker participation, and labour relations involve greater employer commitment and inter-firm relationships than in deregulated market economies (see Chapter 7). SWS scholars believe that many positive work environments and organizational systems already exist, and that research and practice will identify innovative organizations where there is a dual emphasis on quality of work life and competitive organizational performance. High quality of work life includes attention to the intellectual, emotional and physical needs of every individual and consideration of relationships and influences outside the organizational context. The theme of reproduction and development of human resources pervades the emerging SWS theory.

Requirements for a new design process

SWS authors and consultants do not currently agree on many design process matters, and it is not likely that a single theoretical perspective on process will emerge. As with socio-technical systems and other design approaches, design processes will emerge separately by country contexts and by the nature of the industry and firm. Still, it is possible to articulate requirements for the design process under SWS thinking. By 'requirements' we mean the pressures that stem from external and internal business conditions – the things that require changes (Lillrank *et al.* 1998). Requirements are not the same as *design criteria*, but they eventually lead to development of criteria that will guide different organizational change programmes.

Reflexive design

Reflexive design principles have been addressed in other chapters and only a few highlights related to design process are provided below. SWS is a *reflexive* methodology of intervention – a type of enlightened, self-critical redesign that accepts differences in science and practice (see Chapter 15). By definition, reflexive design means to mirror or direct back the redesign work. Thus, the following are key requirements for the design process:

- Exploring alternative design models with participants during the design process. The clients investigate and choose among redesign approaches that fit their unique situation (see Figure 17.1).
- That participants' self-apply theory, methods, practices. In keeping with self-design values, clients take ownership of the change process through high involvement at all stages. In a spirit of enquiry, all parties including consultants consider both theory and practice, and deliberate on ways to link them.
- Encouraging participants to identify and explore the meanings and implications of possible dilemmas – for example that team-centred design can foster work intensity.
- Emphasis on the iterative nature of design activities. Deliberations among stakeholders

occur throughout the process to ensure that redesign produces the desired balanced out-comes. Self-design and learning from experience are facilitated.

- Work and organization designs are subject to continuous modification and improve-ment. Transitions require evaluation checkpoints and design modifications reflecting feedback and new information.
- Exploration and awareness of 'side effects' – that good design work can have unin-tended consequences. All parties are sensitive to the idea that even self-design can produce work intensity.

Design criteria

SWS theory advocates local control of design processes and high participant involvement in creation of design criteria. Design criteria are statements that describe, in ideal terms, those functions that the organization design should perform. Design criteria usually have an action verb; they state that the design should facilitate, promote, encourage, provide for, or motivate (Nadler and Tushman 1988). Design criteria reflect the values of the different stakeholders and are written in response to competitive conditions, the tasks to be executed, the collective sense of current problems and perceived cause of problems, and other constraints. There is a question of who ought to be included in the creation of design criteria. Increasingly, there are calls to include suppliers, customers, unions or works councils, and other employees along with managers. In the past, design criteria have most often been established by top leaders and then modified by steering groups and design team members. This has the drawback of point-ing the redesign effort in the direction of intensive work systems rather than sustainable work systems. Design criteria drive the entire decision-making process and provide links to strategy, technology integration and the development process that occurs in design cycles.

Since design criteria provide the fundamental values and assumptions behind redesign work, they can be used to assess whether the programme is on track. However, with greater stakeholder involvement, it is sometimes difficult to achieve consensus on design criteria. Conflict is often rampant as perspectives clash. Yet this discussion sets the stage for dialogue throughout the redesign process. It is worthwhile to spend time on both criteria language and prioritization, so that a guideline exists to help with the inevitable trade-offs that occur during the redesign process. For example, in a major redesign of Kaiser Permanente (Nadler and

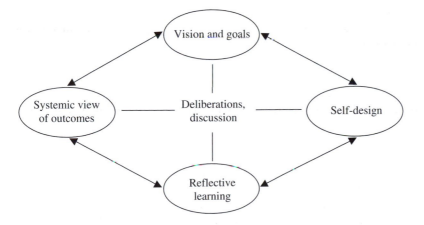

Figure 17.1 Reflective design requirements.

Tushman 1997), the design team generated thirteen criteria including:

- The design alternatives should drive the organization towards customer focus.
- The designs should enhance partnerships with patients, members, suppliers, purchasers, communities, and labour unions.
- Maximize capacity for organizational learning.
- Reduce the hierarchy to ensure those serving the customer have information, resources, and freedom to act.
- Support individual and team accountability for results.

In the Kaiser example, managers alone developed the list of criteria. The list did not directly include reference to meaningful work for employees or other dimensions of quality of work life. Employee and customer perspectives emerged in later stages of the redesign project and became part of the guiding change philosophy; they were missing at the outset. SWS theory is an enhancement over the example in that the design process provides high involvement at all stages including the front end. In many cases, high involvement results in creation of a long list of criteria. Experience to date suggests that a *ranking* of criteria helps the designers stay on track. A sense of priorities is crucial when alternative designs are created and compared, and when impact analyses are conducted of effects on various stakeholders (Nadler and Tushman 1997).

Collective design

There is considerable agreement among SWS authors that the design process must consider individual and team capacity to cope with changing work. One of the most compelling aspects of SWS redesign is the emphasis on personal support, learning and individual capacity to deal with workplace stresses (see Chapter 3). During redesign, individual experimentation takes place within the context of group work and inter-group relationships. Change cannot occur without social support mechanisms. Successful redesign work thus requires the active involvement of those who must live with the changes as well as support so that work intensity is not the result. Accordingly, SWS can be characterized as 'collaborative design'.

In our view, *collaborative design* means that greater attention is given to different stakeholders; there is genuine participation of stakeholders at various stages of the change process. The design team that usually leads the effort is composed of both organizational members and outside experts. The designers are alert to workplace implications of design changes, and individuals are supported as they attempt to change work processes and job content. The probability that design will produce work intensity is reduced if stakeholders hold to the established design criteria and discuss the implications of changes along the way.

Work-based learning

SWS design processes provide time for learning and development of competence in work. This includes deliberations within the normal project stages as well as time for spontaneous and unplanned learning and reflection. The focus is on learning that takes place among people through deliberations and discussion. The process of change centres on the knowledge and experience of those who are closest to the work at hand (see e.g. Chapters 8, 9, 15 and 16).

Learning, coping capacity and other individual capabilities support people as they experiment with new roles, relationships and work activities. Successful transformation depends upon effort, individual capabilities and sound facilitation of the overall SWS change process.

Recognizing and transcending existing design models

Three developments in the field of organization change have had enormous impact on contemporary organization redesign: action research, socio-technical systems and self-design theories. At a basic level, design processes follow a general action research sequence. Planning, diagnostic and experimental phases seem to be included in most organized change efforts. Fundamental concepts advanced by Lewin, Shepard, Beckhard and other pioneers are still evident in practice today (see e.g. Reason and Bradbury 2001). A similar history exists with socio-technical systems, in that STS thinking underlies many of the current change methodologies. And while STS was originally developed to work in production settings it has been significantly modified to work in services (Adler and Docherty 1998) and non-routine situations (Pava 1983; Stebbins and Shani 1995; Pasmore 1997). STS change processes have been invented to extend the reach of redesign to include current issues such as knowledge transfer and work-based learning (Raelin 2000). The third development is self-design. Self-design, considered an outgrowth of STS, provides a highly developed redesign process that is particularly suited to knowledge work settings (Weick 1977; Mohrman and Cummings 1989). Following an action research schema that relies on design iterations, self-design positions the organization for continuous adjustment and redesign.

Action research

Kurt Lewin introduced the general notion of action research in 1946 as an innovative process for changing behaviour. His attempts to resolve social problems using data collection and feedback approaches were pioneering and are the foundation for much organizational development theory and practice (Susman and Evered 1978; Stebbins, Hawley and Rose 1982; Cummings and Worley 2001). Lewin, John Collier and William Whyte found that research needed to be closely linked to action if organizational members were to use it to manage change. Action research is thus viewed as an emergent enquiry process, embedded in partnership between researchers and organizational members, for the purpose of solving organizational problems and simultaneously generating scientific knowledge (Shani and Pasmore 1985). Furthermore, action research seeks to improve the organization's ability to understand and help itself (Friedlander and Brown 1974; Pasmore and Friedlander 1982).

Action research projects also identify issues related to the survival and growth of the organization as a system and therefore address sustainability. Gustavsen (2001) notes that in Norway and Sweden, the labour market partners began in the 1980s to hold search conferences on how to deal with issues such as work organization and regional/local co-operation. The idea was to share goals, ideas, visions and to consider how to go about pursuing them. The search conferences methodology – developed by Emery in community building efforts – was not based on a particular theoretical platform but instead was focused more on relationship building and mediating between theory and practice (Emery and Purser 1996). While few cases of substantial change emerged, the search conferences set the stage for new dialogue in the 1990s and beyond economic–industrial development on a regional basis (Ennals and Gustavsen 1998).

Socio-technical systems design

In the European context, STS interventions rely on the original work by Eric Trist and his associates in the 1950s. Trist first met Lewin in 1933 and studied under his direction in the United States. He then began his career as an applied psychologist, building on and extending Lewin's theories in collaboration with his colleagues at the Tavistock Institute in London. Tavistock would become dedicated to action research, with equal emphasis on the advancement of knowledge, the resolution of practical problems and the commitment for democratizing the workplace. An account of the early development of STS thinking is beyond the scope of this chapter. Suffice it to say that STS rests on pioneering work by Lewin, Bion, Trist, Bamforth, Mumford, Rice, Thorsrud, Emery and others. Strong STS efforts in Britain, Norway, Sweden and eventually Holland have been documented in the STS literature (see e.g. Pasmore *et al.* 1982; Taylor and Felten 1993; van Eijnatten 1994).

The early emphasis on people and their reactions to work, particularly individual outcomes related to job satisfaction and mental health, is noteworthy. SWS design theory claims to focus first and foremost on the individual, but this has been advanced much earlier with STS and quality of working life (QWL) theories. In the 1970s, Davis and Cherns (1975) identified development of human capacities, growth and use of knowledge and skills in future assignments, the opportunity to interact and dialogue with others in the workplace, and the balance between life at work and life at home as criteria affecting individual outcomes (see also Chapter 14). Clearly, then, SWS thinking is an extension of STS design.

Some are criticizing STS by arguing that STS has not kept pace with changes in the work environment (Adler and Docherty 1998). Yet, a broadening of STS theory to include open systems scanning and strategic matters (Hanna 1988; Shani and Elliott 1989; Taylor and Felten 1993) proved helpful. Also, advances by Pava (1983) and others allow creative investigation of the technical system in knowledge work. With the enhancements, STS shows promise for application in the white collar world (Stebbins and Shani 1995; Raelin 2000).

Self-design

Self-design is an outgrowth of STS theory and practice. First proposed by Karl Weick (1977), self-design was applied as an academic exercise to the NASA Skylab situation, offering a dramatic look at the possibilities for self-control versus mission control of astronaut daily work and routines. In Weick's scenario, the astronauts might redefine the mission and alter priorities in response to missed experiments, space station jiggles or pure fascination. This in fact happened with Apollo 3 on a modest level. However, Apollo 3 was far from a self-designing system where astronauts could determine the length of the mission, ask additional persons to join them, shut off communications with mission control, or turn their work over to robots. Apollo 3 also involved relatively little planning.

For Weick, self-designing systems value improvisation and looking for opportunities, inventing solutions that fit local situations, dialogue and argument, the pursuit of contradictions, and performance assessment systems beyond accounting (Weick 1977). In sum, organizations must value things that they used to disparage. This type of thinking is also used in SWS design (see Chapters 15 and 17).

Weick's pioneering thoughts on self-design have been captured and enhanced by Mohrman and Cummings (1989). The ideas of design as an ongoing process and design as a recipe are pursued with vigour. In this case, recipe does not mean a blueprint, but rather recipes that require varying amounts of improvisation. Emphasis is on the processes that are responsible for creating new designs rather than the designs themselves. Through action learning and iterative processes that involve multiple stakeholders, the organization is prepared for continuous adjustment and significant redesign.

Self-design begins with a mutual learning phase involving all stakeholders. The participants work together to create a guiding conceptual model. Special emphasis is placed on the identification of the skills and training required for the successful implementation of the programme. In SWS redesign, a similar phase is needed, but would be modified to include evaluation of multiple redesign models and local choice and modification of the process to be used. In self-design theory, the design team conducts diagnostic activities to identify institutional, work and organization issues. This would be enhanced under SWS to include home grown creation of diagnostic tools and involvement of diverse stakeholders in the diagnosis. Identification of design criteria would follow and this would again involve a dialogue of stakeholders as an SWS enhancement. The benefits of self-design can be seen in the following case example.

Lessons from the field – IDEO case

While the SWS journey has just begun and the identification of design principles is therefore problematic, certain patterns are emerging in 'model' firms. Not surprisingly, many of these firms are in high technology settings with external environments ranging from fiercely competitive and time-paced, to insulated and relaxed. IDEO Product Development of Palo Alto, California, is an example of the latter environment. IDEO was founded by a Stanford University engineering professor and is now the largest firm of its type in the US with a mission of helping client companies develop new products and become more innovative. IDEO employs over 400 engineers, industrial designers and human factors specialists who work on projects that average ten to twelve months in duration. Services range from rough sketches of products to complete new products. Employees work out of offices in diverse locations including San Francisco, Boston, London and Tokyo in order to serve customers in the respective locations. The firm has won numerous awards for design work, and has been acclaimed 'the world's most celebrated design firm' (Sutton and Kelley 1997).

The founders of IDEO wish to create an environment that supports good relationships and creativity. Accordingly, the physical layout is purposely centred on small buildings with open facilities design. There is no visible administration – the buildings all have a reception desk for visitors, and the rest of the space is devoted to the engineers and laboratories where prototypes are created. The small buildings and limited number of employees eliminate the need for extensive security and employees know each other and know who should and should not be present. The psychological climate at IDEO incorporates many features associated with ideal conditions for knowledge workers. In general, unspoken norms take the place of policies and rules. There is little or no structure; the management encourages employees to take the initiative and use their knowledge and skills. For example, employees design their own workplaces, consistent with the idea of periodic movement to new projects and work locations in the building. Office designs are open, featuring distinctive partitions such as a DC-3 wing suspended from the ceiling. Most work locations also offer space to work alone in peace and quiet on a given day if the open environment begins to intrude.

Given IDEO's reputation and its commitment to learning, tours and interviews are an ongoing part of employee life. Most employees participate in showing visitors the work in progress. Employees say that a common topic of interviews is 'how to maintain energy and creativity as the small firm grows'. The secret is apparently in employee involvement in a selection of clients and projects, and allowing employees to gravitate to projects or client companies that fit their interests. Clients participate in an estimated 20 per cent of brainstorming sessions, and clients work side by side with the staff for one or two weeks at a time to observe, learn and try out IDEO work practices. In some cases, clients are co-located at IDEO for up to a year where long-term alliances are desired. The staff meet separately in separate buildings once a week for an hour, sitting on the floor in a large circle to share information on team activities, discuss new technologies, demonstrate new products, and give very brief updates on progress and setbacks – on products for fifteen to forty clients. They also take time out once a week for an organized bike ride through the hills of Palo Alto.

Much of the work is team-based. IDEO employees are trained in facilitation techniques and all brainstorming sessions in design teams are facilitator-led. Team members also host special sessions to demonstrate new work practices and technologies to others in the building. An example is the frequent practice of running involvement workshops to teach other staff to observe users, brainstorm new designs and build working models. IDEO employees are experts at teaching rapid prototyping, and are frequent contributors to Silicon Valley engineering and business school programmes.

Interviews indicate that IDEO employees are not there for the money, but rather remain with the company because of the unique working environment. As relatively young people with advanced degrees in engineering and related fields, they are well paid but could do better elsewhere. Compensation is not on a 'merit' or performance increase basis, but rather increases with time and market conditions. Management believes that typical merit schemes create a competitive environment, and are 'not nurturing'. When employees leave, it is often for a sabbatical or to gain advanced education.

Case implications for SWS design process

In the IDEO case, the founders wished to preserve freedoms that they enjoyed as inventors and entrepreneurs when the company was small. With growth, they were careful to create simple forms of structure supported in part by the limitations on the size of offices and laboratories. A small company atmosphere was maintained by growing new units in separate office buildings. Moreover, employees influenced strategy by creating their own projects and having a say in outside projects that IDEO might select. In some ways, projects take the place of formal structures and managerial processes. Employees participate in all aspects of the business including training others in IDEO work practices. Consistent with SWS thinking, employees have a sense of security and personal support. Turnover is very low despite attractive outside opportunities in the Silicon Valley area. High quality of work life, solid financial performance and other indicators suggest that IDEO is a sustainable work system.

The change approach involves strategy, structure and support processes. The overall change process is incremental: gaining agreement on promising areas for growth; replicating the simple structure with each formal move to new facilities; and building a positive work climate in the new office and laboratory units. Emphasis is on lean structures and managerial processes that support the individual.

Eclectic self-design

In the spirit of the IDEO case, we propose that the change process is eclectic self-design (Stebbins and Shani 1995). As depicted in Table 17.1, SWS design has some familiar programme phases, but with minimal constraints. That is, the phases or steps are merely

Table 17.1 Eclectic self-design

Steps
1   Preliminary project planning with clients
2   Reviewing alternative design models and change processes
3   Motivating the change effort and involving stakeholders
4   Establishing design criteria
5   Creating the parallel design mechanism – starting with the establishment of a steering body and continuing with creating the network of redesign teams
6   Building personal and social support for work design experimentation
7   Comprehensive impact analysis
8   Extending prototypes and work processes to other work units
9   Documenting SWS outcomes and providing feedback

guidelines and exist to support invention, experimentation, reflection/assessment and adjustments. The change process is tailored to each client situation. In keeping with self-design theory and practice, design activities can recycle to earlier phases as different stakeholders join the design process. Design teams are created and their efforts must mesh with work conducted by other teams.

Self-design theory provides insights on change process dynamics. For example, it is a tactical issue whether to bring stakeholders together from the outset or whether to include them at later phases. Regardless of this, the articulation of needs, goals and design criteria must reflect diversity of the work system. When agreement on design criteria has been established, design teams can proceed to consider different design models and to proceed with strategic and operational matters. Selection of a particular model provides basic guidelines for the change process. For example, under self-design, educational and diagnostic activities occur before invention and experimentation. Checkpoints are established to allow reflection/assessment before new designs are extended to other work groups. Design is not at all superficial, but instead allows maximum freedom for individuals and work groups to reconfigure core work processes. The 'magic' of SWS redesign is regeneration of resources – learning and enhanced capabilities through active experimentation, assessment and work adjustments.

One of the compelling issues in SWS design is how to orchestrate the change process so that work intensity is not the result, and so that employees have support for local efforts. A parallel learning design configuration (Bushe and Shani 1991; Shani and Docherty 2002) can co-ordinate design activities and gauge training needs at different phases. Training activities would emphasize simulation and other experiential methods that increase employee capacity to cope with change. We suggest the following:

- Simulation activities that increase the individual's capacity to create order and meaning in a seemingly disordered situation.
- Brainstorming sessions, with emphasis on forces that promote manageability and meaning in work.
- Relationship building conferences and exercises that promote goodwill and problem solving by different stakeholders in the transformation process.
- Person-centred training interventions that focus on (a) managing the personal work environment: time management, task variation, overload avoidance; (b) lifestyle management: maintaining a balance, taking time off from work; and (c) response-directed options such as relaxation, meditation, physical outlets and emotional outlets.

As shown in Table 17.1, as the design work unfolds, the steering group must provide opportunities for comprehensive *impact analysis* (Nadler and Tushman 1988). This analysis tracks outcomes for different stakeholders and the larger environment. It also increases the probability that new designs can be extended to other groups and locations within the organization. The IDEO case provides help here, in that it shows that a strategic design can be replicated if sufficient freedom is provided for work groups to self-design activities within the new work unit.

Research issues and future projects

From university and science perspectives, action research, socio-technical systems and self-design are preferred over traditional management consulting change processes (Cummings and Worley 2001). Regarding research on change, it is recognized that organizations and communities are often complex entities and cannot be solely studied using traditional reduction methods. Field experiments, ethnography and case studies appear often in social science journals, and the situation is much improved over the 1950s' climate when resistance to these methods was so strong (Pasmore 2001). SWS seeks to continue the action research-based tradition even though the price of high involvement SWS design can be delays, competing perspectives and chaos. The thinking is that involvement and dialogue with a purpose will raise human needs above the technical and economic pressures that consume organizations in post-industrial society.

SWS redesign rooted in action research and self-design concepts possesses the ability to anticipate and deal with many obstacles. But it is not foolproof. The notion of SWS is based on the premise that companies and managers will be drawn to it because it focuses on development of human resources and capabilities at all levels. Certainly it will be received more positively where the labour market is tight and where employers seek to be recognized as 'employers of choice'. Here, employers are motivated to create positive working conditions and environments as they must compete to retain scarce human resources. In keeping with STS and QWL foundations, they will further hope to create enriched and manageable jobs and healthy work teams, to support both knowledge creation and knowledge transfer, and to subscribe to a philosophy of continuous learning. It is obvious that these conditions do not exist in much of post-industrial society, but they are consistent with what many organizations hope to accomplish in 'old economy' and knowledge work settings. Research is needed to discover the extent to which SWS has appeal to all parties, within different economic sectors, industries and employee groups.

As SWS scholars begin to study non-routine organizations such as IDEO, they are likely to focus on problems reported in the literature. Regarding new product development (NPD), work process dynamics are often difficult to study. In such settings, companies are preoccupied with time to market and with expediting development processes. Participants may not have time to engage in action research projects that explore NPD processes. Moreover, front-end NPD work is always uncertain. It involves activities such as investigating alternative technologies and evaluating the market potential for an initial product concept. Tracking such activities requires new research methods. These difficulties have many implications for the SWS design process.

Since the context is so difficult with knowledge work, the SWS redesign process must be adjusted. The SWS process calls for major time commitments and training in SWS concepts and tools, and this poses a conflict. At the same time, the promise of improved NPD processes, increased individual capabilities and inter-project learning might make the time spent worthwhile.

In production and services settings, an investment in SWS redesign is less controversial.

There is already a huge body of empirical evidence that action research, STS and self-design produces improvements in workflow and jobs. We expect that SWS will continue this tradition. SWS builds on these modern approaches and the redesign process itself is a vehicle for uncovering and resolving problems along the way. In ideal form, SWS requires dedication of support resources (training, budgets for experimentation, creation of measurement systems, ergonomic analysis and the like). Given history, the worry is that SWS will fail in the context of competitive work systems, and in full implementation of concepts that produce qualitatively better conditions for employees and the community. What is needed is redesign of 'an emancipatory' or critical form. Emancipatory action research seeks to improve outcomes and the self-understanding of participants, as well as provide a critique of the larger social and work setting (Kemmis 2001).

Pasmore (2001) argues that most organizations are firmly caught in the grasp of technological determinism and scientific positivism. Therefore, any approach that promises to push human needs to the forefront is welcome. SWS is one way to challenge the dominant development paradigm. The challenge of SWS redesign is to build a comprehensive theory that includes design process. This chapter has articulated some of the design process requirements based on reflexive concepts. We have offered an eclectic change process that should be useful to those hoping to try SWS design. We have also explored some foundation approaches and concepts that will undoubtedly play out in future SWS thinking, albeit in ways that mesh with the rapidly changing post-industrial context.

References

Adler, N. and Docherty, P. (1998) 'Bringing business into sociotechnical theory and practice', *Human Relations*, 51, 3, 319–45.

Bradbury, H. and Clair, J. (1999) 'Promoting sustainable organizations with Sweden's natural step', *Academy of Management Executive*, 13, 4, 63–73.

Bushe, G.R. and Shani, A.B. (Rami) (1991) *Parallel Learning Structures. Increasing Innovation in Bureaucracies*, Boston: Addison-Wesley.

Cummings, T. and Worley, C. (2001) *Organization Development and Change*, Cincinnati, OH: South-Western Publishing.

Davis, L. and Cherns A.B. (1975) *The Quality of Working Life*, New York: Free Press.

Eijnatten, F.M. van (1994) *The Paradigm that Changed the Work Place*, Assen/Stockholm: Van Gorcum/Arbetslivscentrum.

Emery, F. (1959) *Characteristics of Socio-Technical Systems*, London: Tavistock, document 527.

Emery, F. and Trist, E. (1978) 'Analytical model for sociotechnical systems', in W.A. Pasmore and J.J. Sherwood (eds) *Sociotechnical Systems. A Sourcebook*, La Jolla, CA: University Associates.

Emery, M. and Purser, R.E. (1996) *The Search Conference*, San Francisco: Jossey-Bass.

Ennals, R. and Gustavsen, B. (1998) *Work Organization and Europe as a Development Coalition*, Amsterdam: John Benjamins.

Friedlander, F. and Brown, L.D. (1974) 'Organization development', *Annual Review of Psychology*, 25, 313–41.

Galbraith, J.R. (1994) *Competing with Flexible Lateral Organizations*, Boston: Addison-Wesley.

Gustavsen, B. (2001) 'Theory and practice. The mediating discourse', in P. Reason and H. Bradbury (eds), *Handbook of Action Research. Participative Inquiry and Practice*, London: Sage, pp. 13–26.

Hanna, D. (1988) *Designing Organizations for High Performance*, Boston: Addison-Wesley.

Kemmis, S. (2001) 'Exploring the relevance of critical theory for action research. Emancipatory action research in the footsteps of Jurgen Habermas', in P. Reason and H Bradbury (eds), *Handbook of Action Research. Participative Inquiry and Practice*, London: Sage, pp. 91–102.

Lewin, K. (1951) *Field Theory in Social Science. Selected Theoretical Papers*, New York: Harper & Row.

Lillrank, P., Shani, A.B. (Rami), Kolodny, H., Stymne, B., Figuera, J.R. and Liu, M. (1998) 'Learning from the success of continuous improvement change programs. An international comparative study', in R. Woodman and W. Pasmore (eds) *Research in Organization Change and Development*, Vol. 13, Greenwich, CT: JAI Publications, pp. 47–72.

Mackenzie, K.D. (1986) *Organization Design. The Organizational Audit and Analysis Technology*, New York: Ablex.

Mohrman, S.A. and Cummings, T.G. (1989) *Self-Designing Organizations. Learning How to Create High Performance*, Boston: Addison-Wesley.

Nadler, D.A. and Tushman, M.L. (1988) *Strategic Organization Design. Concepts, Tools, and Processes*, New York: HarperCollins.

Nadler, D.A. and Tushman, M.L. (1997) *Competing by Design. The Power of Organizational Architecture*, Oxford: Oxford University Press.

Pasmore, W.A. (1997) 'Managing organization deliberations in non-routine work', in R. Katz (ed.) *The Human Side of Managing Technological Innovation*, Oxford: Oxford University Press.

Pasmore, W.A. (2001) 'Action research in the workplace. The socio-technical perspective', in P. Reason and H. Bradbury (eds), *Handbook of Action Research. Participative Inquiry and Practice*, London: Sage.

Pasmore, W.A., Francis, C. and Shani, A.B. (Rami) (1982) 'Sociotechnical systems. A North American reflection on empirical studies of the seventies', *Human Relations*, 35, 12, 1179–204.

Pasmore, W.A. and Friedlander, F. (1982) 'An action research program for increasing employee involvement in problem solving', *Administrative Science Quarterly*, 27, 343–62.

Pava, C.H. (1983) *Managing New Office Technology. An Organizational Strategy*, New York: Free Press.

Raelin, J.A. (2000) *Work-Based Learning. The New Frontier of Management Development*, Englewood Cliffs, NJ: Prentice-Hall.

Reason, P. and Bradbury, H. (eds) (2001) *Handbook of Action Research. Participative Inquiry and Practice*, London: Sage.

Shani, A.B. (Rami) and Docherty, P. (2002) *Learning by Design*, Oxford: Blackwell (in press).

Shani, A. B. (Rami) and Elliott, O. (1989) 'Sociotechnical system design in transition', in W. Sikes *et al.* (eds) *The Emerging Practice of Organization Development*, La Jolla, CA: University Associates, pp. 187–99.

Shani, A.B. (Rami) and Mitki, Y. (2000) 'Creating the learning organization. Beyond mechanisms', in R. Golembiewski (ed.) *Handbook of Organizational Consultation*, New York: Marcel Dekker, pp. 911–19.

Shani, A.B. (Rami) and Pasmore, W.A. (1985) 'Organization inquiry. Towards a new model of the action research process', in D. Warrick (ed.) *Contemporary Organization Development*, Glenview, IL: Scott, Foresman & Company, pp. 438–48.

Shani, A.B. (Rami), Sena, J. and Stebbins, M.W. (2000) 'Knowledge work teams and groupware technology. Learning from Seagate's experience', *Journal of Knowledge Management*, 4, 2, 111–24.

Stebbins, M.W., Hawley, J. and Rose, A. (1982) 'Long-term action research. The most effective way to improve complex health care organizations', in N. Margulies and J. Adams (eds) *Organizational Development in Health Care Organizations*, Boston: Addison-Wesley.

Stebbins, M.W. and Shani, A.B. (Rami) (1995) 'Organization design and the knowledge worker', *Leadership and Organization Development*, 16, 1, 23–30.

Stebbins, M.W. and Shani, A.B. (Rami) (1998) 'Business process reengineering at Blue Shield of California. The integration of multiple change initiatives', *Journal of Organizational Change Management*, 11, 3, 216–232.

Stebbins, M.W. and Snow, C.C. (1983) 'Processes and payoffs of programmatic action research', *Journal of Applied Behavioral Science*, 18, 1, 69–86.

Susman, G.I. and Evered, R.D. (1978) 'An assessment of the scientific merits of action research', *Administrative Science Quarterly*, 23, 583–603.

Sutton, R.I. and Kelley, T.A. (1997) 'Creativity doesn't require isolation. Why product designers bring visitors "backstage" ', *California Management Review*, 40, 1, 75–91.

Taylor, J.C. and Felten, D.F. (1993) *Performance by Design. Sociotechnical Systems in North America*, Englewood Cliffs, NJ: Prentice-Hall.

Trist, E. (1981) *The Evolution of Sociotechnical Systems*, London: Tavistock.

Weick, K.E. (1977) 'Organization design. Organizations and self-designing systems', *Organizational Dynamics*, 6, 30–46.

18 Sustainable work systems

Lessons and challenges

Peter Docherty, Jan Forslin and A.B. (Rami) Shani

Introduction

When this group of authors came together four years ago, it was with a sense of urgency. Many of us had been involved with workplace development for many years and there was now a feeling that the world was moving in a wrong direction. There were many indicators of increased pressures in work and we found that the notion of intensive work systems captured the essence of the situation. During the years that have passed the problems have worsened and remedies for a situation in which we, as humans, seem caught in a trap of increasing work demands and diminishing resources are nowadays high on the political agenda. Soon we came to the conclusion that formulating an alternative for the future was maybe more important than analysing the past. So with the adoption of the concept of sustainable work systems, we felt that we had at least an expression for an antipode that not only encompassed the abolishing of the sources of intensity, but more bravely saw work as a possible source of enjoyment and invigoration while still being high achieving.

Work intensity we believed to be able to understand reasonably well with our experiences of work and organizational life. But to understand what sustainable work systems look like was a much tougher challenge. To move into this virgin territory, we thought we had better get rid of some of our intellectual luggage, review our extensive experience and question our conventional wisdom. There was a certain enthusiasm at being provided with a reason and opportunity to start afresh, to speculate and to formulate deviating perspectives – an intellectual rebirth.

Without being apologetic, we think that with this explorative and tentative approach, the normal custom for a concluding chapter to summarize the findings presented and to come out with a few solid conclusions is hardly applicable in this case. The eighteen chapters that make up the book, written by nineteen researchers representing different academic disciplines from twelve institutions and nine European countries and the United States cover a great amount of diverse material. The range of disciplinary perspectives, illustrations, development and change orientations and the current state of knowledge about the emerging phenomenon of sustainability of work systems we have so far not been able to put together into a neat organizational model. Thus, this final but non-concluding chapter should rather be viewed as a deeper level of reflection on this collective four year endeavour.

Perspectives and concepts

The principal objectives, motives and framing for this book were laid out in some detail in Chapter 1 and need only a brief recapitulation in this chapter. The emerging context of work sets the stage for two central concepts of our study, namely intensive and sustainable work systems.

Although the notion of sustainable systems here is borrowed from ecology, the caring and efficient use of natural resources in general is not the topic of this book. What is common, though, is the awareness that resources – in our case human and social – are finite and the need exists to develop towards less consuming but still competitive production forms. The industrial society has an infamous record of creating wealth through the ruthless exploitation of resources. Nature can hardly fight back – not in the short term at least. Maltreated humans can object to and change a malfunctioning and resource consuming system. The ambition here is to contribute to this change.

An intensive work system, in this book, is seen as a system that maintains productivity only by depleting human and social resources. Following the generic definition that we have adopted, a sustainable work system is a system where human and social resources are instead regenerated through the process of work while still maintaining productivity and a competitive edge. Such a generic definition gives room for the specific and unique, but little guidance. By presenting several theoretical perspectives and reviewing empirical lessons, we have tried to make up for this.

As this is a production of scholars with differing experiences and disciplinary backgrounds from different cultures, the understanding of work intensity and sustainable work has varying points of theoretical departure. In Table 18.1 we have summarized the essence of five disciplinary perspectives that were developed and utilized throughout this book.

Table 18.1 Main concepts of work intensity and sustainable work systems

Disciplinary perspective	*Foundation*	*Key analytical concepts*
Individual	psychology stress research	sense of coherence, stress, coping, flow, salutogenes, resource regeneration, competence
Resources	sociology social economy	human and social resources, autonomy, stress, context, values, contradictory job requirements
Work organization	sociology management	confinement, prescriptive design, cognitive and relational resources
Complexity	socio-technical systems chaos theory	chaos, network, holon, chaordic organization
Institutional	political science sociology	labour law, union–employer agreement, market strategy

The individual-based perspective, as can be seen in Table 18.1, is anchored predominantly in the psychological domain. As such, concepts like stress, coping, balance between personal resources and work requirements, sense of coherence, flow, competence development stand out as both essential to understanding intensity and as contributions to regeneration of resources and salutary work.

The foundation for the resource-based perspective can be found in the fields of sociology, social economy and management strategy. Interestingly, the importance of stress and autonomy again stands out, although to be understood as contradictory job requirements and in the contextual embeddedness of work and guiding values. With a relational view the concept of resources becomes social resources, which reside in the relations among individuals, social groups and institutional actors. The management and organizational perspectives are enforced with focusing on work design as central to the issue of work intensity with dimensions such as work prescription and work confinement, cognitive and relational competence, but also self-management. Socio-technical system theory seems to be an influencing theoretical base both in this perspective and with complexity as the foundation for understanding the major drivers of work intensity. The complexity-based perspective is further enforced by borrowing from physics and chaos theory concepts such as chaordic organizations, holons and network.

Work autonomy and power are central to several of the perspectives here as well as with the institutional-based perspective. The latter defines institutions as both legal and quasi-legal frameworks that need to address the constraints imposed by the presence of a variety of actors, such as labour unions, works councils and employee associations. Thus, the level of work intensity is related to the industrial relations system, but also to type of market strategy.

Facets of sustainability

The basic problem at the individual level, which we address in this book, is the growth in the level of work intensity and the growth in the prevalence of this condition in working life. Our aim is to examine what different academic perspectives can contribute conceptually and theoretically to the development of ideas on sustainability and what good practice can also contribute to our understanding of these issues. In this section, we present our reflections on the practical illustrations of efforts to realize facets of sustainability that were presented in Chapters 8 to 13. These reflections are made, first, in the light of the disciplinary perspectives presented in Chapters 3 to 7 and, second, in the light of the development processes presented in Chapters 14 to 17.

Observations through the perspective lens

The illustrations were generated through an extensive discussion among a group of senior American and European researchers with long experience of fieldwork in many sectors and a long personal commitment to this area. The examples selected were all taken from ongoing research in the group. All the cases come from the United States and northern Europe. They illustrate that sustainability can be thought of, designed and managed in many ways. Each example illustrates a particular feature of sustainability, while not addressing others. Several of the cases illustrate the difficulties in maintaining sustainability at different levels, not least due to changes in an organization's surroundings or context. Utilizing the different disciplinary perspectives reveals some unique insights into the holistic nature and complexity of sustainability. No a priori decision was made to apply or utilize a specific perspective or multiple perspectives for a specific example. Table 18.2 provides a summary of the examination of the examples from the specific perspectives, to see how they are explained with the different disciplinary lenses. The discussion serves as a way to examine both the similarities and differences among the illustrations, as well as the potential insight gained by utilizing a specific or multiple disciplinary perspectives.

Considering the individual perspectives' relevance to the illustrations presented, the *individual-focused perspective* can help shed light on the sustainability dynamics in the banking case to a major extent, in the software development, network and regional network to a moderate extent and to a limited extent in the car manufacturing case. The *resource-based perspective* helps shed light in the software development and the network cases to a major extent, in the banking, car manufacturing and regional development to a moderate extent and to a limited extent in the telecom case. The *work organization-based perspective* can help shed light in the soft-ware development, telecom and car manufacturing cases to a major extent, banking to a moderate extent and to a limited extent in the network and regional development cases. The *complexity-based perspective* seems to shed light to a moderate extent in the software and telecom cases and to a limited extent in the banking, car manufacturing, network and regional devel-opment cases. Finally, the *institutional-based perspective* sheds light to a major extent in the regional development case, to a moderate extent in the banking and network cases and in the software development, telecom and car manufacturing cases to a limited extent.

As this retrospective analysis indicates, the different perspectives seem to be relevant to varying degrees for each case. For example, while the individual-based perspective seems to shed light to a major extent in the banking case, the resource-based perspective seems to be the most relevant for the network case, the work organization-based perspective for the soft-ware development, telecom and car manufacturing cases and the institutional-based perspective for the regional development case.

A careful examination of Table 18.2 also reveals that while some disciplinary perspectives seem more relevant for a specific example, a combination of perspectives – multiple per-spectives – has the potential of providing a more comprehensive and holistic insight into the phenomenon of sustainability, its context, mechanisms and dynamics. For example, an exam-ination of the software development case from the individual-based perspective reveals a better understanding of the effect that the interaction between individuals and their work has on how they experience work and the coping mechanisms that individuals developed. An examination of the case from a resource-based perspective reveals the mechanisms that were developed by the organization to develop the capacity to continuously develop human resources by nurturing a special long-term partnership with a neighbouring university. A reflection on the example from a work organization-based perspective reveals the platform-based design that was developed as an organizational mechanism to facilitate the utilization and generation of organizational knowledge. Through the complexity-based perspective we can learn about the emergent properties of the software development firm such as the spon-taneous and mutual alignment of individuals and tasks/projects based on changing needs. Finally, the institutional-based perspective reveals insights into the market characteristics that foster a culture and mentality of continuous change as an integral component of work life.

Observations through the development process lens

In writing the illustrations, the contributors' main focus in the cases was on the perspectives. In some cases the key processes contributing to learning are not captured in the texts pre-sented here. This is partly because learning has not been the main message of the case and partly because the learning processes have not been so perceptible to the contributors. Table 18.3 presents the presence of the learning-oriented processes as they can be gleaned from the cases. In the table, the columns represent the cases (Chapters 8 to 13) and the rows represent the development sub-processes (Chapters 14 to 17). The evaluations are our general impres-sions, based on the routines and organizational mechanisms described. A three point scale has been used to indicate the level of development: high, moderate and low. The brackets around some evaluations indicate uncertainty in the evaluation. The course of the regional develop-ment case changed radically in midstream and thus the two major phases in that illustration are evaluated separately.

The columns in Table 18.3 reflect the organizational learning cycles in the cases. A first observation is that the feedback process is generally the most developed element or phase

Table 18.2 A comparative synopsis of the illustrations

Illustrating cases

Perspectives	Essence of the illustration / Software development (Ch. 8)	Telecom products (Ch. 9)	Banking (Ch. 10)	Car manufacturing (Ch. 11)	SME network (Ch. 12)	Regional development (Ch. 13)
Essence of the illustration	Sustainability through the development of capability to continuously generate resources	Sustainability through the design mechanism of project-based self-design work and organization	Sustainability through the active balancing mechanism of stakeholder interests	Sustainability through the extension of democratic and integrative principles of work group design	Sustainability through a network-based mechanism to generate development resources for SMEs	Sustainability through a coalition with resources and competence to support development
Individual (Ch. 3)	to a moderate extent	to a limited extent	to a major extent	to a limited extent	to a moderate extent	to a moderate extent
Resources (Ch. 4)	to a major extent	to a limited extent	to a moderate extent	to a moderate extent	to a major extent	to a moderate extent
Work organization (Ch. 5)	to a major extent	to a major extent	to a moderate extent	to a major extent	to a limited extent	to a limited extent
Complexity (Ch. 6)	to a moderate extent	to a moderate extent	to a limited extent	to a limited extent	to a limited extent	to a limited extent
Institutional (Ch. 7)	to a limited extent	to a limited extent	to a moderate extent	to a limited extent	to a moderate extent	to a major extent

Table 18.3 Analysis of the development processes in the illustrations from a learning perspective

	Software development (Ch. 8)	Telecom products (Ch. 9)	Banking (Ch. 10)	Car manufacturing (Ch. 11)	SME network (Ch. 12)	Regional development (Ch. 13)
Feedback (Ch. 14)	Moderate	Low/ Moderate	High	High	Moderate	1. Moderate 2. Low
Reflexivity (Ch. 15)	Low	Low	Moderate	Moderate	Low	1. High 2. Low
Learning (Ch. 16)	Moderate	Moderate	Moderate	(Moderate)	(Moderate)	1. Moderate 2. Low
Eclectic design (Ch. 17)	High	High	(Moderate)	(Low)	Low	High Low

of the process. This is the element most supported by the planning and control methods and structures emerging from management accounting and production engineering. Many work situations now have local planning systems that provide workers with regular and detailed feedback on their work performance. Feedback is closely followed by the design phase regarding level of development. Design has also had the benefit of high status professional groups in organizations engaged in the development of tools and methods and who eagerly assist in their application at all levels in organizations. Reflexivity and learning appear less developed in the illustrations. This may well reflect that less attention is focused as yet on these issues in organizations. Considering the four phases in the Kolb circle, the reported focus on design and feedback or 'action/experience' reflects the classic practitioner sub-optimization (Ramnarayan *et al.* 1989). The main formal learning efforts referred to in the cases concern formal training. Without underestimating the value of such efforts they focus on 'single-loop' learning. In general there is a need to focus more on the systematic support of reflexivity and learning in general and 'double-loop' and 'deuterolearning' in particular.

The rows in Table 18.3 concern the separate stages in the learning process. Regarding feedback, many cases reported the systematic and regular availability of production data at the individual and team levels, irrespective of whether they were permanent or temporary (project) teams. In several cases there were also clear evaluation routines, i.e. the 'who, when and how' of the evaluation process were specified. Regarding reflexivity, the illustrations mainly name the arenas that have been formed in this context: workplace meetings for teams, 'continuous improvement' activities and temporary development projects on the shop or office floor. In individual cases, performance data are also displayed on whiteboards in the coffee rooms for informal discussions.

Regarding learning, some cases made reference to the informal professional discussions of the evaluation of structural and process changes in practice in one context or another – behaviour that may be said to constitute development in a 'community of practice' (COP). Similarly there were examples of professional networks that had been established between different workplaces in the same organization, between different teams and between companies. Again, these developments had, with the exception of the inter-company networks, grown and functioned very informally.

Regarding design, half the cases pointed out the role of self-design in teams and project groups and the formation of cross-level groups. The existence of a shared vision and shared goals was a key base for these design processes. In one case, work organization was covered by a joint agreement between management and unions.

Returning to a question posed earlier, who benefits? Or in this case, who learns? The illustrations indicate that the developments in HR practices in formal training are such that, at least in major corporations, they reach down to the broad majority of personnel on the shop or office floor. Learning in networks and temporary (project) organizations is now the focus of attention, though we know relatively little about the nature of the processes. Cross-level and cross-boundary learning is less common. Formal networks seldom manage to realize their potential. (Both a positive and negative example are presented here.)

Considering the use of feedback for control or dialogue/learning, there is clear evidence in the cases of the use of feedback in dialogue both for joint learning and joint decision-making. This is reported between teams and between levels in the hierarchy and between the social partners in some instances. Dialogues between functions or along the value chain appear less common.

Finally, considering learning on the job, in the workplace at an individual or group level or even organizational level, such things are reported – they happen, but seldom with the planned and considered support of those in the organization.

Directions for practice and research

In this chapter we have attempted to capture retrospectively some of our learning from this project. Due to the emergent nature of the field, its scope, context, mechanisms and dynamics it is impossible to provide a comprehensive path for research and practice. Yet, in this section of the chapter our objective is to identify a few areas that we view as critical for both research and practice.

The practice challenge

The trends and challenges arising in business and commerce and in the labour market are being met constructively, enthusiastically and successfully by people at all levels in organizations in all sectors of the economy (Beer and Nohria 2000). Many of the lessons the illustrations present us today are lessons that others learned a long time ago. It is not simply a case of forgetfulness or time pressure or that pathway of good intentions that may explain our *déja vu* feeling. Many of the most pertinent lessons today regarding efforts to realize sustainable work systems may require a shift in attitudes or even values that has not yet occurred since the 'old' lessons were first formulated.

Without an exhaustive checklist, we present half a dozen practical principles. The majority start with the word 'active.' This word means that there must be a conscious, considered, committed decision on a principal path of action, on the part of all the members in the organization, from the top down, to follow, implement and develop the tenet, principle, strategy concerned. Paradigms are not shifted by lip service.

Active choice of sustainable workplaces

The decision to initiate the process to develop and maintain sustainable work systems (SWS) needs to be a strategic, long-term choice that will function as an important criterion in the conscious decision-making on other issues: 'How will this decision affect our strategic goal of social sustainability?' SWS can be difficult to reconcile with certain 'tactical', short-term behaviours. It cannot be reconciled with the 'quarterly mentality' of many stock market analysts who exert a dominating influence on many managers. Top management must not only just make such strategic choices, they must be seen to-be-made and seen to-be-meant (see e.g. Chapter 10). There are many examples of top management decisions being neutralized by other managers or of decisions that have not penetrated the consciousness of the majority of the members of an organization (Dilschmann *et al.* 1994). The choice must be embedded, understood and accepted by the members of the organization.

Active value creation for all constituencies

The legitimate needs and aspirations of all the constituencies involved, personnel, customers, shareholders, even suppliers and society, should be addressed by the organization (see for example Chapter 8). Again, this is not simply a case of making a policy statement. The constituencies must be able to monitor their position through information provided by the organization. In many cases this will require tailor-made information systems. As has been stated previously, meeting these aspirations will usually enhance the reciprocal exchange with the constituency in question. Ensuring the security, health, well-being, respect, identity and development of the personnel with such measures as high trust, high involvement, 'high road' policies will usually be reciprocated with their commitment, trust, creativity, readiness for change and personal development. Organizations need the commitment of all their members, e.g. in scanning developments of relevance to the organization in its environment (Hamrefors 1999).

Wide vision and variable design focus for sustainability

Considering all the main constituencies requires management to create a very broad spectrum of goals and indicators to be considered in people's work situations (Beer 2000, 2001). This broad field functions as the overall backcloth to a person's activities and organized work. As we have seen in Chapters 8–13, sustainable work can be achieved in a variety of ways. From a work and organization design perspective, we have proposed an eclectic self-design approach as a way to address the varied and continuously changing design requirements (see Chapter 17). Furthermore, we advanced a set of nine steps that build the organizational capacity for continuous redesign process – in line with the need for social and organizational sustainability.

Sustainability through active balance and integration

There usually exist mismatches and conflicts between the strong needs and aspirations of different constituencies and the various aspects of internal and external, and static and dynamic efficiency may well be non-reconcilable. Trade-offs must be arrived at. This requires an active balancing process in which trade-offs on the extent and sequencing order of goal realization must be determined. This is an ever ongoing process necessary for maintaining sustainability. This interfaces with the field of corporate social responsibility and social accounting in the balance among the economic, social and ecological spheres and the due consideration to societal laws, guidelines and ethical directives (see Chapter 14). At the same time, integration entails combining several goals, activities, actors and resources to reduce complexity and increase resources and efficiency through synergy effects. Balancing and problem solution are achieved within the holon, be it a work team, project, alliance, coalition or network (see Chapter 6). The cases presented earlier indicate that integrated work groups often function to all intents and purposes as small enterprises. These integrated units or holons, which provide a foundation for sustainability, require careful planning and grouping with respect to their goals, tasks, resources and responsibilities.

Sustainability through active experimentation, learning mechanisms and reflexivity

The integration of static and dynamic effectiveness and internal and external efficiency may be achieved by continuous experimentation in the workplace. Personnel are not only involved in problem solving activities but also in these activities. These development activities may concern the incremental developments in such systems as continuous improvement, or in the participation in projects entailing radical developments in products and production processes. These projects entail continuous learning at the individual, group and organizational levels and strengthen readiness for change and new ideas. From a design and learning perspective, some type of legitimate forum for exchanges of ideas and action through conversations is an essential feature (see Chapters 15, 16 and 17). The forum is seen as a mechanism with a structural configuration and processes that are devoted to sustainability (Shani and Docherty 2002). As can be seen in the illustrations, the types and dynamics of the learning mechanisms vary widely and are subject to the strategic and design choices, goals and emergent system dynamics and context (see Chapters 8–13). These measures are basically reflections of a different set of values.

The research challenge

As can be seen from the different disciplinary perspectives on sustainability and the illustrations described and examined in this book, sustainability is an emerging complex phenomenon and a field of study that is in need of much research and discussion. What follows is a discussion of five research areas: the critical pursuit of multi-level interdisciplinary research; the critical pursuit of multiple contexts and levels of analysis; the scientific process of creating actionable knowledge about sustainability; the nature of partnership in sustainable work systems; and reflexivity, learning and sustainability.

The critical pursuit of multi-level interdisciplinary research on sustainable work systems

The complexity of sustainable work systems coupled with the emergent nature of the theoretical knowledge calls for a holistic, interdisciplinary and multi-level perspective. The previous chapters in this book and the observations on the illustrations with respect to the theoretical perspectives and developmental processes in this chapter showed the insights that can be generated using this approach. Yet, we have to develop ways that will allow the conduct of such complex research projects – the result of which is likely to be a clearer definition of the field of study.

Disciplines tend to develop theories and knowledge-based ways of thinking that are distinct. Many disciplines advocate a specific level of analysis and tend to develop distinct approaches to enquiry that are not always complementary. Our study documents that when continuous dialogue between researchers from different disciplines takes place over time, as the research projects get formulated, carried out and analysed, a true interdisciplinary perspective can emerge. Achieving the interdisciplinary perspective requires a major commitment of all the parties involved and the willingness to work through some very difficult disagreements that are both of theoretical and methodological nature.

The critical pursuit of research on sustainable work systems in multiple contexts and on multiple levels of analysis

The level of analysis of the set of empirical studies reported in this book can be viewed as sustainable episodes, structures or processes. From such studies much was learned about the features of sustainability, its dynamics and possible drivers and inhibitors in particular settings at particular points in time. Yet, less was learned about the temporal and spatial contextual factors that were shaping those particular events, episodes, structures or processes.

The recent rise of contextualism as a scientific theory and method provides a possible new approach to the study of change and sustainability (Pettigrew, Woodman and Cameron 2001). Based on the results from the study reported in this book, we advocate that future research on sustainability should explore the contexts, content and process of sustainability together with their interconnections over time (see Chapters 9, 12 and 13). This kind of approach presents a few challenges to scholars: to attempt to catch reality at a particular point in time, and to study long-term processes in their contexts in order to elevate embeddedness to a principle of method.

The argument that we have advanced in this book – that the processes and mechanisms of sustainability are embedded in contexts and can only be studied as such – requires the need to conceptualize and study the interactive fields within which sustainability emerges over time. Pursuing this kind of research approach will further require key analytical decisions about how many levels of analysis to include in the treatment of the context and which processes or mechanisms should be included or excluded from the study, e.g. individual, group, organization, network or region. The complexity of such an approach is evident, not least as the concept of sustainability will be different at different levels. However, the combination of the chosen levels of contexts, the processes and the interaction field brought into an analysis are likely to generate new insights into the phenomenon of sustainability.

The scientific process of creating actionable knowledge about sustainability

The lack of a coherent theory, disciplinary base and methodological foundation of sustainable work systems creates an opportunity for the creation of new actionable knowledge. Actionable knowledge is viewed as knowledge that can simultaneously serve the needs of science and the living systems (i.e. units, organizations, networks, societies). Some scholars argue that any attempt to increase the actionable value has a major risk for the academic value of the research. Others argue that meeting the needs of both is not only critical and doable but generates a more meaningful insight into the phenomenon that is being studied (Reason and Bradbury 2001). The issues of sustainability are, however, of such critical social, economic and ecological importance that the development of actionable knowledge must be on the research agenda and actors in workplaces and organizations should participate in the research process.

Our study suggests that careful attention to the enquiry process allows the creation of actionable knowledge that meets the needs of the academy and the living systems. The focus on sustainability lends itself to the exploration and utilization of different alternative participative enquiry approaches. While some of these approaches were identified throughout the book (see Chapters 15, 16 and 17), they also include other varieties of action research forms such as participative enquiry, action science, intervention research, clinical field research, development action enquiry, appreciative enquiry and table-tennis research (Adler and Shani 2001).

This research points towards the possibility that the scientific process chosen is likely to be an enabler of the further development of the system under investigation and thus enhance its sustainable nature. Yet, much more research is needed in order to explore the relative relevance of the different participative research forms as well as the possible causal relationship between the participative research forms and the facilitation of system sustainability.

The nature of partnership in sustainable work systems

Our research indicates that sustainable work systems seem to be based on true partnership and joint efforts among organizational members. As can be derived from our study, the basic foundation for sustainable systems is that the state of continuous regeneration of resources and the promotion and development of working life and competitive performance might be achieved as a result of joint commitment and collaborative effort of management and organizational members. Joint effort demands that productive dialogue based on mutual respect and understanding is established (see Chapters 15 and 17). Yet, our theoretical knowledge of true partnership, its key features and its dynamics – in the context of creating sustainable work systems – is limited.

For the processes of development, creation and change of sustainable work systems to take hold, heavy investment in time, energy and resources is required. If partnership is a possible critical element of such attempts and desires, enquiry into the developmental nature of partnerships and the possible cause-and-effect relationship between the partnership stage of development and sustainability processes and outcomes is of vital importance at this stage of theory development. There is growing evidence of cross-level interactions between forms of direct and representational participation in organizations and their positive impacts on organizational processes and outcomes (see Chapter 14).

Reflexivity, learning and sustainability

One of the areas explored in this study is the nature of sustainable change processes for renewal and learning. In Chapter 1, we argued that in the context of the increasingly volatile business environment, sustainability means creating liberating, emancipatory mechanisms and building up internal capabilities to carry through reorganizations and continuous change successfully and to facilitate learning. In Chapters 14 to 17, we devoted attention to sustainability from a development and change perspective. As such, the theoretical points of departure included socio-technical system theory, action research, self-design theory, organization development and change theory, organization learning theory and organization design theory.

'Security is in the change' was already the war cry of the 1970s, but despite all initiatives for change, organizations manifest a remarkable stability. Interventions from outside experts, perpetually enthusiastic HRM champions, recurrent OD projects, alternating union–management campaigns, new personnel policies, stacks of transparencies and government reforms appear to have little effect on the reality of shop or office floors. An impatient owner will not wait for the effects. A new top manager has met another consultant. Too few invested resources make the expectations unrealistic. Internal politics prevent changes of the status quo. The wind of change has soon blown by and business is 'resumed as usual', often after a considerable waste of resources. Repeated change projects with no clear benefit demoralize – and are in fact a basic cause of such negative phenomena as burnout (Barklöf 2000).

With a mechanistic ideal, change means moving from one steady state to another and single-loop learning. Theories of the learning organization have been concerned with the (lack of) capacity for double-loop learning. What actually is the issue at stake with a sustainability perspective comes close to deutero-learning with an integrated and built in capacity for innovation (see Chapter 16).

The processes of learning and development in organizations, regarding experiential learning, tacit knowledge, communities of practice, creativity and development in organizations have all been acknowledged as of great importance but are still enigmatic and require much further research.

Integrating the issues of economic, social and ecological sustainability

There is a long established political awareness of the need for societies to be 'sustainable and competitive', as stated for example in the EU's fifth framework programme for research and development. However, this was followed in 2001 by the EU green paper on 'Corporate Social Responsibility'. The green paper addresses economic, social and ecological responsibility. These three topics have been pursued by professionals with different disciplinary backgrounds as three separate disciplinary tracts. Business has always been interested in economic sustainability. Political parties and specific movements have emphasized ecological aspects. Unions and sectors of the public services have been interested in social aspects, especially in working life. Social aspects have been focused on in this book as they have received less attention than the others in society – a clear reason for the emergence of work life intensity.

There is a pressing need for the political and social involvement of society in 'social responsibility' to ensure both that the generation of knowledge in these three disciplines may develop at comparable rates and that the issue integrating them is allotted due attention and resources. There is a real risk that knowledge regarding the social dimension will fall behind.

In our earlier treatment of sustainability from a work systems perspective, we identified several dimensions in social auditing which are common to the three types of responsibility, namely the inclusion of all constituencies, the inclusion of outcomes and processes, the inclusion of organizations and their contexts and the inclusion of static and dynamic effectiveness (see Chapter 14, Table 14.3). These are all issues of critical importance requiring further research.

Last, the issues of social responsibility concern values and ethics. Previously in the book we have broached the fact that choices and changes to establish sustainability have a strong value base. We repeat two earlier quotations on this issue.

> Without the acceptance on the part of business of a wider notion of accountability and its underpinning concepts of auditing, accounting and public reporting, the advancement of the holistic sustainable development agenda will suffer.
>
> (Sillanpää 1999, p. 537)

> Sustainability and sustainable development remain elusive concepts. They have been variously referred to as 'vision expression', 'value change', 'moral development' or 'transformational process'.
>
> (Gladwin *et al.* 1995, p. 877)

These underline this issue, which widens the research field on sustainability to the values, culture and ethical sphere.

We started by wrestling with the heritage of Fredrick Winslow Taylor. He ended life rather embittered and, as he saw himself, misunderstood and opposed by his contemporaries. Like many of today's OD consultants, he complained about the narrowness and conservatism of his time.

> Scientific management does not exist and cannot exist until there has been a complete mental revolution on the part of the workmen working under it, as to their duties toward themselves and toward their employers, and a complete mental revolution in the outlook for the employers, toward their duties, toward themselves, and toward their workmen.
>
> (Frederick Taylor, *The Principles of Scientific Management*, 1911)

Taylor was scornful of a wasteful management. However, he did, at least posthumously, manage to change the mental set-up of the whole industrialized world. Maybe the mental revolution that Taylor demanded was the rationality of modernism and a final break with the conceptions and value system of the agricultural past. Now, ninety years later, we feel that realizing sustainable work systems may well demand another mental revolution. Taylor's problem was to go from one state of mind to another. The challenge is now probably of a different kind; not a movement from one state to another, but rather establishing a dynamic flexibility as sustainability is a process not a state.

References

Adler, N. and Shani, A.B. (Rami), (2001) 'In search of an alternative framework for the creation of actionable knowledge. Table-tennis research at Ericsson', in W. Pasmore and R.W. Woodman (eds) *Research in Organizational Change and Development*, Vol. 13, Greenwich, CT: JAI Publications, pp. 43–79.

Barklöf, K. (2000) *Magra organisationer* (Lean Organizations), Stockholm: Swedish Council for Work Life Research.

Beer, M. (2000) 'Research that will break the code of change. The role of useful normal science and usable action science – a commentary on Van den Ven and Argyris', in M. Beer and N. Nohria (eds) *Breaking the Code of Change*, Boston: Harvard Business School Press.

Beer, M. (2001) 'How to develop an organization capable of sustained high performance', *Organizational Dynamics*, 29, 4, 233–47.

Beer, M. and Nohira, N. (2000) 'Resolving the tension between theories E and O of change', in M. Beer and N. Nohria (eds) *Breaking the Code of Change*, Boston: Harvard Business School Press.

Dilschmann, A., Docherty, P. and Stjernberg, T. (1994) *Kompetensstrategier – bärande lärdomar* (Competence Strategies. Principal Lessons), Stockholm: Arbetsgivarverket.

European Union Commission (2001) *Corporate Social Responsibility*, Brussels: EU green paper.

Gladwin, T.N., Kennelly, J.J. and Krause, T.S. (1995), 'Shifting paradigms for sustainable development. Implications for management theory and research', *Academy of Management Review*, 20, 4, 847–907.

Hamrefors, S. (1999) *Spontaneous Environmental Scanning. Putting 'Putting into Perspective' into Perspective*, Stockholm: Economic Research Institute at the Stockholm School of Economics.

Pettigrew, A.M., Woodman, R.W. and Cameron, K.S. (2001) 'Studying organizational change and development. Challenges for future research', *Academy of Management Journal*, 44, 4, 697–713.

Ramnarayan, S. and Mohan Reddy, N. (1989) 'Institutional learning. The essence of strategic management', *Vikalpa*, 14, 1, 21–33.

Reason, P. and Bradbury, H. (eds) (2001) *Handbook of Action Research*, London: Sage.

Shani, A.B. (Rami) and Docherty, P (2002) *Learning by Design*, Oxford: Blackwell (in press).

Sillanpää, M. (1999) 'Taking the social dimension seriously', in M. Bennett and P. James (eds) *Sustainable Measures. Evaluation and Reporting of Environmental and Social Performance*, Sheffield: Greenleaf Publishing, pp. 535–68.

Index

References to figures and tables are in *italics*; those for notes are followed by n